A WORLD OF DIFFERENCE

A World of Difference

An Anthology of Short Stories from Five Continents

EDITED BY

LYNDA PRESCOTT

palgrave
macmillan

First published 2008 by
PALGRAVE MACMILLAN in association with THE OPEN UNIVERSITY

THE OPEN UNIVERSITY, Walton Hall, Milton Keynes, MK7 6AA, United Kingdom

PALGRAVE MACMILLAN, Houndmills, Basingstoke, Hampshire RG21 6XS and
175 Fifth Avenue, New York, N.Y. 10010
Companies and representatives throughout the world

PALGRAVE MACMILLAN is the global academic imprint of the Palgrave
Macmillan division of St. Martin's Press, LLC and of Palgrave Macmillan Ltd.
Macmillan® is a registered trademark in the United States, United Kingdom
and other countries. Palgrave is a registered trademark in the European
Union and other countries.

ISBN-13: 978–0–230–20208–5 paperback
ISBN-10: 0–230–20208–X paperback

This book forms part of an Open University course AA100 *The Arts Past and
Present*. Details of this and other Open University courses can be obtained
from the Student Registration and Enquiry Service, The Open University,
PO Box 197, Milton Keynes, MK7 6BJ, United Kingdom:
tel. +44 (0)845 300 60 90, email general-enquiries@open.ac.uk
http://www.open.ac.uk

This book is printed on paper suitable for recycling and made from fully
managed and sustained forest sources. Logging, pulping and manufacturing
processes are expected to conform to the environmental regulations of the
country of origin.

A catalogue record for this book is available from the British Library.

A catalog record for this book is available from the Library of Congress.

Contents

Acknowledgements

The editor and publishers wish to thank the following for permission to use copyright material:

Peter Carey, for 'American Dreams' from *Collected Stories* by Peter Carey (Faber and Faber, 1995). Copyright © 1995 Peter Carey, by permission of Rogers, Coleridge & White Ltd on behalf of the author;

Raymond Carver, for 'What Do You Do in San Francisco?' from *Where I'm Calling From: The Collected Stories* by Raymond Carver (Harvill Press, 1993). Copyright © 1976, 1988 by Raymond Carver, by permission of The Random House Group Ltd and Grove/Atlantic, Inc.;

Mavis Gallant, for 'The End of the World' from *The End of the World and Other Stories* by Mavis Gallant (McClelland & Stewart, 1974), by permission of David Higham Associates on behalf of the author;

Lorna Goodison, for 'Bella Makes Life' from *Baby Mother and the King of Swords* by Lorna Goodison (Longman, 1990), by permission of Pearson Education Ltd;

Nadine Gordimer, for 'The Ultimate Safari' from *Jump and Other Stories* by Nadine Gordimer (Bloomsbury, 1991). Copyright © 1991 by Felix Licensing BV, by permission of A. P. Watt on behalf of Felix Licensing BV, Farrar Straus and Giroux, LLC and Penguin Group (Canada), a division of Pearson Canada Inc.;

Romesh Gunesekera, for 'Storm Petrel' from *Monkfish Moon* by Romesh Gunesekera, *Granta* (1992). Copyright © Romesh Gunesekera 1990, by permission of A. M. Heath & Co. Ltd on behalf of the author;

Bernard Malamud, for 'The Last Mohican' from *The Magic Barrel* by Bernard Malamud (Chatto & Windus, 1958). Copyright © 1950, 1958, renewed 1977, 1986 by Bernard Malamud, by permission of The Random House Group Ltd and Farrar, Straus and Giroux LLC;

Ana Menéndez, for 'In Cuba I was a German Shepherd' from *In Cuba I was a German Shepherd* by Ana Menéndez (Grove Press, 2001). Copyright © 2001 by Ana Menéndez, by permission of Headline Publishing Group Ltd and Grove/Atlantic, Inc.;

Rohinton Mistry, for 'Squatter' from *Tales from Firozsha Baag* by Rohinton Mistry (1992), by permission of Faber and Faber Ltd;

V. S. Naipaul, for 'One out of Many' from *In a Free State* by V. S. Naipaul (Penguin, 1973). Copyright © 1971 V. S. Naipaul, by permission of Aitken Alexander Associates on behalf of the author, Knopf Canada and Alfred A. Knopf, a division of Random House Inc.;

Roxana Robinson, for 'Mr Sumarsono' from *Asking for Love* by Roxana Robinson (Bloomsbury, 1996), by permission of PFD on behalf of the author;

Alan Sillitoe, for 'Pit Strike' from *Men, Women and Children* by Alan Sillitoe (W. H. Allen, 1975). Copyright © Alan Sillitoe 1975, by permission of Sheil Land Associates Ltd on behalf of the author;

Zadie Smith, for 'Martha, Martha', *Granta* 81, by permission of A. P. Watt Ltd on behalf of the author;

Amy Tan, for the extract from *The Joy Luck Club* (Vintage, 1998). Copyright © 1989 by Amy Tan, by permission of Abner Stein Ltd on behalf of the author and G. P. Putnam's Sons, a division of Penguin Group (USA) Inc.;

William Trevor, for 'The Distant Past' from *Collected Stories* by William Trevor (Penguin Books, 1992), by permission of PFD on behalf of the author;

Judy Axenson, for the image of Ana Menéndez on p. 16;

Corbis Images UK Ltd, for images of Raymond Carver on p. 64, Mavis Gallant on p. 122 and Bernard Malamud on p. 94;

Getty Images, for images of Zadie Smith on p. 176 and Amy Tan on p. 38;

Lebrecht Music & Arts, for the image of V. S. Naipaul on p. 258;

Rex Features Ltd, for images of Nadine Gordimer on p. 2, Romesh Gunesekera on p. 220, Rohinton Mistry on p. 230, Alan Sillitoe on p. 196 and William Trevor on p. 134;

Ellen Warner, for the image of Roxana Robinson on p. 76;

Writer Pictures, for the image of Peter Carey on p. 148.

Every effort has been made to trace the copyright holders but if any have been inadvertently overlooked the publishers will be pleased to make the necessary arrangement at the first opportunity.

Preface

A key theme of this anthology, as the title suggests, is difference, and the stories collected here represent many variations on this theme. Certain limits have been set to give the collection coherence: although the stories come from many different parts of the world, they were all written in English, within the last fifty years. And, most importantly, they all have something to say about cultural encounters, often arising from experiences of displacement, migration or uprooting – common enough human experiences throughout history, but increasingly prominent in the world we inhabit now. In tone and mood these fifteen stories are as varied as in their geographical settings, and readers who choose to follow the stories in sequence from the beginning to the end of the collection will find different kinds of responses called forth as they move from story to story. But before we become absorbed in variety, a few generalizations may help to set the stories in context.

To begin with, here are three very broad general points about the short story itself. First, it is worth reminding ourselves that the short story is one of the most popular of all literary forms. With its roots in simpler narratives, stretching back to oral tales and legends, it is a form that most readers are likely to have encountered, often without a consciousness of 'literariness'. It is also extremely popular with writers. All over the world, many writers and aspiring writers find their distinctive voices and hone their literary skills within the confines of the short story. Some of these writers will regard themselves primarily as novelists or poets; perhaps only a few would describe themselves as, first and foremost, short story writers. This suggests a second general point about the short story: that it is not an especially prestigious literary form. Poetry may declare itself as something special because its language and its shapes stand apart from the everyday; drama may claim the status of a public event once it is performed, as well as having a literary existence on the page; the novel and longer prose narratives such as memoirs may fill whole books; but short stories often make their initial appearance in relatively ephemeral media, sitting alongside journalism in magazines or sandwiched between news broadcasts on radio. The short story is thus 'popular' in two different senses, being both familiar and accessible, and also being regarded as somehow inferior. Paradoxically – and this is the third general point about the short story – it is also critically regarded as one of the most exacting of literary forms. Although there is no universal agreement as to the length of a short story, the idea of compactness is implicit in the genre, and this in turn generates a closeness of focus, an intensity, and, in the best short stories, a resonance that will create significance out of small-scale, glancing effects.

The stories in this anthology often demonstrate this resonance in ways that transcend the particularities of their settings. Many of the stories involve characters who have journeyed from their homeland to another place, and consequently we see different worlds colliding, overlapping, or existing alongside each other. But whatever geographical distances these fictional characters travel, far or near, the tightness of the short story's form can throw into sharp focus the effects of psychological or emotional distance. Often the short story strips away the protective membrane that normally insulates our own world from other people's by offering the reader access to an off-centre viewpoint. With just a few characters in the frame, 'outsider' figures have as much prominence as those who might be more firmly rooted in a particular place or society. Historically the short story has built up an association with, instead of 'heroes', members of what the Irish short story writer Frank O'Connor calls 'submerged population groups'.[1] The identity of people in such groups will differ from writer to writer, but often they inhabit the edges of a larger world that the short story only indirectly acknowledges. In this collection a number of the stories are told from the point of view of characters who are outsiders because they have moved from one place to another, or because they have been left behind.

In these stories, then, we become aware of the tides of migration and internal displacement that have become such a common aspect of human experience across the globe, especially during the last half-dozen decades. In some of the stories here, global mobility in the shape of tourism also forms part of the background. Movement and travel have, of course, been perennial elements in human history, and literary expressions of journeying have deep roots in a variety of narrative forms. But writers seeking to give voice to experiences of exile, diaspora and other forms of uprooting do often seem to have found the short story form sympathetic and malleable to their needs. So through the anthology as a whole we may hear more than the individual voices of displaced figures, outsiders or travellers. Sometimes the larger fact of shifting populations is a quiet pulse in the background of a story, sometimes we can hear the political noise of such movements loud and clear in the foreground. At the same time, because all these stories are written in English, we are also aware of the ties and tensions in a common language, and the histories embedded in it.

It might be more accurate, in fact, to speak of different Englishes, since the varieties of English used across the world as well as within the British Isles can be quite distinct from each other. In some of the stories here, traces of other languages are woven into the speech of characters whose very names as well as their vocabularies tell of past and present movements of peoples. At a more local level, different dialects sometimes convey a sense of identity too precise to be contained within the broader definitions of nationality. But whether we think of 'English' as singular or plural, the language is sufficiently protean to offer us a subtle range of linguistic pleasures as we thread our way, via these stories, from one country and one continent to another. The American writer Richard Ford, introducing his *Granta Book of the American Short Story* in 1992, puts his finger on some of the qualities that make 'written in English' a more open category than might at first appear:

English for all its restrictive, complicated, colonial aspects, is a remarkable adaptable and accepting literary language, full of nuance, flexibility, minute coloration as well as the possibility of growth from without.[2]

So although this anthology's 'written in English' criterion excludes the stories of some great and influential practitioners of the genre, such as the Argentinian Jorge Luis Borges or the Egyptian Naguib Mahfouz, it does still permit a very varied international selection.

Having mentioned Ford's collection of American short stories, this seems a good place to acknowledge the prominence of North American writing in the current volume. The short story has always been a popular form in American literature, from the early nineteenth-century tales of Washington Irving, Nathaniel Hawthorne and Edgar Allan Poe onwards, and publication outlets in the USA, particularly in mass-circulation magazines, have provided important (and often profitable) platforms for short story writers. Even if Frank O'Connor was exaggerating slightly when he suggested that the short story is America's 'national art form',[3] the sheer range and quality of American short story writing is undeniable.

There is another reason, though, why this anthology features a significant proportion of stories from North America, and that relates to the theme of 'difference'. The identities of a number of the American writers represented here are often expressed in duple terms: so, we find Bernard Malamud described as Jewish-American, Amy Tan as Chinese-American, Ana Menéndez as Cuban-American. And as a single nation, the USA includes not only multiple nationalities but also vast differences deriving from sheer geographical spread. The small-town perspectives established in the stories by Raymond Carver in the Pacific North-West and Roxana Robinson on the North-Eastern Atlantic coast are metaphorically as well as literally many miles apart, and newcomers step into them as into new worlds. Venturing northwards on the same continent, we find distinguished Canadian writers who also embody in their lives and writings 'worlds of difference': Mavis Gallant, born in French-speaking Quebec, has lived most of her writing life in France, whilst Rohinton Mistry, born in Bombay, is now a naturalized Canadian citizen. Cultural encounters of various kinds are almost in-built features of some of these writers' works.

Of course, as the introductions to each of the individual stories in this collection show, the North American writers do not have a monopoly on plural identities or appreciation of multicultural complexities. Many of the writers represented here have inherited or lived through some kind of 'transplanting', and for this reason each introduction begins with a brief profile of the author, outlining his or her background as well as literary career. Then the chosen story is set within the context of the writer's work, and something of the story's publication history is outlined. In the final part of each introduction the focus narrows to the story itself, with one or two pointers or explanatory notes to prepare the ground for the reading experience to follow.

One of the interesting points that emerges from tracing the publication history of short stories, even partially, is that although initial publication is often in the relatively neutral context of magazines or literary journals, it is usually not long before a strong story gathers another context around itself. Discrete, free-standing stories may be collected by the author into a single volume for book publication, but in a number of cases the stories are part of a larger literary conception with some linking features. In the following introductions to the stories by Menéndez, Tan, Malamud, Mistry and Naipaul we glimpse various ways in which the architecture of linked stories can be built. Reading the individual stories within this larger context does produce slightly different effects, since we are reading, in part, with an eye to the author's overall design. But when the larger, book-length context for a particular story originates not with the author but with an editor or anthologist, other emphases may foreground themselves. The focus might be nationality (no anthology of contemporary Australian writing would seem to be complete without Peter Carey), gender (for example, the stories by Lorna Goodison and Roxana Robinson have reached wide readerships in collections of women's writing), age (Zadie Smith appears in the latest of *Granta's* ten-yearly 'Best of Young British Novelists' lists) or some other grouping-factor. For the present anthology, of course, the major principle of selection is thematic, but, like any other anthologist, having selected the stories, I have then been faced with the question of organization.

A major virtue of anthologies is that they *can* be read selectively – a reader should be able to dip into a volume like this one at just about any point and still have a coherent, pleasurable reading experience. But since the stories must be presented consecutively, and may be read that way, 'difference' again comes into play, this time as an ordering principle. Just as a music album is enriched by variations in mood and tempo from track to track, this particular sequence of stories aims to offer a reading dynamic enriched by shifts in tone, structure, narrative approach, pace and so on, that will work for anyone who approaches the stories in sequence, as well as for the reader who 'dips in' more or less randomly. At the same time, consecutive reading of the stories will, I hope, offer some readerly pleasure by way of the links, thematic and geographical, that loosely hold the sequence together.

We begin, then, in Africa, with Nadine Gordimer's story 'The Ultimate Safari', a vivid and moving evocation of the experience of Mozambican refugees fleeing their war-torn homeland. Our second continent is North America, and forced exile is the link between Gordimer's story and first Ana Menéndez' 'In Cuba I Was a German Shepherd', set in Miami, with traces of Cuba, then Amy Tan's 'The Joy Luck Club', exploring generational differences in the Chinese-American community of northern California. In terms of miles, it is not far from Amy Tan's San Francisco to Raymond Carver country, but to the postman-narrator of the next story, 'What Do You Do in San Francisco?' in-comers from the Californian city might almost belong to a different world, so vast are the gulfs of understanding and communication between them. The visitor in Roxana Robinson's 'Mr Sumarsono' really does come from a different part of the world, Indonesia, but the narrative movement here is towards rather than away from understanding and awareness. In the last of this set of stories from the USA, Bernard Malamud's 'The Last Mohican', the central character, Arthur Fidelman, leaves America for Europe, Italy in this case. A similar journey is undertaken, much less willingly, by Mavis Gallant's protagonist Billy Apostolesco, as he goes from Canada to his dying father's bedside in France in 'The End of the World'. According to Billy, 'One of the advantages of having an Old Country in the family is you can always say the relations that give you trouble have gone there.' But no such escape or excuse is available for the Anglo-Irish brother and sister in William Trevor's 'The Distant Past', so inextricably have their family's fortunes become enmeshed with those of the small southern Irish town near which they live.

After this brief stay in Europe, we move to our fourth continent, Australasia. The pairing of William Trevor's Ireland with Peter Carey's Australia brings different kinds of colonial residues into juxtaposition, but the small-town perspectives of 'The Distant Past' and 'American Dreams' may also remind us of Raymond Carver's and Roxana Robinson's stories, with 'insiders' and 'outsiders' clearly separated. The American dreams of Carey's story are, of course, dreams of prosperity, and these are the dreams that, initially at least, also galvanize the adventurous Jamaican woman in the next story, by Lorna Goodison, 'Bella Makes Life', which takes us back to the Americas. In Goodison's part-epistolary comic tale, we follow the changes that New York brings about in Bella through the eyes of her stay-at-home husband. In Zadie Smith's 'Martha, Martha', it is a stranger, a real estate agent, who provides the reader's perspective on another young black woman – British, this time – who has fetched up, rather mysteriously, in the North-East USA. Then we move back to Britain, and back a generation, for Alan Sillitoe's story of Nottinghamshire miners drawn into picketing duties in the – to them – foreign country south of the River Thames in 'Pit Strike'. Sillitoe's event-packed narrative contrasts sharply with Romesh Gunesekera's brief, conversational story of Sri Lankan exiles in London, but the sunny atmosphere of 'Storm Petrel' is over-shadowed, as the title hints, by violence on a scale undreamt-of at the story's opening. Having approached our fifth continent indirectly with Gunesekera, we settle more firmly in South Asia as Rohinton Mistry's Bombay story-teller, Nariman Hansotia, recounts a story of failed emigration in 'Squatter'. The anthology's last, and longest, story, V. S. Naipaul's 'One out of Many', also begins in Bombay, and Naipaul's Santosh is, like Mistry's Sarosh, something of a dreamer, but the mood of the two stories, sharply distinguished in their narrative techniques, could hardly be more different. Santosh's attempts to adapt to life in Washington, DC, reveal some of the dangers of difference as he becomes a casualty of freedom.

Opening and closing the anthology with stories by Nadine Gordimer and V. S. Naipaul, both of whom have been awarded Nobel Prizes for Literature, establishes certain claims for the significance, as well as the literary value, of the stories collected here. Fittingly, this anthology also features a number of writers whose distinguished reputations rest very largely on their short stories: Mavis Gallant, William Trevor, and the late Raymond Carver. But the vitality of the short story as a genre is, I hope, reinforced by the inclusion of other writers, some of whom are still establishing their reputations and some who are known primarily for their work in other literary forms. It perhaps goes without saying that there are many more writers who could equally well have appeared within these pages, taking forward the theme of 'a world of difference' in their short stories.

In conclusion, though, perhaps it *does* need to be said that other kinds of short stories could have been used to illustrate this theme besides the predominantly realist stories collected here. Although science fiction, or metafiction, or fabulation can tell us a great deal about 'difference', stories that explore cultural encounters using techniques of literary realism allow us to make a relatively direct connection between the world of the story and the world we live in. And one of the virtues of this direct connection is that it also enables us to see the literary short story in relation to stories more generally. The term 'story' has always had a generous range, but recently, sometimes in the guise of 'narrative', it has begun to seep into much academic as well as non-academic discourse. We can now find the concept of narrative, and thus stories, being widely used in social psychology, health studies, cultural anthropology, and a number of other cognate fields. 'Storying', says Susan Lohafer, 'is a way of processing experience in the interests of human well-being.'[4] Literary 'storying' adds another dimension to this process, foregrounding verbal texture and the flow of a story's structure. So whilst the realist narratives of cultural encounters gathered here may claim some kind of kinship with nonfictional stories of the kind that shape our understanding of ourselves and our world, they may also offer us, through their attention to shape, to texture, to rhythm, insights that are richer for being felt through the experience of reading.

Lynda Prescott

Notes

1. F. O'Connor, *The Lonely Voice: A Study of the Short Story* (Hoboken, NJ: Melville House, 2004 [1963]), p. 17.

2. R. Ford, *The Granta Book of the American Short Story* (London: Granta, 1992), p. xv.
3. O'Connor, *The Lonely Voice*, p. 39.
4. S. Lohafer, 'A Cognitive Approach to Storyness', in C. E. May (ed.), *The New Short Story Theories* (Athens, OH: Ohio University Press, 1994), p. 310.

The Ultimate Safari

Nadine Gordimer

Introduction

Nadine Gordimer was born in Springs, a mining town near Johannesburg, South Africa, in 1923. Both her parents were immigrants. Her father, Isidore, had left Latvia, which was then part of Tsarist Russia, when he was thirteen; her mother, Nan Myers, had emigrated as a child from England to South Africa with her parents. Isidore, a watchmaker and jeweller by trade, established a successful business, and Nan was active in the local (white) community. Despite their Jewish parentage, Nadine and her older sister were sent to a nearby convent school run by Dominican nuns. Because of supposedly frail health, Nadine was educated at home for several years, but later attended the University of the Witwatersrand for one year.

Gordimer began writing in childhood, and her first adult fiction, a short story titled 'Come Again Tomorrow', was published in a Johannesburg journal in 1939. By the 1950s she was writing stories for the *New Yorker* and other American magazines as well as publishing novels. So her writing career was already underway when the Afrikaner National Party came to power in South Africa in 1948 and established the policy of racial segregation (*apartheid*) that lasted until the early 1990s, when Nelson Mandela, leader of the African National Congress, was released from prison and subsequently became President of South Africa. Gordimer's fiction engages closely with the politics of her time, dramatizing the tensions between private and public worlds in a prose style that is unsentimental, taut and subtle. Her explorations of liberal white South African experience, in novels such as *The Late Bourgeois World* (1966) and *Burger's Daughter* (1979), are urgent and innovative. Some of her work, including these two novels, was banned for a time in South Africa, and Gordimer has been as consistent an opponent of censorship as she has of *apartheid*.

Apart from a brief period spent in Zambia in the mid-1960s, Gordimer has lived all her life in South Africa, though she has travelled widely and has held visiting lectureships at a number of American universities. Her fiction has been translated into many languages and she has won prizes and awards all over the world, including, in 1991, the Nobel Prize for Literature. She has also published essays, and a work of criticism, *The Black Interpreters* (1973), and made television documentaries. Although her literary reputation rests mainly on her novels, Gordimer's contribution to the short story genre is widely recognized, and she herself has argued that the short story is *the* form for our age, being well suited to representing the fragmentary nature of much contemporary experience.[1]

From her first published short story onwards, Gordimer has been remarkable for her ability to inhabit a viewpoint that may be far from her own perspective. In a recent interview with Hermione Lee, discussing the narrative techniques that allow a writer to depart from the personal, she quoted the novelist and short story writer Graham Greene, who said: 'we see things happen in people's lives or we catch a glimpse and then we see an alternate life for them'. The suggestion is, then, that the writer 'taps into stories which are somehow out there'.[2]

'The Ultimate Safari', told from the perspective of a young black girl, was first published in the British literary quarterly *Granta*, in September 1989. It was subsequently collected in *Jump and Other Stories* (1991), Gordimer's tenth collection of short stories, and she later included it in an international anthology of stories, *Telling Tales*, that she edited in 2004. The profits from this volume were directed to Treatment Action Campaign, a voluntary organization for HIV/AIDS preventive education and medical treatment. The *Telling Tales* stories themselves are not about HIV/AIDS, but Gordimer's portrayal of orphaned Mozambican refugees in 'The Ultimate Safari' conveys a sense of fragility that fits the collection's underlying purpose.

Notes

1. See Nadine Gordimer, 'The International Symposium on the Short Story', *Kenyon Review*, 30 (1968), 457–63.
2. S. Nasta (ed.), *Writing Across Worlds* (London: Routledge, 2004), p. 324, p. 326.

The Ultimate Safari

The African Adventure Lives On . . . You can do it!
The ultimate safari or expedition
With leaders who know *Africa.*

– Travel advertisement,
Observer, London, 27/11/88

That night our mother went to the shop and she didn't come back. Ever. What happened? I don't know. My father also had gone away one day and never come back; but he was fighting in the war. We were in the war, too, but we were children, we were like our grand-mother and grandfather, we didn't have guns. The people my father was fighting – the bandits, they are called by our government – ran all over the place and we ran away from them like chickens chased by dogs. We didn't know where to go. Our mother went to the shop because someone said you could get some oil for cooking. We were happy because we hadn't tasted oil for a long time; perhaps she got the oil and someone knocked her down in the dark and took that oil from her. Perhaps she met the bandits. If you meet them, they will kill you. Twice they came to our village and we ran and hid in the bush and when they'd gone we came back and found they had taken everything; but the third time they came back there was nothing to take, no oil, no food, so they burned the thatch and the roofs of our houses fell in. My mother found some pieces of tin and we put those up over part of the house. We were waiting there for her that night she never came back.

We were frightened to go out, even to do our business, because the bandits did come. Not into our house – without a roof it must have looked as if there was no one in it, everything gone – but all through the village. We heard people screaming and running. We were afraid even to run, without our mother to tell us where. I am the middle one, the girl, and my little brother clung against my stomach with his arms round my neck and his legs round my waist like a baby monkey to its mother. All night my first-born brother kept in his hand a broken piece of wood from one of our burnt house-poles. It was to save himself if the bandits found him.

We stayed there all day. Waiting for her. I don't know what day it was; there was no school, no church any more in our village, so you didn't know whether it was a Sunday or a Monday.

When the sun was going down, our grandmother and grandfather came. Someone from our village had told them we children were alone, our mother had not come back. I say 'grandmother' before 'grandfather' because it's like that: our grandmother is big and strong, not yet old, and our grandfather is small, you don't know where he is, in his loose trousers, he smiles but he hasn't heard what you're saying, and his hair looks as if he's left it full of soap suds. Our grandmother took us – me, the baby, my first-born brother, our grandfather – back to her house and we were all afraid (except the baby, asleep on our grandmother's back) of meeting the bandits on the way. We waited a long time at our grandmother's place. Perhaps it was a month. We were hungry. Our mother never came. While we were waiting for her to fetch us our grandmother had no food for us, no food for our grandfather and herself. A woman with milk in her breasts gave us some for my little brother, although at our house he used to eat porridge, same as we did. Our grandmother took us to look for wild spinach but everyone else in her village did the same and there wasn't a leaf left.

Our grandfather, walking a little behind some young men, went to look for our mother but didn't find her. Our grandmother cried with other women and I sang the hymns with them. They brought a little food – some beans – but after two days there was nothing again. Our grandfather used to have three sheep and a cow and a vegetable garden but the bandits had long ago taken the sheep and the cow, because they were hungry, too; and when planting time came our grandfather had no seed to plant.

So they decided – our grandmother did; our grandfather made little noises and rocked from side to side, but she took no notice – we would go away. We children were pleased. We wanted to go away from where our mother wasn't and where we were hungry. We wanted to go where there were no bandits and there was food. We were glad to think there must be such a place; away.

Our grandmother gave her church clothes to someone in exchange for some dried mealies and she boiled them and tied them in a rag. We took them with us when we went and she thought we would get water from the rivers but we didn't come to any river and we got so thirsty we had to turn back. Not all the way to our grandparents' place but to a village where there was a pump. She opened the basket where she carried some clothes and the mealies and she sold her shoes to buy a big plastic container for water. I said, *Gogo*, how will you go to church now even without shoes, but she said we had a long journey and too much to carry. At that village we met other people who were also going away. We joined them because they seemed to know where that was better than we did.

To get there we had to go through the Kruger Park. We knew about the Kruger Park. A kind of whole country of animals – elephants, lions, jackals, hyenas, hippos, crocodiles, all kinds of animals. We had some of them in our own country, before the war (our grandfather remembers; we children weren't born yet) but the bandits kill the elephants and sell their tusks, and the bandits and our soldiers have eaten all the buck. There was a man in our village without legs – a crocodile took them off, in our river; but all the same our country is a country of people, not animals. We knew about the Kruger Park because some of our men used to leave home to work there in the places where white people come to stay and look at the animals.

So we started to go away again. There were women and other children like me who had to carry the small ones on their backs when the women got tired. A man led us into the Kruger Park; are we there yet, are we there yet, I kept asking our grandmother. Not yet, the man said, when she asked him for me. He told us we had to take a long way to get round the fence, which he explained would kill you, roast off your skin the moment you touched it, like the wires high up on poles that give electric light in our towns. I've seen that sign of a head without eyes or skin or hair on an iron box at the mission hospital we used to have before it was blown up.

When I asked the next time, they said we'd been walking in the Kruger Park for an hour. But it looked just like the bush we'd been walking through all day, and we hadn't seen any animals except the monkeys and birds which live around us at home, and a tortoise that, of course, couldn't get away from us. My first-born brother and the other boys brought it to the man so it could be killed and we could cook and eat it. He let it go because he told us we could not make a fire; all the time we were in the Park we must not make a fire because the smoke would show we were there. Police, wardens, would come and send us back where we came from. He said we must move like animals among the animals, away from the roads, away from the white people's camps. And at that moment I heard – I'm sure I was the first to hear – cracking branches and the sound of something parting grasses and I almost squealed because I thought it was the police, wardens – the people he was telling us to look out for – who had found us already. And it was an elephant, and another elephant, and more elephants, big blots of dark moved wherever you looked between the trees. They were curling their trunks round the red leaves of the Mopane trees and stuffing them into their mouths. The babies leant against their mothers. The almost grown-up ones wrestled like my first-born brother with his friends – only they used trunks instead of arms. I was so interested I forgot to be afraid. The man said we should just stand still and be quiet while the elephants passed. They passed very slowly because elephants are too big to need to run from anyone.

The buck ran from us. They jumped so high they seemed to fly. The warthogs stopped dead, when they heard us, and swerved off the way a boy in our village used to zigzag on the bicycle his father had brought back from the mines. We followed the animals to where they drank. When they had gone, we went to their water-holes. We were never thirsty without finding water, but the animals ate, ate all the time. Whenever you saw them they were eating, grass, trees, roots. And there was nothing for us. The mealies were finished. The only food we could eat was what the baboons ate, dry little figs full of ants that grow along the branches of the trees at the rivers. It was hard to be like the animals.

When it was very hot during the day we would find lions lying asleep. They were the colour of the grass and we didn't see them at first but the man did, and he led us back and a long way round where they slept. I wanted to lie down like the lions. My little brother was getting thin but he was very heavy. When our grandmother looked for me, to put him on my back, I tried not to see. My first-born brother stopped talking; and when we rested he had to be shaken to get up again, as if he was just like our grandfather, he couldn't hear. I saw flies crawling on our grandmother's face and she didn't brush them off; I was frightened. I picked a palm leaf and chased them.

We walked at night as well as by day. We could see the fires where the white people were cooking in the camps and we could smell the smoke and the meat. We watched the hyenas with their backs that slope as if they're ashamed, slipping through the bush after the smell. If one turned its head, you saw it had big brown shining eyes like our own, when we looked at each other in the dark. The wind brought voices in our own language from the compounds where the people who work in the camps live. A woman among us wanted to go to them at night and ask them to help us. They can give us the food from the dustbins, she said, she started wailing and our grandmother had to grab her and put a hand over her mouth. The man who led us had told us that we must keep out of the way of our people who worked at the Kruger Park; if they helped us they would lose their work. If they saw us, all they could do was pretend we were not there; they had seen only animals.

Sometimes we stopped to sleep for a little while at night. We slept close together. I don't know which night it was – because we were walking, walking, any time, all the time – we heard the lions very near. Not groaning loudly the way they did far off. Panting, like we do when we run, but it's a different kind of panting: you can hear they're not running, they're waiting, somewhere near. We all rolled closer together, on top of each other, the ones on the edge fighting to get into the middle. I was squashed against a woman who smelled bad because she was afraid but I was glad to hold tight on to her. I prayed to God to make the lions take someone on the edge and go. I shut my eyes not to see the tree from which a lion might jump right into the middle of us, where I was. The man who led us jumped up instead, and beat on the tree with a dead branch. He had taught us never to make a sound but he shouted. He shouted at the lions like a drunk man shouting at nobody, in our village. The lions went away. We heard them groaning, shouting back at him from far off.

We were tired, so tired. My first-born brother and the man had to lift our grandfather from stone to stone where we found places to cross the rivers. Our grandmother is strong but her feet were bleeding. We could not carry the basket on our heads any longer, we couldn't carry anything except my little brother. We left our things under a bush. As long as our bodies get there, our grandmother said. Then we ate some wild fruit we didn't know from home and our stomachs ran. We were in the grass called elephant grass because it is nearly as tall as an elephant, that day we had those pains, and our grandfather couldn't just get down in front of people like my little brother, he went off into the grass to be on his own. We had to keep up, the man who led us always kept telling us, we must catch up, but we asked him to wait for our grandfather.

So everyone waited for our grandfather to catch up. But he didn't. It was the middle of the day; insects were singing in our ears and we couldn't hear him moving through the grass. We couldn't see him because the grass was so high and he was so small. But he must have been somewhere there inside his loose trousers and his shirt that was torn and our grandmother couldn't sew because she had no cotton. We knew he couldn't have gone far because he was weak and slow. We all went to look for him, but in groups, so we too wouldn't be hidden from each other in that grass. It got into our eyes and noses; we called him softly but the noise of the insects must have filled the little space left for hearing in his ears. We looked and looked but we couldn't find him. We stayed in that long grass all night. In my sleep I found him curled round in a place he had tramped down for himself, like the places we'd seen where the buck hide their babies.

When I woke up he still wasn't anywhere. So we looked again, and by now there were paths we'd made by going through the grass many times, it would be easy for him to find us if we couldn't find him. All that day we just sat and waited. Everything is very quiet when the sun is on your head, inside your head, even if you lie, like the animals, under the trees. I lay on my back and saw those ugly birds with hooked beaks and plucked necks flying round and round above us. We had passed them often where they were feeding on the bones of dead animals, nothing was ever left there for us to eat. Round and round, high up and then lower down and then high again. I saw their necks poking to this side and that. Flying round and round. I saw our grandmother, who sat up all the time with my little brother on her lap, was seeing them, too.

In the afternoon the man who led us came to our grandmother and told her the other people must move on. He said, If their children don't eat soon they will die.

Our grandmother said nothing.

I'll bring you water before we go, he told her.

Our grandmother looked at us, me, my first-born brother, and my little brother on her lap. We watched the other people getting up to leave. I didn't believe the grass would be empty, all around us, where they had been. That we would be alone in this place, the Kruger Park, the police or the animals would find us. Tears came out of my eyes and nose onto my hands but our grandmother took no notice. She got up, with her feet apart the way she puts them when she is going to lift firewood, at home in our village, she swung my little brother onto her back, tied him in her cloth – the top of her dress was torn and her big breasts were showing but there was nothing in them for him. She said, Come.

So we left the place with the long grass. Left behind. We went with the others and the man who led us. We started to go away, again.

There's a very big tent, bigger than a church or a school, tied down to the ground. I didn't understand that was what it would be, when we got there, away. I saw a thing like that the time our mother took us to the town because she heard our soldiers were there and she wanted to ask them if they knew where our father was. In that tent, people were praying and singing. This one is blue and white like that one but it's not for praying and singing, we live in it with other people who've come from our country. Sister from the clinic says we're two hundred without counting the babies, and we have new babies, some were born on the way through the Kruger Park.

Inside, even when the sun is bright it's dark and there's a kind of whole village in there. Instead of houses each family has a little place closed off with sacks or cardboard from boxes – whatever we can find – to show the other families it's yours and they shouldn't come in even though there's no door and no windows and no thatch, so that if you're standing up and you're not a small child you can see into everybody's house. Some people have even made paint from ground rocks and drawn designs on the sacks.

Of course, there really is a roof – the tent is the roof, far, high up. It's like a sky. It's like a mountain and we're inside it; through the cracks paths of dust lead down, so thick you think you could climb them. The tent keeps off the rain overhead but the water comes in at the sides and in the little streets between our places – you can only move along them one person at a time – the small kids like my little brother play in the mud. You have to step over them. My little brother doesn't play. Our grandmother takes him to the clinic when the doctor comes on Mondays. Sister says there's something wrong with his head, she thinks it's because we didn't have enough food at home. Because of the war. Because our father wasn't there. And then because he was so hungry in the Kruger Park. He likes just to lie about on our grandmother all day, òn her lap or against her somewhere, and he looks at us and looks at us. He wants to ask something but you can see he can't. If I tickle him he may just smile. The clinic gives us special powder to make into porridge for him and perhaps one day he'll be all right.

When we arrived we were like him – my first-born brother and I. I can hardly remember. The people who live in the village near the tent took us to the clinic, it's where you have to sign that you've come – away, through the Kruger Park. We sat on the grass and everything was muddled. One Sister was pretty with her hair straightened and beautiful high-heeled shoes and she brought us the special powder. She said we must mix it with water and drink it slowly. We tore the packets open with our teeth and licked it all up, it stuck round my mouth and I sucked it from my lips and fingers. Some other children who had walked with us vomited. But I only felt everything in my belly moving, the stuff going down and around like a snake, and hiccups hurt me. Another Sister called us to stand in line on the verandah of the clinic but we couldn't. We sat all over the place there, falling against each other; the Sisters helped each of us up by the arm and then stuck a needle in it. Other needles drew our blood into tiny bottles. This was against sickness, but I didn't understand, every time my eyes dropped closed I thought I was walking, the grass was long, I saw the elephants, I didn't know we were away.

But our grandmother was still strong, she could still stand up, she knows how to write and she signed for us. Our grandmother got us this place in the tent against one of the sides, it's the best kind of place there because although the rain comes in, we can lift the flap when the weather is good and then the sun shines on us, the smells in the tent go out. Our grandmother knows a woman here who showed her where there is good grass for sleeping mats, and our grandmother made some for us. Once every month the food truck comes to the clinic. Our grandmother takes along one of the cards she signed and when it has been punched we get a sack of mealie meal. There are wheelbarrows to take it back to the tent; my first-born brother does this for her and then he and the other boys have races, steering the empty wheelbarrows back to the clinic. Sometimes he's lucky and a man who's bought beer in the village gives him money to deliver it – though that's not allowed, you're supposed to take that wheelbarrow straight back to the Sisters. He buys a cold drink and shares it with me if I catch him. On another day, every month, the church leaves a pile of old clothes in the clinic yard. Our grandmother has another card to get punched, and then we can choose something: I have two dresses, two pants and a jersey, so I can go to school.

The people in the village have let us join their school. I was surprised to find they speak our language; our grandmother told me, That's why they allow us to stay on their land. Long ago, in the time of our fathers, there was no fence that kills you, there was no Kruger Park between them and us, we were the same people under our own king, right from our village we left to this place we've come to.

Now that we've been in the tent so long – I have turned eleven and my little brother is nearly three although he is so small, only his head is big, he's not come right in it yet – some people have dug up the bare ground around the tent and planted beans and mealies and cabbage. The old men weave branches to put up fences round their gardens. No one is allowed to look for work in the towns but some of the women have found work in the village and can buy things. Our grandmother, because she's still strong, finds work where people are building houses – in this village the people build nice houses with bricks and cement, not mud like we used to have at our home. Our grandmother carries bricks for these people and fetches baskets of stones on her head. And so she has money to buy sugar and tea and milk and soap. The store gave her a calendar she has hung up on our flap of the tent. I am clever at school and she collected advertising paper people throw away outside the store and covered my school-books with it. She makes my first-born brother and me do our homework every afternoon before it gets dark because there is no room except to lie down, close together, just as we did in the Kruger Park, in our place in the tent, and candles are expensive. Our grandmother hasn't been able to buy herself a pair of shoes for church yet, but she has bought black school shoes and polish to clean them with for my first-born brother and me. Every morning, when people are getting up in the tent, the babies are crying, people are pushing each other at the taps outside and some children are already pulling the crusts of porridge off the pots we ate from last night, my first-born brother and I clean our shoes. Our grandmother makes us sit on our mats with our legs straight out so she can look carefully at our shoes to make sure we have done it properly. No other children in the tent have real school shoes. When we three look at them it's as if we are in a real house again, with no war, no away.

Some white people came to take photographs of our people living in the tent – they said they were making a film, I've never seen what that is though I know about it. A white woman squeezed into our space and asked our grandmother questions which were told to us in our language by someone who understands the white woman's.

How long have you been living like this?

She means here? our grandmother said. In this tent, two years and one month.

And what do you hope for the future?

Nothing, I'm here.

But for your children?

I want them to learn so that they can get good jobs and money.

Do you hope to go back to Mozambique – to your own country?

I will not go back.

But when the war is over – you won't be allowed to stay here? Don't you want to go home?

I didn't think our grandmother wanted to speak again. I didn't think she was going to answer the white woman. The white woman put her head on one side and smiled at us.

Our grandmother looked away from her and spoke – There is nothing. No home.

Why does our grandmother say that? Why? I'll go back. I'll go back through that Kruger Park. After the war, if there are no bandits any more, our mother may be waiting for us. And maybe when we left our grandfather, he was only left behind, he found his way somehow, slowly, through the Kruger Park, and he'll be there. They'll be home, and I'll remember them.

In Cuba I Was a German Shepherd

Ana Menéndez

Introduction

Ana Menéndez was born in Los Angeles, California, in 1970. Her Cuban parents (her mother was of Spanish and Lebanese background) fled from Castro's Cuba in the 1960s, finding refuge first in Los Angeles and then later in Florida. Ana and her sister Rose were brought up in the expectation that the family would be returning to Cuba as soon as possible, and spoke only Spanish until they went to school.

Menéndez grew up learning and loving poetry. Her uncle, the award-winning Cuban-American poet Dionisio D. Martinez, introduced her to the work of both American and Cuban poets, and the writing of the nineteenth-century Cuban patriot José Martí was an especially strong influence during her childhood. She began writing herself at an early age, and after taking her bachelor's degree at Florida International University she became a journalist, first at the *Miami Herald* and then in California, at the *Orange County Register*. After six years of journalism, she decided to take a creative writing course at New York University, winning a *New York Times* fellowship. In 1997 she visited Cuba for the first time, and during the late 1990s she also spent periods of time in India, where her husband worked as foreign correspondent for the *Los Angeles Times*. She herself reported from Afghanistan and Kashmir, and now lives partly in Turkey, where her husband is based, and partly in Miami.

Since her move into fiction-writing, Menéndez has taught at various universities, and has been a visiting writer at the University of Texas. Her debut collection of short stories, *In Cuba I Was a German Shepherd* (2001), was an immediate success, and she followed it up in 2003 with a novel, *Loving Che*, which again draws on recent Cuban history and themes. Menéndez's work to date seems to align itself with a tradition of Cuban literature described by recent anthologists as 'one of exile and displacement'.[1]

The germ of the story 'In Cuba I Was a German Shepherd' came from an interview Menéndez conducted with a Cuban-born sculptor when she was a reporter for the *Miami Herald* in the early 1990s. The story itself was published in Francis Ford Coppola's short story magazine *Zoetrope: All-Story*, in 1999, and was awarded a prestigious Pushcart Prize. In addition to appearing in the Pushcart Anthology, the story featured in *Best New American Voices, 2000*. As the title-story of Menéndez's 2001 collection, it is followed by ten more linked tales set in Miami and Havana and focused on the exiled Cuban community.

In the story's present-day, the late 1990s, Bill Clinton was in his second term as President of the USA, and the seemingly indestructible Fidel Castro was nearing the end of his fourth decade as Prime Minister and subsequently President of Cuba. When Castro's rebel forces had ousted the former President, Fulgencia Batista, in 1959, one turbulent period in Cuba's history gave way to even more dramatic upheavals. By 1961, when Castro announced that Cuba had become a communist state, with rapid centralization of the economy on Marxist–Leninist principles, many of the island's citizens, especially middle-class people like the story's Máximo and Raúl, fled to the USA, which had by then broken off all relations with Cuba. The influx to Florida (natural refuge of Cuban exiles right back to the early years of the nineteenth century) continued steadily in the years that followed, with some desperate Cubans even making the hazardous voyage across the Gulf of Mexico to the American coast in small boats or even on rafts. Miami, already a city of immigrants, with numerous Spanish-speakers from Mexico and South America, was an obvious destination for Cuba's city-folk, and the area around Eighth Street where the Cuban exiles tended to settle became known as 'Little Havana'.

Note

1. C. Hospital and J. Cantera (eds), *A Century of Cuban Writers in Florida* (Sarasota, FA: Pineapple Press, 1996), p. 26.

In Cuba I Was a German Shepherd

The park where the four men gathered was small. Before the city put it on its tourist maps, it was just a fenced rectangle of space that people missed on the way to their office jobs. The men came each morning to sit under the shifting shade of a banyan tree, and sometimes the way the wind moved through the leaves reminded them of home.

One man carried a box of plastic dominos. His name was Máximo, and because he was a small man his grandiose name had inspired much amusement all his life. He liked to say that over the years he'd learned a thing or two about the meaning of laughter and his friends took that to mean good humor could make a big man out of anyone. Now, Máximo waited for the others to sit before turning the dominos out on the table. Judging the men to be in good spirits, he cleared his throat and began to tell the joke he had prepared for the day.

"So Bill Clinton dies in office and they freeze his body."

Antonio leaned back in his chair and let out a sigh. "Here we go."

Máximo caught a roll of the eyes and almost grew annoyed. But he smiled. "It gets better."

He scraped the dominos in two wide circles across the table, then continued.

"Okay, so they freeze his body and when we get the technology to unfreeze him, he wakes up in the year 2105."

"Two thousand one hundred and five, eh?"

"Very good," Máximo said. "Anyway, he's curious about what's happened to the world all this time, so he goes up to a Jewish fellow and he says, 'So, how are things in the Middle East?' The guy replies, 'Oh wonderful, wonderful, everything is like heaven. Everybody gets along now.' This makes Clinton smile, right?"

The men stopped shuffling and dragged their pieces across the table and waited for Máximo to finish.

"Next he goes up to an Irishman and he says, 'So how are things over there in Northern Ireland now?' The guy says, 'Northern? It's one Ireland now and we all live in peace.' Clinton is extremely pleased at this point, right? So he does that biting thing with his lip."

Máximo stopped to demonstrate and Raúl and Carlos slapped their hands on the domino table and laughed. Máximo paused. Even Antonio had to smile. Máximo loved this moment when the men were warming to the joke and he still kept the punch line close to himself like a secret.

"So, okay," Máximo continued, "Clinton goes up to a Cuban fellow and says, 'Compadre, how are things in Cuba these days?' The guy looks at Clinton and he says to the president, 'Let me tell you, my friend, I can feel it in my bones. Any day now Castro's gonna fall.' "

Máximo tucked his head into his neck and smiled. Carlos slapped him on the back and laughed.

"That's a good one, sure is," he said. "I like that one."

"Funny," Antonio said, nodding as he set up his pieces.

"Yes, funny," Raúl said. After chuckling for another moment, he added, "But old."

"What do you mean old?" Antonio said, then he turned to Carlos. "What are you looking at?"

Carlos stopped laughing.

"It's not old," Máximo said. "I just made it up."

"I'm telling you, professor, it's an old one," Raúl said. "I heard it when Reagan was president."

Máximo looked at Raúl, but didn't say anything. He pulled the double nine from his row and laid it in the middle of the table, but the thud he intended was lost in the horns and curses of morning traffic on Eighth Street.

*   *   *

Raúl and Máximo had lived on the same El Vedado street in Havana for fifteen years before the revolution. Raúl had been a government accountant and Máximo a professor at the University, two blocks from his home on L Street. They weren't close friends, but friendly still in that way of people who come from the same place and think they already know the important things about one another.

Máximo was one of the first to leave L Street, boarding a plane for Miami on the eve of the first of January 1961, exactly two years after Batista had done the same. For reasons he told himself he could no longer remember, he said good-bye to no one. He was thirty-six years old then, already balding, with a wife and two young daughters whose names he tended to confuse. He left behind the row house of long shiny windows, the piano, the mahogany furniture, and the pension he thought he'd return to in two years' time. Three if things were as serious as they said.

In Miami, Máximo tried driving a taxi, but the streets were a web of foreign names and winding curves that could one day lead to glitter and another to the hollow end of a pistol. His Spanish and his University of Havana credentials meant nothing here. And he was too old to cut sugarcane with the younger men who began arriving in the spring of 1961. But the men gave Máximo an idea and after teary nights of promises, he convinced his wife – she of stately homes and multiple cooks – to make lunch to sell to those sugar men who waited, squatting on their heels in the dark, for the bus to Belle Glade every morning. They worked side by side, Máximo and Rosa. And at the end of every day, their hands stained orange from the lard and the cheap meat, their knuckles red and tender where the hot water and the knife blade had worked their business, Máximo and Rosa would sit down to whatever remained of the day's cooking and they would chew slowly, the day unraveling, their hunger ebbing away with the light.

They worked together for seven years like that, and when the Cubans began disappearing from the bus line, Máximo and Rosa moved their lunch packets indoors and opened their little restaurant right on Eighth Street. There, a generation of former professors served black beans and rice to the nostalgic. When Raúl showed up in Miami in the summer of 1971 looking for work, Máximo added one more waiter's spot for his old acquaintance from L Street. Each night, after the customers had gone, Máximo and Rosa and Raúl and Havana's old lawyers and bankers and dreamers would sit around the biggest table and eat and talk and sometimes, late in the night after several glasses of wine, someone would start the stories that began with "In Cuba I remember." They were stories of old lovers, beautiful and round-hipped. Of skies that stretched on clear and blue to the Cuban hills. Of green landscapes that clung to the red clay of Güines, roots dug in like fingernails in a good-bye. In Cuba, the stories always began, life was good and pure. But something always happened to them in the end, something withering, malignant. Máximo never understood it. The stories that opened in sun, always narrowed into a dark place. And after those nights, his head throbbing, Máximo would turn and turn in his sleep and awake unable to remember his dreams.

Even now, five years after selling the place, Máximo couldn't walk by it in the early morning when it was still clean and empty. He'd tried it once. He'd stood and stared into the restaurant and had become lost and dizzy in his own reflection in the glass, the near row of chairs, the tombstone lunch board behind them.

* * *

"Okay. A bunch of rafters are on the beach getting ready to sail off to Miami."

"Where are they?"

"Who cares? Wherever. Cuba's got a thousand miles of coastline. Use your imagination."

"Let the professor tell his thing, for God's sake."

"Thank you." Máximo cleared his throat and shuffled the dominos. "So anyway, a bunch of rafters are gathered there on the sand. And they're all crying and hugging their wives and all the rafts are bobbing on the water and suddenly someone in the group yells, 'Hey! Look who goes there!' And it's Fidel in swimming trunks, carrying a raft on his back."

Carlos interrupted to let out a yelping laugh. "I like that, I like it, sure do."

"You like it, eh?" said Antonio. "Why don't you let the Cuban finish it."

Máximo slid the pieces to himself in twos and continued. "So one of the guys on the sand says to Fidel, 'Compatriota, what are you doing here? What's with the raft?' And Fidel sits on his raft and pushes off the shore and says, 'I'm sick of this place too. I'm going to Miami.' So the other guys look at each other and say, 'Coño, compadre, if you're leaving, then there's no reason for us to go. Here, take my raft too, and get the fuck out of here.'"

Raúl let a shaking laugh rise from his belly and saluted Máximo with a domino piece.

"A good one, my friend."

Carlos laughed long and loud. Antonio laughed too, but he was careful to not laugh too hard and he gave his friend a sharp look over the racket he was causing. He and Carlos were Dominican, not Cuban, and they ate their same foods and played their same games, but Antonio knew they still didn't understand all the layers of hurt in the Cubans' jokes.

*   *   *

It had been Raúl's idea to go down to Domino Park that first time. Máximo protested. He had seen the rows of tourists pressed up against the fence, gawking at the colorful old guys playing dominos.

"I'm not going to be the sad spectacle in someone's vacation slide show," he'd said.

But Raúl was already dressed up in a pale blue guayabera, saying how it was a beautiful day and smell the air.

"Let them take pictures," Raúl said. "What the hell. Make us immortal."

"Immortal," Máximo said like a sneer. And then to himself, The gods' punishment.

It was that year after Rosa died and Máximo didn't want to tell how he'd begun to see her at the kitchen table as she'd been at twenty-five. Watched one thick strand of her dark hair stuck to her morning face. He saw her at thirty, bending down to wipe the chocolate off the cheeks of their two small daughters. And his eyes moved from Rosa to his small daughters. He had something he needed to tell them. He saw them grown up, at the funeral, crying together. He watched Rosa rise and do the sign of the cross. He knew he was caught inside a nightmare, but he couldn't stop. He would emerge slowly, creaking out of the shower and there she'd be, Rosa, like before, her breasts round and pink from the hot water, calling back through the years. Some mornings he would awake and smell peanuts roasting and hear the faint call of the manicero pleading for someone to relieve his burden of white paper cones. Or it would be thundering, the long hard thunder of Miami that was so much like the thunder of home that each rumble shattered the morning of his other life. He would awake, caught fast in the damp sheets, and feel himself falling backwards.

He took the number eight bus to Eighth Street and 15th Avenue. At Domino Park, he sat with Raúl and they played alone that first day, Máximo noticing his own speckled hands, the spots of light through the banyan leaves, a round red beetle that crawled slowly across the table, then hopped the next breeze and floated away.

*   *   *

Antonio and Carlos were not Cuban, but they knew when to dump their heavy pieces and when to hold back the eights for the final shocking stroke. Waiting for a table, Raúl and Máximo would linger beside them and watch them lay their traps, a succession of threes that broke their opponents, an incredible run of fives. Even the unthinkable: passing when they had the piece to play.

Other twosomes began to refuse to play with the Dominicans, said that tipo Carlos gave them the creeps with his giggling and mono-syllables. Besides, any team that won so often must be cheating, went the charge, especially a team one-half imbecile. But really it was that no one plays to lose. You begin to lose again and again and it reminds you of other things in your life, the despair of it all begins to bleed through and that is not what games are for. Who wants to live their whole life alongside the lucky? But Máximo and Raúl liked these blessed Dominicans, appreciated the well-oiled moves of two old pros. And if the two Dominicans, afraid to be alone again, let them win now and then, who would know, who could ever admit to such a thing?

For many months they didn't know much about each other, these four men. Even the smallest boy knew not to talk when the pieces were in play. But soon came Máximo's jokes during the shuffling, something new and bright coming into his eyes like daydreams as he spoke. Carlos's full loud laughter, like that of children. And the four men learned to linger long enough between sets to color an old memory while the white pieces scraped along the table.

One day as they sat at their table closest to the sidewalk, a pretty girl walked by. She swung her long brown hair around and looked in at the men with her green eyes.

"What the hell is she looking at," said Antonio, who always sat with his back to the wall, looking out at the street. But the others saw how he resumed the stare too.

Carlos let out a giggle and immediately put a hand to his mouth.

"In Santo Domingo, a man once looked at –" But Carlos didn't get to finish.

"Shut up, you old idiot," said Antonio, putting his hands on the table like he was about to get up and leave.

"Please," Máximo said.

The girl stared another moment, then turned and left. Raúl rose slowly, flattening down his oiled hair with his right hand.

"Ay, mi niña."

"Sit down, hombre," Antonio said. "You're an old fool, just like this one."

"You're the fool," Raúl called back. "A woman like that . . . " He watched the girl cross the street. When she was out of sight, he grabbed the back of the chair behind him and eased his body down, his eyes still on the street. The other three men looked at one another.

"I knew a woman like that once," Raúl said after a long moment.

"That's right, he did," Antonio said, "in his moist boy dreams – what was it? A century ago?"

"No me jodas," Raúl said. "You are a vulgar man. I had a life all three of you would have paid millions for. Women."

Máximo watched him, then lowered his face, shuffled the dominos.

"I had women," Raúl said.

"We all had women," Carlos said, and he looked like he was about to laugh again, but instead just sat there, smiling like he was remembering one of Máximo's jokes.

"There was one I remember. More beautiful than the rising moon," Raúl said.

"Oh Jesus," Antonio said. "You people."

Máximo looked up, watching Raúl.

"Ay, a woman like that," Raúl said and shook his head. "The women of Cuba were radiant, magnificent, wouldn't you say, professor?"

Máximo looked away.

"I don't know," Antonio said. "I think that Americana there looked better than anything you remember."

And that brought a long laugh from Carlos.

Máximo sat all night at the pine table in his new efficiency, thinking about the green-eyed girl and wondering why he was thinking about her. The table and a narrow bed had come with the apartment, which he'd moved into after selling their house in Shenandoah. The table had come with two chairs, sturdy and polished – not in the least institutional – but he had moved the other chair by the bed.

The landlady, a woman in her forties, had helped Máximo haul up three potted palms. Later, he bought a green pot of marigolds he saw in the supermarket and brought its butter leaves back to life under the window's eastern light. Máximo often sat at the table through the night, sometimes reading Martí, sometimes listening to the rain on the tin hull of the air conditioner.

When you are older, he'd read somewhere, you don't need as much sleep. And wasn't that funny because his days felt more like sleep than ever. Dinner kept him occupied for hours, remembering the story of each dish. Sometimes, at the table, he greeted old friends and awakened with a start when they reached out to touch him. When dawn rose and slunk into the room sideways through the blinds, Máximo walked as in a dream across the thin patterns of light on the terrazzo. The chair, why did he keep the other chair? Even the marigolds reminded him. An image returned again and again. Was it the green-eyed girl?

And then he remembered that Rosa wore carnations in her hair and hated her name. And that it saddened him because he liked to roll it off his tongue like a slow train to the country.

"Rosa," he said, taking her hand the night they met at La Concha while an old danzón played.

"Clavel," she said, tossing her head back in a crackling laugh. "Call me clavel."

She pulled her hand away and laughed again. "Don't you notice the flower in a girl's hair?"

He led her around the dance floor, lined with chaperones, and when they turned he whispered that he wanted to follow her laughter to the moon. She laughed again, the notes round and heavy as summer raindrops, and Máximo felt his fingers go cold where they touched hers. The danzón played and they turned and turned and the faces of the chaperones and the moist warm air – and Máximo with his cold fingers worried that she had laughed at him. He was twenty-four and could not imagine a more sorrowful thing in all the world.

Sometimes, years later, he would catch a premonition of Rosa in the face of his eldest daughter. She would turn toward a window or do something with her eyes. And then she would smile and tilt her head back and her laughter connected him again to that night, made him believe for a moment that life was a string you could gather up in your hands all at once.

He sat at the table and tried to remember the last time he saw Marisa. In California now. An important lawyer. A year? Two? Anabel, gone to New York? Two years? They called more often than most children, Máximo knew. They called often and he was lucky that way.

*   *   *

"Fidel decides he needs to get in touch with young people."

"Ay, ay, ay."

"So his handlers arrange for him to go to a school in Havana. He gets all dressed up in his olive uniform, you know, puts conditioner on his beard and brushes it one hundred times, all that."

Raúl breathed out, letting each breath come out like a puff of laughter. "Where do you get these things?"

"No interrupting the artist anymore, okay?" Máximo continued. "So after he's beautiful enough, he goes to the school. He sits in on a few classes, walks around the halls. Finally, it's time for Fidel to leave and he realizes he hasn't talked to anyone. He rushes over to the assembly that is seeing him off with shouts of 'Comandante!' and he pulls a little boy out of a row. 'Tell me,' Fidel says, 'what is your name?' 'Pepito,' the little boy answers. 'Pepito – what a nice name,' Fidel says. 'And tell me, Pepito, what do you think of the revolution?' 'Comandante,' Pepito says, 'the revolution is the reason we are all here.' 'Ah, very good, Pepito. And tell me, what is your favorite subject?' Pepito answers, 'Comandante, my favorite subject is mathematics.' Fidel parts the little boy on the head. 'And tell me, Pepito, what would you like to be when you grow up?' Pepito smiles and says, 'Comandante, I would like to be a tourist.' "

Máximo looked around the table, a shadow of a smile on his thin white lips as he waited for the laughter.

"Ay," Raúl said. "That is so funny it breaks my heart."

* * *

Máximo grew to like dominos, the way each piece became part of the next. After the last piece was laid down and they were tallying up the score, Máximo liked to look over the table as an artist might. He liked the way the row of black dots snaked around the table with such free-flowing abandon it was almost as if, thrilled to be let out of the box, the pieces choreographed a fresh dance of gratitude every night. He liked the straightforward contrast of black on white. The clean, fresh scrape of the pieces across the table before each new round. The audacity of the double nines. The plain smooth face of the blank, like a newborn unetched by the world to come.

"Professor," Raúl began. "Let's speed up the shuffling a bit, sí?"

"I was thinking," Máximo said.

"Well, that shouldn't take long," Antonio said.

"Who invented dominos, anyway?" Máximo said.

"I'd say it was probably the Chinese," Antonio said.

"No jodas," Raúl said. "Who else could have invented this game of skill and intelligence but a Cuban?"

"Coño," said Antonio without a smile. "Here we go again."

"Ah, bueno," Raúl said with a smile stuck between joking and condescending. "You don't have to believe it if it hurts."

Carlos let out a long laugh.

"You people are unbelievable," said Antonio. But there was something hard and tired behind the way he smiled.

* * *

It was the first day of December, but summer still hung about in the brightest patches of sunlight. The four men sat under the shade of the banyan tree. It wasn't cold, not even in the shade, but three of the men wore cardigans. If asked, they would say they were expecting a chilly north wind and doesn't anybody listen to the weather forecasts anymore. Only Antonio, his round body enough to keep him warm, clung to the short sleeves of summer.

Kids from the local Catholic high school had volunteered to decorate the park for Chirstmas and they dashed about with tinsel in their hair, bumping one another and laughing loudly. Lucinda, the woman who issued the dominos and kept back the gambling, asked them to quiet down, pointing at the men. A wind stirred the top branches of the banyan tree and moved on without touching the ground. One leaf fell to the table.

Antonio waited for Máximo to fetch Lucinda's box of plastic pieces. Antonio held his brown paper bag to his chest and looked at the Cubans, his customary sourness replaced for a moment by what in a man like him could pass for levity. Máximo sat down and began to dump the plastic pieces on the table as he always did. But this time, Antonio held out his hand.

"One moment," he said and shook his brown paper bag.

"Qué pasa, chico?" Máximo said.

Antonio reached into the paper bag as the men watched. He let the paper fall away. In his hand he held an oblong black leather box.

"Coñooo," Raúl said.

He set the box on the table, like a magician drawing out his trick. He looked around to the men and finally opened the box with a flourish to reveal a neat row of big heavy pieces, gone yellow and smooth like old teeth. They bent in closer to look. Antonio tilted the box gently and the pieces fell out in one long line, their black dots facing up now like tight dark pupils in the sunlight.

"Ivory," Antonio said. "And ebony. It's an antique. You're not allowed to make them anymore."

"Beautiful," Carlos said and clasped his hands.

"My daughter found them for me in New Orleans," Antonio continued, ignoring Carlos.

He looked around the table and lingered on Máximo, who had lowered the box of plastic dominos to the ground.

"She said she's been searching for them for two years. Couldn't wait two more weeks to give them to me," he said.

"Coñooo," Raúl said.

A moment passed.

"Well," Antonio said, "what do you think, Máximo?"

Máximo looked at him. Then he bent across the table to touch one of the pieces. He gave a jerk with his head and listened for the traffic. "Very nice," he said.

"Very nice?" Antonio said. "Very nice?" He laughed in his thin way. "My daughter walked all over New Orleans to find this and the Cuban thinks it's 'very nice?'" He paused, watching Máximo. "Did you know my daughter is coming to visit me for Christmas, Máximo? Maybe you can tell her that her gift was very nice, but not as nice as some you remember, eh?"

Máximo looked up, his eyes settling on Carlos, who looked at Antonio and then looked away.

"Calm down, hombre," Carlos said, opening his arms wide, a nervous giggle beginning in his throat. "What's gotten into you?"

Antonio waved his hand and sat down. A diesel truck rattled down Eighth Street, headed for downtown.

"My daughter is a district attorney in Los Angeles," Máximo said after the noise of the truck died. "December is one of the busiest months."

He felt a heat behind his eyes he had not felt in many years.

"Feel one in your hand," Antonio said. "Feel how heavy that is."

*   *   *

When the children were small, Máximo and Rosa used to spend Nochebuena with his cousins in Cárdenas. It was a five-hour drive from Havana in the cars of those days. They would rise early on the twenty-third and arrive by mid-afternoon so Máximo could help the men kill the pig for the feast the following night. Máximo and the other men held the squealing, squirming animal down, its wiry brown coat cutting into their gloveless hands. But God, they were intelligent creatures. No sooner did it spot the knife than the animal bolted out of their arms, screaming like Armageddon. It had become the subtext to the Nochebuena tradition, this chasing of the terrified pig through the yard, dodging orange trees and rotting fruit underneath. The children were never allowed to watch, Rosa made sure. They sat indoors with the women and stirred the black beans. With loud laughter, they shut out the shouts of the men and the hysterical pleadings of the animal as it was dragged back to its slaughter.

*   *   *

"Juanito the little dog gets off the boat from Cuba and decides to take a little stroll down Brickell Avenue."

"Let me make sure I understand the joke. Juanito is a dog. Bowwow."

"That's pretty good."

"Yes, Juanito is a dog, goddamn it."

Raúl looked up, startled.

Máximo shuffled the pieces hard and swallowed. He swung his arms across the table in wide, violent arcs. One of the pieces flew off the table.

"Hey, hey, watch it with that, what's wrong with you?"

Máximo stopped. He felt his heart beating. "I'm sorry," he said. He bent over the edge of the table to see where the piece had landed. "Wait a minute."

He held the table with one hand and tried to stretch to pick up the piece.

"What are you doing?"

"Just wait a minute." When he couldn't reach, he stood up, pulled the piece toward him with his foot, sat back down, and reached for it again, this time grasping it between his fingers and his palm. He put it facedown on the table with the others and shuffled, slowly, his mind barely registering the traffic.

"Where was I – Juanito the little dog, right, bowwow." Máximo took a deep breath. "He's just off the boat from Cuba and is strolling down Brickell Avenue. He's looking up at all the tall and shiny buildings. 'Coñoo,' he says, dazzled by all the mirrors. 'There's nothing like this in Cuba.'"

"Hey, hey, professor. We had tall buildings."

"Jesus Christ!" Máximo said. He pressed his thumb and fore-finger into the corners of his eyes. "This is after Castro, then. Let me just get it out for Christ's sake."

He stopped shuffling. Raúl looked away.

"Ready now? Juanito the little dog is looking up at all the tall buildings and he's so happy to finally be in America because all his cousins have been telling him what a great country it is, right? You know, they were sending back photos of their new cars and girl friends."

"A joke about dogs who drive cars – I've heard it all."

"Hey, they're Cuban superdogs."

"All right, they're sending back photos of their new owners or the biggest bones any dog has ever seen. Anything you like. Use your imaginations." Máximo stopped shuffling. "Where was I?"

"You were at the part where Juanito buys a Rolls-Royce."

The men laughed.

"Okay, Antonio, why don't you three fools continue the joke." Máximo got up from the table. "You've made me forget the rest of it."

"Aw, come on, chico, sit down, don't be so sensitive."

"Come on, professor, you were at the part where Juanito is so glad to be in America."

"Forget it. I can't remember the rest now."

Máximo rubbed his temple, grabbed the back of the chair, and sat down slowly, facing the street. "Just leave me alone, I can't remember it."

He pulled at the pieces two by two. "I'm sorry. Look, let's just play."

The men set up their double rows of dominos, like miniature barricades before them.

"These pieces are a work of art," Antonio said and laid down a double eight.

The banyan tree was strung with white lights that were lit all day. Colored lights twined around the metal poles of the fence, which was topped with a long loping piece of gold tinsel garland.

The Christmas tourists began arriving just before lunch as Máximo and Raúl stepped off the number eight. Carlos and Antonio were already at the table, watched by two groups of families. Mom and Dad with kids. They were big; even the kids were big and pink.

The mother whispered to the kids and they smiled and waved. Raúl waved back at the mother.

"Nice legs, yes," he whispered to Máximo.

Before Máximo looked away, he saw the mother take out a little black pocket camera. He saw the flash out of the corner of his eye. He sat down and looked around the table; the other men stared at their pieces.

The game started badly. It happened sometimes – the distribution of the pieces went all wrong and out of desperation one of the men made mistakes and soon it was all they could do not to knock all the pieces over and start fresh. Raúl set down a double three and signaled to Máximo it was all he had. Carlos passed. Máximo surveyed his last five pieces. His thoughts scattered to the family outside. He looked to find the tallest boy with his face pressed between the iron slats, staring at him.

"You pass?" Antonio said.

Máximo looked at him, then at the table. He put down a three and a five. He looked again, the boy was gone. The family had moved on.

The tour groups arrived later that afternoon. First the white buses with the happy blue letters WELCOME TO LITTLE HAVANA. Next, the fat women in white shorts, their knees lost in an abstraction of flesh. Máximo tried to concentrate on the game. The worst part was how the other men acted out for them. Dominos are supposed to be a quiet game. And now there they were shouting at each other and gesturing. A few of the men had even brought cigars, and they dangled now, unlit, from their mouths.

"You see, Raúl," Máximo said. "You see how we're a spectacle?" He felt like an animal and wanted to growl and cast about behind the metal fence.

Raúl shrugged. "Doesn't bother me."

"A goddamn spectacle. A collection of old bones," Máximo said.

The other men looked up at Máximo.

"Hey, speak for yourself, cabrón," Antonio said.

Raúl shrugged again.

Máximo rubbed his knuckles and began to shuffle the pieces. It was hot, and the sun was setting in his eyes, backlighting the car exhaust like a veil before him. He rubbed his temple, feeling the skin move over the bone. He pressed the inside corners of his eyes, then drew his hand back over the pieces.

"Hey, you okay there?" Antonio said.

* * *

An open trolley pulled up and parked on the curb. A young man with blond hair, perhaps in his thirties, stood up in the front, holding a microphone. He wore a guayabera. Máximo looked away.

"This here is Domino Park," came the amplified voice in English, then Spanish. "No one under fifty-five allowed, folks. But we can sure watch them play."

Máximo heard shutters click, then convinced himself he couldn't have heard, not from where he was.

"Most of these men are Cuban and they're keeping alive the tradition of their homeland," the amplified voice continued, echoing against the back wall of the park. "You see, in Cuba, it was very common to retire to a game of dominos after a good meal. It was a way to bond and build community. Folks, you here are seeing a slice of the past. A simpler time of good friendships and unhurried days."

Maybe it was the sun. The men later noted that he seemed odd. The tics. Rubbing his bones.

First Máximo muttered to himself. He shuffled automatically. When the feedback on the microphone pierced through Domino Park, he could no longer sit where he was, accept things as they were. It was a moment that had long been missing from his life.

He stood and made a fist at the trolley.

"Mierda!" he shouted. "Mierda! That's the biggest bullshit I've ever heard."

He made a lunge at the fence. Carlos jumped up and restrained him. Raúl led him back to his seat.

The man of the amplified voice cleared his throat. The people on the trolley looked at him and back at Máximo; perhaps they thought this was part of the show.

"Well." The man chuckled. "There you have it, folks."

Lucinda ran over, but the other men waved her off. She began to protest about rules and propriety. The park had a reputation to uphold.

It was Antonio who spoke.

"Leave the man alone," he said.

Máximo looked at him. His head was pounding. Antonio met his gaze briefly, then looked to Lucinda.

"Some men don't like to be stared at is all," he said. "It won't happen again."

She shifted her weight, but remained where she was, watching.

"What are you waiting for?" Antonio said, turning now to Máximo, who had lowered his head into the white backs of the dominos. "Let's play."

The night Máximo was too tired to sit at the pine table. He didn't even prepare dinner. He slept and in his dreams he was a green and yellow fish swimming in warm waters, gliding through the coral, the only fish in the sea and he was happy. But the light changed and the sea darkened suddenly and he was rising through it, afraid of breaking the surface, afraid of the pinhole sun on the other side, afraid of drowning in the blue vault of sky.

*   *   *

"Let me finish the story of Juanito the little dog."

No one said anything.

"Is that okay? I'm okay. I just remembered it. Can I finish it?"

The men nodded, but still did not speak.

"He is just off the boat from Cuba. He is walking down Brickell Avenue. And he is trying to steady himself, see, because he still has his sea legs and all the buildings are so tall they are making him dizzy. He doesn't know what to expect. He's maybe a little afraid. And he's thinking about a pretty little dog he knew once and he's wondering where she is now and he wishes he were back home."

He paused to take a breath. Raúl cleared his throat. The men looked at one another, then at Máxmo. But his eyes were on the blur of dominos before him. He felt a stillness around him, a shadow move past the fence, but he didn't look up.

"He's not a depressive kind of dog, though. Don't get me wrong. He's very feisty. And when he sees an elegant white poodle striding toward him, he forgets all his worries and exclaims, 'O Madre de Dios, si cocinas como caminas . . . ' "

The men let out a small laugh. Máximo continued.

" 'Si cocinas como caminas . . . ,' Juanito says, but the white poodle interrupts and says, 'I beg your pardon? This is America – kindly speak English.' So Juanito pauses for a moment to consider and says in his broken English, 'Mamita, you are one hot doggie, yes? I would like to take you to movies and fancy dinners.' "

"One hot doggie, yes?" Carlos repeated, then laughed. "You're killing me."

The other men smiled, warming to the story as before.

"So Juanito says, 'I would like to marry you, my love, and have gorgeous puppies with you and live in a castle.' Well, all this time the white poodle has her snout in the air. She looks at Juanito and says, 'Do you have any idea who you're talking to? I am a refined breed of considerable class and you are nothing but a short, insignificant mutt.' Juanito is stunned for a moment, but he rallies for the final shot. He's a proud dog, you see and he's afraid of his pain. 'Pardon me, your highness,' Juanito the mangy dog says. 'Here in America, I may be a short, insignificant mutt, but in Cuba I was a German shepherd.' "

Máximo turned so the men would not see his tears. The afternoon traffic crawled eastward. One horn blasted, then another. He remembered holding his daughters days after their birth, thinking how fragile and vulnerable lay his bond to the future. For weeks, he carried them on pillows, like jeweled china. Then, the blank spaces in his life lay before him. Now he stood with the gulf at his back, their ribbony youth aflutter in the past. And what had he salvaged from the years? Already, he was forgetting Rosa's face, the precise shade of her eyes.

Carlos cleared his throat and moved his hand as if to touch him, then held back. He cleared his throat again.

"He was a good dog," Carlos said and pressed his lips together.

Antonio began to laugh, then fell silent with the rest. Máximo started shuffling, then stopped. The shadow of the banyan tree worked a kaleidoscope over the dominos. When the wind eased, Máximo tilted his head to listen. He heard something stir behind him, someone leaning heavily on the fence. He could almost feel the breath. His heart quickened.

"Tell them to go away," Máximo said. "Tell them, no pictures."

The Joy Luck Club

Amy Tan

Introduction

Amy Tan was born in Oakland, California, in 1952. Her parents were Chinese immigrants who had met in China during the Second World War. Her paternal grandfather was an English-speaking Presbyterian minister from Canton, married to a Chinese traditional healer. Her father, John, spoke English, Cantonese and Mandarin, and worked for the US Information Service in China. After the war he travelled to the United States, but instead of taking up his scholarship at the Massachusetts Institute of Technology he enrolled in the Berkeley Baptist Divinity School. Her mother, Du Ching (Daisy), had been married to an abusive husband when she first met John Tan, and had three daughters from her first marriage. She lost custody of these daughters when she divorced, and so was forced to leave them behind when she fled Shanghai just before the Communists took over the city in 1949. In California, far away from the Chinese Civil War, John and Daisy married. They settled near San Francisco, home of one of the largest Chinese-American communities in the USA, and raised three children, Amy and her two brothers.

Daisy Tan's harrowing experiences in China, and those of *her* mother, Gu Jingmai, a young widow who had been forced into concubinage then killed herself by swallowing raw opium, would subsequently become important stimuli for Amy Tan's fiction. But more tragedies befell the family in America: John and his older son died within a year of each other, both of brain tumours. Daisy sold the family house and took her surviving children to Europe. Amy completed her secondary education at an international school in Montreux, Switzerland.

Back in America, Amy Tan studied English and linguistics, her final course being an uncompleted PhD at the University of California, Berkeley. She tried a variety of jobs, including freelance business writing, then in 1985 began writing short stories. In 1987 she went to China for the first time, in the company of her mother, with whom she had always had a difficult relationship. It proved to be a pivotal experience: 'I hated it and I loved it. And when I returned home, I began to write stories about her life.'[1] The outcome was a set of sixteen interlocking tales about four Chinese mothers and their Chinese-American daughters, *The Joy Luck Club*. Some individual stories had been published in magazines (the title story appeared in the *Ladies' Home Journal*) but the complete volume quickly became one of the best-selling books of 1989. Often described as 'a novel', *The Joy Luck Club* transferred to the screen in 1993. As co-screenwriter and co-producer of the film, Tan hoped it would 'change Hollywood's mind that movies about Asian-Americans can't be successful', whilst rejecting the idea that 'the raison d'être of any story with an ethnic angle is to provide an educational lesson on culture'.[2]

Tan has written several novels since The Joy Luck Club, including The Kitchen God's Wife (1991) and The Bonesetter's Daughter (2001), and has collected numerous literary awards. But she is also an eloquent supporter of the short story: as guest editor of The Best American Short Stories 1999, she emphasized the importance of a story's rhythm, its kinship with poetry, and the ability of a good story to quietly lift readers 'out of our skins'.[3] In 'The Joy Luck Club' contrasting worlds – domestic, dream-like and unspeakably tragic – are brought into fragile connection around a mah jong table. Mah jong is a traditional Chinese game involving both skill and luck; it was banned by China's Communist government in 1949, being associated with gambling and therefore capitalism (and in Tan's story this association is perfectly evident). The game, which has always had a strongly social character, is played with tiles that are often things of beauty themselves, some representing winds, flowers and seasons. In the last, haunting line of the story the everyday poetry of the game gently suggests continuity, harmony and acceptance.

Notes

1. Amy Tan, 'What I Would Remember', in The Opposite of Fate (London: Penguin, 2003), p. 359.
2. Amy Tan, 'Joy Luck and Hollywood', in The Opposite of Fate, p. 191.
3. Amy Tan, 'The Best Stories', in The Opposite of Fate, p. 354.

The Joy Luck Club

My father has asked me to be the fourth corner at the Joy Luck Club. I am to replace my mother, whose seat at the mah jong table has been empty since she died two months ago. My father thinks she was killed by her own thoughts.

'She had a new idea inside her head,' said my father. 'But before it could come out of her mouth, the thought grew too big and burst. It must have been a very bad idea.'

The doctor said she died of a cerebral aneurysm. And her friends at the Joy Luck Club said she died just like a rabbit: quickly and with unfinished business left behind. My mother was supposed to host the next meeting of the Joy Luck Club.

The week before she died, she called me, full of pride, full of life: 'Auntie Lin cooked red bean soup for Joy Luck. I'm going to cook black sesame-seed soup.'

'Don't show off,' I said.

'It's not showoff.' She said the two soups were almost the same, *chabudwo*. Or maybe she said *butong*, not the same thing at all. It was one of those Chinese expressions that means the better half of mixed intentions. I can never remember things I didn't understand in the first place.

My mother started the San Francisco version of the Joy Luck Club in 1949, two years before I was born. This was the year my mother and father left China with one stiff leather trunk filled only with fancy silk dresses. There was no time to pack anything else, my mother had explained to my father after they boarded the boat. Still his hands swam frantically between the slippery silks, looking for his cotton shirts and wool pants.

When they arrived in San Francisco, my father made her hide those shiny clothes. She wore the same brown-checked Chinese dress until the Refugee Welcome Society gave her two hand-me-down dresses, all too large in sizes for American women. The society was composed of a group of white-haired American missionary ladies from the First Chinese Baptist Church. And because of their gifts, my parents could not refuse their invitation to join the church. Nor could they ignore the old ladies' practical advice to improve their English through Bible study class on Wednesday nights and,

later, through choir practice on Saturday mornings. This was how
my parents met the Hsus, the Jongs, and the St Clairs. My mother
could sense that the women of these families also had unspeakable
tragedies they had left behind in China and hopes they couldn't
begin to express in their fragile English. Or at least, my mother
recognized the numbness in these women's faces. And she saw how
quickly their eyes moved when she told them her idea for the Joy
Luck Club.

Joy Luck was an idea my mother remembered from the days of
her first marriage in Kweilin, before the Japanese came. That's why
I think of Joy Luck as her Kweilin story. It was the story she would
always tell me when she was bored, when there was nothing to
do, when every bowl had been washed and the Formica table had
been wiped down twice, when my father sat reading the newspaper
and smoking one Pall Mall cigarette after another, a warning not to
disturb him. This is when my mother would take out a box of old ski
sweaters sent to us by unseen relatives from Vancouver. She would
snip the bottom of a sweater and pull out a kinky thread of yarn,
anchoring it to a piece of cardboard. And as she began to roll with
one sweeping rhythm, she would start her story. Over the years, she
told me the same story, except for the ending, which grew darker,
casting long shadows into her life, and eventually into mine.

'I dreamed about Kweilin before I ever saw it,' my mother began,
speaking Chinese. 'I dreamed of jagged peaks lining a curving river,
with magic moss greening the banks. At the tops of these peaks were
white mists. And if you could float down this river and eat the moss
for food, you would be strong enough to climb the peak. If you
slipped, you would only fall into a bed of soft moss and laugh. And
once you reached the top, you would be able to see everything and
feel such happiness it would be enough to never have worries in
your life ever again.

'In China, everybody dreamed about Kweilin. And when I arrived,
I realized how shabby my dreams were, how poor my thoughts.
When I saw the hills, I laughed and shuddered at the same time.
The peaks looked like giant fried fish heads trying to jump out of a
vat of oil. Behind each hill, I could see shadows of another fish, and
then another and another. And then the clouds would move just

a little and the hills would suddenly become monstrous elephants marching slowly toward me! Can you see this? And at the root of the hill were secret caves. Inside grew hanging rock gardens in the shapes and colors of cabbage, winter melons, turnips, and onions. These were things so strange and beautiful you can't ever imagine them.

'But I didn't come to Kweilin to see how beautiful it was. The man who was my husband brought me and our two babies to Kweilin because he thought we would be safe. He was an officer with the Kuomintang, and after he put us down in a small room in a two-story house, he went off to the northwest, to Chungking.

'We knew the Japanese were winning, even when the newspapers said they were not. Every day, every hour, thousands of people poured into the city, crowding the sidewalks, looking for places to live. They came from the East, West, North, and South. They were rich and poor, Shanghainese, Cantonese, northerners, and not just Chinese, but foreigners and missionaries of every religion. And there was, of course, the Kuomintang and their army officers who thought they were top level to everyone else.

'We were a city of leftovers mixed together. If it hadn't been for the Japanese, there would have been plenty of reason for fighting to break out among these different people. Can you see it? Shanghai people with north-water peasants, bankers with barbers, rickshaw pullers with Burma refugees. Everybody looked down on someone else. It didn't matter that everybody shared the same sidewalk to spit on and suffered the same fast-moving diarrhea. We all had the same stink, but everybody complained someone else smelled the worst. Me? Oh, I hated the American air force officers who said habba-habba sounds to make my face turn red. But the worst were the northern peasants who emptied their noses into their hands and pushed people around and gave everybody their dirty diseases.

'So you can see how quickly Kweilin lost its beauty for me. I no longer climbed the peaks to say, How lovely are these hills! I only wondered which hills the Japanese had reached. I sat in the dark corners of my house with a baby under each arm, waiting with nervous feet. When the sirens cried out to warn us of bombers, my neighbors and I jumped to our feet and scurried to the deep caves to hide like wild animals. But you can't stay in the dark for so long. Something inside of you starts to fade and you become like a starving person, crazy-hungry for light. Outside I could hear the bombing. Boom! Boom! And then the sound of raining rocks. And inside I was no longer hungry for the cabbage or the turnips of the hanging rock garden. I could only see the dripping bowels of an ancient hill that might collapse on top of me. Can you imagine how it is, to want to be neither inside nor outside, to want to be nowhere and disappear?

'So when the bombing sounds grew farther away, we would come back out like newborn kittens scratching our way back to the city. And always, I would be amazed to find the hills against the burning sky had not been torn apart.

'I thought up Joy Luck on a summer night that was so hot even the moths fainted to the ground, their wings were so heavy with the damp heat. Every place was so crowded there was no room for fresh air. Unbearable smells from the sewers rose up to my second-story window and the stink had nowhere else to go but into my nose. At all hours of the night and day, I heard screaming sounds. I didn't know if it was a peasant slitting the throat of a runaway pig or an officer beating a half-dead peasant for lying in his way on the sidewalk. I didn't go to the window to find out. What use would it have been? And that's when I thought I needed something to do to help me move.

'My idea was to have a gathering of four women, one for each corner of my mah jong table. I knew which women I wanted to ask. They were all young like me, with wishful faces. One was an army officer's wife, like myself. Another was a girl with very fine manners from a rich family in Shanghai. She had escaped with only a little money. And there was a girl from Nanking who had the blackest hair I have ever seen. She came from a low-class family, but she was pretty and pleasant and had married well, to an old man who died and left her with a better life.

'Each week one of us would host a party to raise money and to raise our spirits. The hostess had to serve special *dyansyin* foods to bring good fortune of all kinds – dumplings shaped like silver money ingots, long rice noodles for long life, boiled peanuts for conceiving sons, and of course, many good-luck oranges for a plentiful, sweet life.

'What fine food we treated ourselves to with our meager allowances! We didn't notice that the dumplings were stuffed mostly with stringy squash and that the oranges were spotted with wormy holes. We ate sparingly, not as if we didn't have enough, but to protest how we could not eat another bite, we had already bloated ourselves from earlier in the day. We knew we had luxuries few people could afford. We were the lucky ones.

'After filling our stomachs, we would then fill a bowl with money and put it where everyone could see. Then we would sit down at the mah jong table. My table was from my family and was of a very fragrant red wood, not what you call rosewood, but *hong mu*, which is so fine there's no English word for it. The table had a very thick pad, so that when the mah jong *pai* were spilled onto the table the only sound was of ivory tiles washing against one another.

'Once we started to play, nobody could speak, except to say "*Pung!*" or "*Chr!*" when taking a tile. We had to play with seriousness and think of nothing else but adding to our happiness through winning. But after sixteen rounds, we would again feast, this time to celebrate our good fortune. And then we would talk into the night until the morning, saying stories about good times in the past and good times yet to come.

'Oh, what good stories! Stories spilling out all over the place! We almost laughed to death. A rooster that ran into the house screeching on top of dinner bowls, the same bowls that held him quietly in pieces the next day! And one about a girl who wrote love letters for two friends who loved the same man. And a silly foreign lady who fainted on a toilet when firecrackers went off next to her.

'People thought we were wrong to serve banquets every week while many people in the city were starving, eating rats and, later, the garbage that the poorest rats used to feed on. Others thought we were possessed by demons – to celebrate when even within our own families we had lost generations, had lost homes and fortunes, and were separated, husband from wife, brother from sister, daughter from mother. Hnnnh! How could we laugh, people asked.

'It's not that we had no heart or eyes for pain. We were all afraid. We all had our miseries. But to despair was to wish back for something already lost. Or to prolong what was already unbearable. How much can you wish for a favorite warm coat that hangs in the closet of a house that burned down with your mother and father inside of it? How long can you see in your mind arms and legs hanging from telephone wires and starving dogs running down the streets with half-chewed hands dangling from their jaws? What was worse, we asked among ourselves, to sit and wait for our own deaths with proper somber faces? Or to choose our own happiness?

'So we decided to hold parties and pretend each week had become the new year. Each week we could forget past wrongs done to us. We weren't allowed to think a bad thought. We feasted, we laughed, we played games, lost and won, we told the best stories. And each week, we could hope to be lucky. That hope was our only joy. And that's how we came to call our little parties Joy Luck.'

My mother used to end the story on a happy note, bragging about her skill at the game. 'I won many times and was so lucky the others teased that I had learned the trick of a clever thief,' she said. 'I won tens of thousands of *yuan*. But I wasn't rich. No. By then paper money had become worthless. Even toilet paper was worth more. And that made us laugh harder, to think a thousand-*yuan* note wasn't even good enough to rub on our bottoms.'

I never thought my mother's Kweilin story was anything but a Chinese fairy tale. The endings always changed. Sometimes she said she used that worthless thousand-*yuan* note to buy a half-cup of rice. She turned that rice into a pot of porridge. She traded that gruel for two feet from a pig. Those two feet became six eggs, those eggs six chickens. The story always grew and grew.

And then one evening, after I had begged her to buy me a transistor radio, after she refused and I had sulked in silence for an hour, she said, 'Why do you think you are missing something you never had?' And then she told me a completely different ending to the story.

'An army officer came to my house early one morning,' she said, 'and told me to go quickly to my husband in Chungking. And I knew he was telling me to run away from Kweilin. I knew what happened to officers and their families when the Japanese arrived. How could I go? There were no trains leaving Kweilin. My friend from Nanking, she was so good to me. She bribed a man to steal a wheelbarrow used to haul coal. She promised to warn our other friends.

'I packed my things and my two babies into this wheelbarrow and began pushing to Chungking four days before the Japanese marched into Kweilin. On the road I heard news of the slaughter from people running past me. It was terrible. Up to the last day, the Kuomintang insisted that Kweilin was safe, protected by the Chinese army. But later that day, the streets of Kweilin were strewn with newspapers reporting great Kuomintang victories, and on top of these papers, like fresh fish from a butcher, lay rows of people – men, women, and children who had never lost hope, but had lost their lives instead. When I heard this news, I walked faster and faster, asking myself at each step, Were they foolish? Were they brave?

'I pushed toward Chungking, until my wheel broke. I abandoned my beautiful mah jong table of *hong mu*. By then I didn't have enough feeling left in my body to cry. I tied scarves into slings and put a baby on each side of my shoulder. I carried a bag in each hand, one with clothes, the other with food. I carried these things until deep grooves grew in my hands. And I finally dropped one bag after the other when my hands began to bleed and became too slippery to hold onto anything.

'Along the way, I saw others had done the same, gradually given up hope. It was like a pathway inlaid with treasures that grew in value along the way. Bolts of fine fabric and books. Paintings of ancestors and carpenter tools. Until one could see cages of ducklings now quiet with thirst and, later still, silver urns lying in the road, where people had been too tired to carry them for any kind of future hope. By the time I arrived in Chungking I had lost everything except for three fancy silk dresses which I wore one on top of the other.'

'What do you mean by "everything"?' I gasped at the end. I was stunned to realize the story had been true all along. 'What happened to the babies?'

She didn't even pause to think. She simply said in a way that made it clear there was no more to the story: 'Your father is not my first husband. You are not those babies.'

When I arrive at the Hsus' house, where the Joy Luck Club is meeting tonight, the first person I see is my father. 'There she is! Never on time!' he announces. And it's true. Everybody's already here, seven family friends in their sixties and seventies. They look up and laugh at me, always tardy, a child still at thirty-six.

I'm shaking, trying to hold something inside. The last time I saw them, at the funeral, I had broken down and cried big gulping sobs. They must wonder now how someone like me can take my mother's place. A friend once told me that my mother and I were alike, that we had the same wispy hand gestures, the same girlish laugh and sideways look. When I shyly told my mother this, she seemed insulted and said, 'You don't even know little percent of me! How can you be me?' And she's right. How can I be my mother at Joy Luck?

'Auntie, Uncle,' I say repeatedly, nodding to each person there. I have always called these old family friends Auntie and Uncle. And then I walk over and stand next to my father.

He's looking at the Jongs' pictures from their recent China trip. 'Look at that,' he says politely, pointing to a photo of the Jongs' tour group standing on wide slab steps. There is nothing in this picture that shows it was taken in China rather than San Francisco, or any other city for that matter. But my father doesn't seem to be looking at the picture anyway. It's as though everything were the same to him, nothing stands out. He has always been politely indifferent. But what's the Chinese word that means indifferent because you can't *see* any differences? That's how troubled I think he is by my mother's death.

'Will you look at that,' he says, pointing to another nondescript picture.

The Hsus' house feels heavy with greasy odors. Too many Chinese meals cooked in a too small kitchen, too many once fragrant smells compressed onto a thin layer of invisible grease. I remember how my mother used to go into other people's houses and restaurants and wrinkle her nose, then whisper very loudly: 'I can see and feel the stickiness with my nose.'

I have not been to the Hsus' house in many years, but the living room is exactly the same as I remember it. When Auntie An-mei and Uncle George moved to the Sunset district from Chinatown twenty-five years ago, they bought new furniture. It's all there, still looking mostly new under yellowed plastic. The same turquoise couch shaped in a semicircle of nubby tweed. The colonial end tables made out of heavy maple. A lamp of fake cracked porcelain. Only the scroll-length calendar, free from the Bank of Canton, changes every year.

I remember this stuff, because when we were children, Auntie An-mei didn't let us touch any of her new furniture except through the clear plastic coverings. On Joy Luck nights, my parents brought me to the Hsus'. Since I was the guest, I had to take care of all the younger children, so many children it seemed as if there were always one baby who was crying from having bumped its head on a table-leg.

'You are responsible,' said my mother, which meant I was in trouble if anything was spilled, burned, lost, broken, or dirty. I was responsible, no matter who did it. She and Auntie An-mei were dressed up in funny Chinese dresses with stiff stand-up collars and blooming branches of embroidered silk sewn over their breasts. These clothes were too fancy for real Chinese people, I thought, and too strange for American parties. In those days, before my mother told me her Kweilin story, I imagined Joy Luck was a shameful Chinese custom, like the secret gathering of the Ku Klux Klan or the tom-tom dances of TV Indians preparing for war.

But tonight, there's no mystery. The Joy Luck aunties are all wearing slacks, bright print blouses, and different versions of sturdy walking shoes. We are all seated around the dining room table under a lamp that looks like a Spanish candelabra. Uncle George puts on his bifocals and starts the meeting by reading the minutes:

'Our capital account is $24,825, or about $6,206 a couple, $3,103 per person. We sold Subaru for a loss at six and three-quarters. We bought a hundred shares of Smith International at seven. Our thanks to Lindo and Tin Jong for the goodies. The red bean soup was especially delicious. The March meeting had to be canceled until further notice. We were sorry to have to bid a fond farewell to our dear friend Suyuan and extended our sympathy to the Canning Woo family. Respectfully submitted, George Hsu, president and secretary.'

That's it. I keep thinking the others will start talking about my mother, the wonderful friendship they shared, and why I am here in her spirit, to be the fourth corner and carry on the idea my mother came up with on a hot day in Kweilin.

But everybody just nods to approve the minutes. Even my father's head bobs up and down routinely. And it seems to me my mother's life has been shelved for new business.

Auntie An-mei heaves herself up from the table and moves slowly to the kitchen to prepare the food. And Auntie Lin, my mother's best friend, moves to the turquoise sofa, crosses her arms, and watches the men still seated at the table. Auntie Ying, who seems to shrink even more every time I see her, reaches into her knitting bag and pulls out the start of a tiny blue sweater.

The Joy Luck uncles begin to talk about stocks they are interested in buying. Uncle Jack, who is Auntie Ying's younger brother, is very keen on a company that mines gold in Canada.

'It's a great hedge on inflation,' he says with authority. He speaks the best English, almost accentless. I think my mother's English was the worst, but she always thought her Chinese was the best. She spoke Mandarin slightly blurred with a Shanghai dialect.

'Weren't we going to play mah jong tonight?' I whisper loudly to Aunti Ying, who's slightly deaf.

'Later,' she says, 'after midnight.'

'Ladies, are you at this meeting or not?' says Uncle George.

After everybody votes unanimously for the Canada gold stock, I go into the kitchen to ask Auntie An-mei why the Joy Luck Club started investing in stocks.

'We used to play mah jong, winner take all. But the same people were always winning, the same people always losing,' she says. She is stuffing wonton, one chopstick jab of gingery meat dabbed onto a thin skin and then a single fluid turn with her hand that seals the skin into the shape of a tiny nurse's cap. 'You can't have luck when someone else has skill. So long time ago, we decided to invest in the stock market. There's no skill in that. Even your mother agreed.'

Auntie An-mei takes count of the tray in front of her. She's already made five rows of eight wonton each. 'Forty wonton, eight people, ten each, five row more,' she says aloud to herself, and then continues stuffing. 'We got smart. Now we can all win and lose equally. We can have stock market luck. And we can play mah jong for fun, just for a few dollars, winner take all. Losers take home leftovers! So everyone can have some joy. Smart-hanh?'

I watch Auntie An-mei make more wonton. She has quick, expert fingers. She doesn't have to think about what she is doing. That's what my mother used to complain about, that Auntie An-mei never thought about what she was doing.

'She's not stupid,' said my mother on one occasion, 'but she has no spine. Last week, I had a good idea for her. I said to her, Let's go to the consulate and ask for papers for your brother. And she almost wanted to drop her things and go right then. But later she talked to someone. Who knows who? And that person told her she can get her brother in bad trouble in China. That person said FBI will put her on a list and give her trouble in the U.S. the rest of her life. That person said, You ask for a house loan and they say no loan, because your brother is a communist. I said, You already have a house! But still she was scared.

'Auntie An-mei runs this way and that,' said my mother, 'and she doesn't know why.'

As I watch Auntie An-mei, I see a short bent woman in her seventies, with a heavy bosom and thin, shapeless legs. She has the flattened soft fingertips of an old woman. I wonder what Auntie An-mei did to inspire a lifelong stream of criticism from my mother. Then again, it seemed my mother was always displeased with all her friends, with me, and even with my father. Something was always missing. Something always needed improving. Something was not in balance. This one or that had too much of one element, not enough of another.

The elements were from my mother's own version of organic chemistry. Each person is made of five elements, she told me.

Too much fire and you had a bad temper. That was like my father, whom my mother always criticized for his cigarette habit and who always shouted back that she should keep her thoughts to herself. I think he now feels guilty that he didn't let my mother speak her mind.

Too little wood and you bent too quickly to listen to other people's ideas, unable to stand on your own. This was like my Auntie An-mei.

Too much water and you flowed in too many directions, like myself, for having started half a degree in biology, then half a degree in art, and then finishing neither when I went off to work for a small ad agency as a secretary, later becoming a copywriter.

I used to dismiss her criticisms as just more of her Chinese superstitions, beliefs that conveniently fit the circumstances. In my twenties, while taking Introduction to Psychology, I tried to tell her why she shouldn't criticize so much, why it didn't lead to a healthy learning environment.

'There's a school of thought,' I said, 'that parents shouldn't criticize children. They should encourage instead. You know, people rise to other people's expectations. And when you criticize, it just means you're expecting failure.'

'That's the trouble,' my mother said. 'You never rise. Lazy to get up. Lazy to rise to expectations.'

'Time to eat,' Auntie An-mei happily announces, bringing out a steaming pot of the wonton she was just wrapping. There are piles of food on the table, served buffet style, just like at the Kweilin feasts. My father is digging into the chow mein, which still sits in an oversize aluminum pan surrounded by little plastic packets of soy sauce. Auntie An-mei must have bought this on Clement Street. The wonton soup smells wonderful with delicate sprigs of cilantro floating on top. I'm drawn first to a large platter of *chaswei*, sweet barbecued pork cut into coin-sized slices, and then to a whole assortment of what I've always called finger goodies – thin-skinned pastries filled with chopped pork, beef, shrimp, and unknown stuffings that my mother used to describe as 'nutritious things.'

Eating is not a gracious event here. It's as though everybody had been starving. They push large forkfuls into their mouths, jab at more pieces of pork, one right after the other. They are not like the ladies of Kweilin, who I always imagined savored their food with a certain detached delicacy.

And then, almost as quickly as they started, the men get up and leave the table. As if on cue, the women peck at last morsels and then carry plates and bowls to the kitchen and dump them in the sink. The women take turns washing their hands, scrubbing them vigorously. Who started this ritual? I too put my plate in the sink and wash my hands. The women are talking about the Jongs' China trip, then they move toward a room in the back of the apartment. We pass another room, what used to be the bedroom shared by the four Hsu sons. The bunk beds with their scuffed, splintery ladders are still there. The Joy Luck uncles are already seated at the card table. Uncle George is dealing out cards, fast, as though he learned this technique in a casino. My father is passing out Pall Mall cigarettes, with one already dangling from his lips.

And then we get to the room in the back, which was once shared by the three Hsu girls. We were all childhood friends. And now they've all grown and married and I'm here to play in their room again. Except for the smell of camphor, it feels the same – as if Rose, Ruth, and Janice might soon walk in with their hair rolled up in big orange-juice cans and plop down on their identical narrow beds, the white chenille bedspreads are so worn they are almost translucent. Rose and I used to pluck the nubs out while talking about our boy problems. Everything is the same, except now a mahogany-colored mah jong table sits in the center. And next to it is a floor lamp, a long black pole with three oval spotlights attached like the broad leaves of a rubber plant.

Nobody says to me, 'Sit here, this is where your mother used to sit.' But I can tell even before everyone sits down. The chair closest to the door has an emptiness to it. But the feeling doesn't really have to do with the chair. It's her place on the table. Without having anyone tell me, I know her corner on the table was the East.

The East is where things begin, my mother once told me, the direction from which the sun rises, where the wind comes from.

Auntie An-mei, who is sitting on my left, spills the tiles onto the green felt tabletop and then says to me, 'Now we wash tiles.' We swirl them with our hands in a circular motion. They make a cool swishing sound as they bump into one another.

'Do you win like your mother?' asks Auntie Lin across from me. She is not smiling.

'I only played a little in college with some Jewish friends.'

'Annh! Jewish mah jong,' she says in disgusted tones. 'Not the same thing.' This is what my mother used to say, although she could never explain exactly why.

'Maybe I shouldn't play tonight, I'll just watch,' I offer.

Auntie Lin looks exasperated, as though I were a simple child: 'How can we play with just three people? Like a table with three legs, no balance. When Auntie Ying's husband died, she asked her brother to join. Your father asked you. So it's decided.'

'What's the difference between Jewish and Chinese mah jong?' I once asked my mother. I couldn't tell by her answer if the games were different or just her attitude toward Chinese and Jewish people.

'Entirely different kind of playing,' she said in her English explanation voice. 'Jewish mah jong, they watch only for their own tile, play only with their eyes.'

Then she switched to Chinese: 'Chinese mah jong, you must play using your head, very tricky. You must watch what everybody else throws away and keep that in your head as well. And if nobody plays well, then the game becomes like Jewish mah jong. Why play? There's no strategy. You're just watching people make mistakes.'

These kinds of explanations made me feel my mother and I spoke two different languages, which we did. I talked to her in English, she answered back in Chinese.

'So what's the difference between Chinese and Jewish mah jong?' I ask Auntie Lin.

'Aii-ya,' she exclaims in a mock scolding voice. 'Your mother did not teach you anything?'

Auntie Ying pats my hand. 'You a smart girl. You watch us, do the same. Help us stack the tiles and make four walls.'

I follow Auntie Ying, but mostly I watch Auntie Lin. She is the fastest, which means I can almost keep up with the others by watching what she does first. Auntie Ying throws the dice and I'm told that Auntie Lin has become the East wind. I've become the North wind, the last hand to play. Auntie Ying is the South and Auntie An-mei is the West. And then we start taking tiles, throwing the dice, counting back on the wall to the right number of spots where our chosen tiles lie. I rearrange my tiles, sequences of bamboo and balls, doubles of colored number tiles, odd tiles that do not fit anywhere.

'Your mother was the best, like a pro,' says Auntie An-mei while slowly sorting her tiles, considering each piece carefully.

Now we begin to play, looking at our hands, casting tiles, picking up others at an easy, comfortable pace. The Joy Luck aunties begin to make small talk, not really listening to each other. They speak in their special language, half in broken English, half in their own Chinese dialect. Auntie Ying mentions she bought yarn at half price, somewhere out in the avenues. Auntie An-mei brags about a sweater she made for her daughter Ruth's new baby. 'She thought it was store-bought,' she says proudly.

Auntie Lin explains how mad she got at a store clerk who refused to let her return a skirt with a broken zipper. 'I was *chiszle*,' she says, still fuming, 'mad to death.'

'But Lindo, you are still with us. You didn't die,' teases Auntie Ying, and then as she laughs Auntie Lin says '*Pung!*' and '*Mah jong!*' and then spreads her tiles out, laughing back at Auntie Ying while counting up her points. We start washing tiles again and it grows quiet. I'm getting bored and sleepy.

'Oh, I have a story,' says Auntie Ying loudly, startling everybody. Auntie Ying has always been the weird auntie, someone lost in her own world. My mother used to say, 'Auntie Ying is not hard of hearing. She is hard of listening.'

'Police arrested Mrs Emerson's son last weekend,' Auntie Ying says in a way that sounds as if she were proud to be the first with this big news. 'Mrs Chan told me at church. Too many TV sets found in his car.'

Auntie Lin quickly says, 'Aii-ya, Mrs Emerson good lady,' meaning Mrs Emerson didn't deserve such a terrible son. But now I see this is also said for the benefit of Auntie An-mei, whose own youngest son was arrested two years ago for selling stolen car stereos. Auntie An-mei is rubbing her tile carefully before discarding it. She looks pained.

'Everybody has TVs in China now,' says Auntie Lin, changing the subject. 'Our family there all has TV sets – not just black-and-white, but color and remote! They have everything. So when we asked them what we should buy them, they said nothing, it was enough that we would come to visit them. But we bought them different things anyway, VCR and Sony Walkman for the kids. They said, No, don't give it to us, but I think they liked it.'

Poor Auntie An-mei rubs her tiles ever harder. I remember my mother telling me about the Hsus' trip to China three years ago. Auntie An-mei had saved two thousand dollars, all to spend on her brother's family. She had shown my mother the insides of her heavy suitcases. One was crammed with See's Nuts & Chews, M & M's, candy-coated cashews, instant hot chocolate with miniature marsh-mallows. My mother told me the other bag contained the most ridiculous clothes, all new: bright California-style beachwear, base-ball caps, cotton pants with elastic waists, bomber jackets, Stanford sweatshirts, crew socks.

My mother had told her, 'Who wants those useless things? They just want money.' But Auntie An-mei said her brother was so poor and they were so rich by comparison. So she ignored my mother's advice and took the heavy bags and their two thousand dollars to China. And when their China tour finally arrived in Hangzhou, the whole family from Ningbo was there to meet them. It wasn't just Auntie An-mei's little brother, but also his wife's stepbrothers and stepsisters, and a distant cousin, and that cousin's husband and that husband's uncle. They had all brought their mothers-in-law and children, and even their village friends who were not lucky enough to have overseas Chinese relatives to show off.

As my mother told it, 'Auntie An-mei had cried before she left for China, thinking she would make her brother very rich and happy by communist standards. But when she got home, she cried to me that everyone had a palm out and she was the only one who left with an empty hand.'

My mother confirmed her suspicions. Nobody wanted the sweatshirts, those useless clothes. The M & M's were thrown in the air, gone. And when the suitcases were emptied, the relatives asked what else the Hsus had brought.

Auntie An-mei and Uncle George were shaken down, not just for two thousand dollars' worth of TVs and refrigerators but also for a night's lodging for twenty-six people in the Overlooking the Lake Hotel, for three banquet tables at a restaurant that catered to rich foreigners, for three special gifts for each relative, and finally, for a loan of five thousand *yuan* in foreign exchange to a cousin's so-called uncle who wanted to buy a motorcycle but who later disappeared for good along with the money. When the train pulled out of Hangzhou the next day, the Hsus found themselves depleted of some nine thousand dollars' worth of goodwill. Months later, after an inspiring Christmastime service at the First Chinese Baptist Church, Auntie An-mei tried to recoup her loss by saying it truly was more blessed to give than to receive, and my mother agreed, her longtime friend had blessings for at least several lifetimes.

Listening now to Auntie Lin bragging about the virtues of her family in China, I realize that Auntie Lin is oblivious to Auntie An-mei's pain. Is Auntie Lin being mean, or is it that my mother never told anybody but me the shameful story of Auntie An-mei's greedy family?

'So, Jing-mei, you go to school now?' says Auntie Lin.

'Her name is June. They all go by their American names,' says Auntie Ying.

'That's okay,' I say, and I really mean it. In fact, it's even becoming fashionable for American-born Chinese to use their Chinese names.

'I'm not in school anymore, though,' I say. 'That was more than ten years ago.'

Auntie Lin's eyebrows arch. 'Maybe I'm thinking of someone else daughter,' she says, but I know right away she's lying. I know my mother probably told her I was going back to school to finish my degree, because somewhere back, maybe just six months ago, we were again having this argument about my being a failure, a 'college drop-off,' about my going back to finish.

Once again I had told my mother what she wanted to hear: 'You're right. I'll look into it.'

I had always assumed we had an unspoken understanding about these things: that she didn't really mean I was a failure, and I really meant I would try to respect her opinions more. But listening to Auntie Lin tonight reminds me once again: My mother and I never really understood one another. We translated each other's meanings and I seemed to hear less than what was said, while my mother heard more. No doubt she told Auntie Lin I was going back to school to get a doctorate.

Auntie Lin and my mother were both best friends and arch enemies who spent a lifetime comparing their children. I was one month older than Waverly Jong, Auntie Lin's prized daughter. From the time we were babies, our mothers compared the creases in our belly buttons, how shapely our earlobes were, how fast we healed when we scraped our knees, how thick and dark our hair, how many shoes we wore out in one year, and later, how smart Waverly was at playing chess, how many trophies she had won last month, how many newspapers had printed her name, how many cities she had visited.

I know my mother resented listening to Auntie Lin talk about Waverly when she had nothing to come back with. At first my mother tried to cultivate some hidden genius in me. She did house-work for an old retired piano teacher down the hall who gave me lessons and free use of a piano to practice on in exchange. When I failed to become a concert pianist, or even an accompanist for the church youth choir, she finally explained that I was late-blooming, like Einstein, who everyone thought was retarded until he discovered a bomb.

Now it is Auntie Ying who wins this hand of mah jong, so we count points and begin again.

'Did you know Lena move to Woodside?' asks Auntie Ying with obvious pride, looking down at the tiles, talking to no one in particular. She quickly erases her smile and tries for some modesty. 'Of course, it's not best house in neighborhood, not million-dollar house, not yet. But it's good investment. Better than paying rent. Better than somebody putting you under their thumb to rub you out.'

So now I know Auntie Ying's daughter, Lena, told her about my being evicted from my apartment on lower Russian Hill. Even though Lena and I are still friends, we have grown naturally cautious about telling each other too much. Still, what little we say to one another often comes back in another guise. It's the same old game, everybody talking in circles.

'It's getting late,' I say after we finish the round. I start to stand up, but Auntie Lin pushes me back down into the chair.

'Stay, stay. We talk awhile, get to know you again,' she says. 'Been a long time.'

I know this is a polite gesture on the Joy Luck aunties' part – a protest when actually they are just as eager to see me go as I am to leave. 'No, I really must go now, thank you, thank you,' I say, glad I remembered how the pretense goes.

'But you must stay! We have something important to tell you, from your mother,' Auntie Ying blurts out in her too-loud voice. The others look uncomfortable, as if this were not how they intended to break some sort of bad news to me.

I sit down. Auntie An-mei leaves the room quickly and returns with a bowl of peanuts, then quietly shuts the door. Everybody is quiet, as if nobody knew where to begin.

It is Auntie Ying who finally speaks. 'I think your mother die with an important thought on her mind,' she says in halting English. And then she begins to speak in Chinese, calmly, softly.

'Your mother was a very strong woman, a good mother. She loved you very much, more than her own life. And that's why you can understand why a mother like this could never forget her other daughters. She knew they were alive, and before she died she wanted to find her daughters in China.'

The babies in Kweilin, I think. I was not those babies. The babies in a sling on her shoulder. Her other daughters. And now I feel as if I were in Kweilin amidst the bombing and I can see these babies lying on the side of the road, their red thumbs popped out of their mouths, screaming to be reclaimed. Somebody took them away. They're safe. And now my mother's left me forever, gone back to China to get these babies. I can barely hear Auntie Ying's voice.

'She had searched for years, written letters back and forth,' says Auntie Ying. 'And last year she got an address. She was going to tell your father soon. Aii-ya, what a shame. A lifetime of waiting.'

Auntie An-mei interrupts with an excited voice: 'So your aunties and I, we wrote to this address,' she says. 'We say that a certain party, your mother, want to meet another certain party. And this party write back to us. They are your sisters, Jing-mei.'

My sisters, I repeat to myself, saying those two words together for the first time.

Auntie An-mei is holding a sheet of paper as thin as wrapping tissue. In perfectly straight vertical rows I see Chinese characters written in blue fountain-pen ink. A word is smudged. A tear? I take the letter with shaking hands, marveling at how smart my sisters must be to be able to read and write Chinese.

The aunties are all smiling at me, as though I had been a dying person who has now miraculously recovered. Auntie Ying is handing me another envelope. Inside is a check made out to June Woo for $1,200. I can't believe it.

'My sisters are sending *me* money?' I ask.

'No, no,' says Auntie Lin with her mock exasperated voice. 'Every year we save our mah jong winnings for big banquet at fancy restaurant. Most times your mother win, so most is her money. We add just a little, so you can go Hong Kong, take a train to Shanghai, see your sisters. Besides, we all getting too rich, too fat.' She pats her stomach for proof.

'See my sisters,' I say numbly. I am awed by this prospect, trying to imagine what I would see. And I am embarrassed by the end-of-the-year-banquet lie my aunties have told to mask their generosity.

I am crying now, sobbing and laughing at the same time, seeing but not understanding this loyalty to my mother.

'You must see your sisters and tell them about your mother's death,' says Auntie Ying. 'But most important, you must tell them about her life. The mother they did not know, they must now know.'

'See my sisters, tell them about my mother,' I say, nodding. 'What will I say? What can I tell them about my mother? I don't know anything. She was my mother.'

The aunties are looking at me as if I had become crazy right before their eyes.

'Not know your own mother?' says Auntie An-mei with disbelief. 'How can you say? Your mother is in your bones!'

'Tell them stories of your family here. How she became success,' offers Auntie Lin.

'Tell them stories she told you, lessons she taught, what you know about her mind that has become your mind,' says Auntie Ying. 'Your mother very smart lady.'

I hear more choruses of 'Tell them, tell them' as each Auntie frantically tries to think what should be passed on.

'Her kindness.'

'Her smartness.'

'Her dutiful nature to family.'

'Her hopes, things that matter to her.'

'The excellent dishes she cooked.'

'Imagine, a daughter not knowing her own mother!'

And then it occurs to me. They are frightened. In me, they see their own daughters, just as ignorant, just as unmindful of all the truths and hopes they have brought to America. They see daughters who grow impatient when their mothers talk in Chinese, who think they are stupid when they explain things in fractured English. They see that joy and luck do not mean the same to their daughters, that to these closed American-born minds 'joy luck' is not a word, it does not exist. They see daughters who will bear grandchildren born without any connecting hope passed from generation to generation.

'I will tell them everything,' I say simply, and the aunties look at me with doubtful faces.

'I will remember everything about her and tell them,' I say more firmly. And gradually, one by one, they smile and pat my hand. They still look troubled, as if something were out of balance. But they also look hopeful that what I say will become true. What more can they ask? What more can I promise?

They go back to eating their soft boiled peanuts, saying stories among themselves. They are young girls again, dreaming of good times in the past and good times yet to come. A brother from Ningbo who makes his sister cry with joy when he returns nine thousand dollars plus interest. A youngest son whose stereo and TV repair business is so good he sends leftovers to China. A daughter whose babies are able to swim like fish in a fancy pool in Woodside. Such good stories. The best. They are the lucky ones.

And I am sitting at my mother's place at the mah jong table, on the East, where things begin.

What Do You Do in San Francisco?

Raymond Carver

Introduction

Raymond Carver was born in Clatskanie, a logging town in Oregon, USA, in 1938. His parents, originally from Arkansas, were poor: his father, Clevie Raymond Carver, also known as Raymond, was a farmhand-turned-labourer who later became a skilled sawmill-worker, and his mother, Ella Casey, was a waitress. Three years after his birth the family moved to Washington State, in the north-western corner of the USA, to be joined later by most of Raymond senior's extended family. The younger Raymond spent most of his life near the Pacific coast, in Washington or California.

Soon after leaving high school he married his sixteen-year-old sweetheart, and took a variety of jobs, including sawmill-worker, janitor and salesman, to support his wife and young children. He later claimed, 'I don't really remember much about my life before I became a parent' (unlike writers who maintain that most of the stuff of their fiction happened to them before they were twenty), and began writing seriously, in his spare time, during his 'ferocious years of parenting'.[1] In 1958 he moved with his wife and two babies to a place called Paradise, in northern California, and enrolled as a part-time student at the nearby Chico State College, to take a course in Creative Writing with the not-yet-famous John Gardner. He continued his education at Humboldt State College, California, where his first short story was published in the college literary magazine and his play *Carnations* was performed.

In 1963, on John Gardner's recommendation, Carver joined the Iowa Writers' Workshop, an acclaimed graduate-level creative writing programme at the University of Iowa. Although he did not graduate from the programme, having gravitated back to California in 1964, he did, ten years later, return there as a visiting lecturer. In those ten years he had worked at a variety of jobs, writing in his spare time. His first volume of poetry was published in 1968, and his first collection of short stories in 1974. But despite the beginnings of literary success, Carver's life during this period was clouded; like his father, he had 'trouble with alcohol'.[2] By 1977 when, with the help of Alcoholics Anonymous, he stopped drinking, he had filed for bankruptcy twice, and his first marriage had ended.

In 1978 he met the poet Tess Gallagher, with whom he lived in various parts of the USA, as their careers took them. They also travelled abroad, making visits to South America, Europe and Australia. Further teaching opportunities opened up for Carver, with a spell at Goddard College, Vermont, and a three-year appointment at Syracuse University, New York State. He had by this time been the recipient of a number of fellowships, and in 1983 the American Academy and Institute of Arts and Letters offered him an award that allowed him to write full-time for the next five years. He continued to write poetry, eight collections in all, as well as essays and short stories; he was also a critic, reviewer and, in 1986, guest editor of that year's *Best American Short Stories*. Carver died in Gallagher's home town of Port Angeles, Washington, in 1988, two months after their marriage.

'I love the swift leap of a good story, the excitement that often commences in the first sentence, the sense of beauty and mystery found in the best of them,' says Carver, in the Author's Foreword to *Where I'm Calling From: The Selected Stories* (1988). The sense of mystery in his own stories often derives from what one obituarist described as 'the strangeness concealed behind the banal'.[3] Carver chronicles the unheroic and often insecure lives of ordinary American blue- and white-collar workers; his style is spare and precise, and his dialogue reveals his characters' frequently limited ability to express themselves. But as the director Robert Altman, who combined nine of Carver's stories and one poem into a 'mosaic' film, *Short Cuts* (1993), noted: 'Raymond Carver made poetry out of the prosaic.'[4]

'What Do You Do in San Francisco?' appeared in Carver's first collection of short stories, *Will You Please Be Quiet, Please?* (1976), and in his later volume of selected stories, *Where I'm Calling From* (1988). The story is set in northern California – the actual town of Arcata is about three hundred miles north of San Francisco.

Notes

1. Raymond Carver, 'Fires', in *Fires* (New York: Vintage, 1989), p. 32, p. 34.
2. Raymond Carver, 'My Father's Life', in *Fires*, p. 20.
3. Peter Kemp, 'The American Chekhov', *The Times*, 7 August 1988.
4. Raymond Carver, *Short Cuts* (London: Harvill Press, 1995), introduction by Robert Altman, p. 7.

What Do You Do in San Francisco?

This has nothing to do with me. It's about a young couple with three children who moved into a house on my route the first of last summer. I got to thinking about them again when I picked up last Sunday's newspaper and found a picture of a young man who'd been arrested down in San Francisco for killing his wife and her boyfriend with a baseball bat. It wasn't the same man, of course, though there was a likeness because of the beard. But the situation was close enough to get me thinking.

Henry Robinson is the name. I'm a postman, a federal civil servant, and have been since 1947. I've lived in the West all my life, except for a three-year stint in the Army during the war. I've been divorced twenty years, have two children I haven't seen in almost that long. I'm not a frivolous man, nor am I, in my opinion, a serious man. It's my belief a man has to be a little of both these days. I believe, too, in the value of work – the harder the better. A man who isn't working has got too much time on his hands, too much time to dwell on himself and his problems.

I'm convinced that was partly the trouble with the young man who lived here – his not working. But I'd lay that at her doorstep, too. The woman. She encouraged it.

Beatniks, I guess you'd have called them if you'd seen them. The man wore a pointed brown beard on his chin and looked like he needed to sit down to a good dinner and a cigar afterward. The woman was attractive, with her long dark hair and her fair complexion, there's no getting around that. But put me down for saying she wasn't a good wife and mother. She was a painter. The young man, I don't know what he did – probably something along the same line. Neither of them worked. But they paid their rent and got by somehow – at least for the summer.

The first time I saw them it was around eleven, eleven-fifteen, a Saturday morning. I was about two-thirds through my route when I turned onto their block and noticed a '56 Ford sedan pulled up in the yard with a big open U-Haul behind. There are only three houses on Pine, and theirs was the last house, the others being the Murchisons, who'd been in Arcata a little less than a year, and the Grants, who'd been here about two years. Murchison worked at Simpson Redwood, and Gene Grant was a cook on the morning shift at Denny's. Those two, then a vacant lot, then the house on the end that used to belong to the Coles.

The young man was out in the yard behind the trailer and she was just coming out the front door with a cigarette in her mouth, wearing a tight pair of white jeans and a man's white undershirt. She stopped when she saw me and she stood watching me come down the walk. I slowed up when I came even with their box and nodded in her direction.

"Getting settled all right?" I asked.

"It'll be a little while," she said and moved a handful of hair away from her forehead while she continued to smoke.

"That's good," I said. "Welcome to Arcata."

I felt a little awkward after saying it. I don't know why, but I always found myself feeling awkward the few times I was around this woman. It was one of the things helped turn me against her from the first.

She gave me a thin smile and I started to move on when the young man – Marston was his name – came around from behind the trailer carrying a big carton of toys. Now, Arcata is not a small town and it's not a big town, though I guess you'd have to say it's more on the small side. It's not the end of the world, Arcata, by any means, but most of the people who live here work either in the lumber mills or have something to do with the fishing industry, or else work in one of the downtown stores. People here aren't used to seeing men wear beards – or men who don't work, for that matter.

"Hello," I said. I put out my hand when he set the carton down on the front fender. "The name's Henry Robinson. You folks just arrive?"

"Yesterday afternoon," he said.

"Some trip! It took us fourteen hours just to come from San Francisco," the woman spoke up from the porch. "Pulling that damn trailer."

"My, my," I said and shook my head. "San Francisco? I was just down in San Francisco, let me see, last April or March."

"You were, were you?" she said. "What did you do in San Francisco?"

"Oh, nothing, really. I go down about once or twice a year. Out to Fisherman's Wharf and to see the Giants play. That's about all."

There was a little pause and Marston examined something in the grass with his toe. I started to move on. The kids picked that moment to come flying out the front door, yelling and tearing for the end of the porch. When that screen door banged open, I thought Marston was going to jump out of his skin. But she just stood there with her arms crossed, cool as a cucumber, and never batted an eye. He didn't look good at all. Quick, jerky little movements every time he made to do something. And his eyes – they'd land on you and then slip off somewheres else, then land on you again.

There were three kids, two little curly-headed girls about four or five, and a little bit of a boy tagging after.

"Cute kids," I said. "Well, I got to get under way. You might want to change the name on the box."

"Sure," he said. "Sure. I'll see about it in a day or two. But we don't expect to get any mail for a while yet, in any case."

"You never know," I said. "You never know what'll turn up in this old mail pouch. Wouldn't hurt to be prepared." I started to go. "By the way, if you're looking for a job in the mills, I can tell you who to see at Simpson Redwood. A friend of mine's a foreman there. He'd probably have something . . . " I tapered off, seeing how they didn't look interested.

"No, thanks," he said.

"He's not looking for a job," she put in.

"Well, goodbye, then."

"So long," Marston said.

Not another word from her.

That was on a Saturday, as I said, the day before Memorial Day. We took Monday as a holiday and I wasn't by there again until Tuesday. I can't say I was surprised to see the U-Haul still there in the front yard. But it did surprise me to see he still hadn't unloaded it. I'd say about a quarter of the stuff had made its way to the front porch – a covered chair and a chrome kitchen chair and a big carton of clothes that had the flaps pulled off the top. Another quarter must have gotten inside the house, and the rest of the stuff was still in the trailer. The kids were carrying little sticks and hammering on the sides of the trailer as they climbed in and out over the tailgate. Their mamma and daddy were nowheres to be seen.

On Thursday I saw him out in the yard again and reminded him about changing the name on the box.

"That's something I've got to get around to doing," he said.

"Takes time," I said. "There's lots of things to take care of when you're moving into a new place. People that lived here, the Coles, just moved out two days before you came. He was going to work in Eureka. With the Fish and Game Department."

Marston stroked his beard and looked off as if thinking of something else.

"I'll be seeing you," I said.

"So long," he said.

Well, the long and the short of it was he never did change the name on the box. I'd come along a bit later with a piece of mail for that address and he'd say something like, "Marston? Yes, that's for us, Marston. . . . I'll have to change the name on that box one of these days. I'll get myself a can of paint and just paint over that other name . . . Cole," all the time his eyes drifting here and there. Then he'd look at me kind of out the corners and bob his chin once or twice. But he never did change the name on the box, and after a time I shrugged and forgot about it.

You hear rumors. At different times I heard that he was an ex-con on parole who come to Arcata to get out of the unhealthy San Francisco environment. According to this story, the woman was his wife, but none of the kids belonged to him. Another story was that he had committed a crime and was hiding out here. But not many people subscribed to that. He just didn't look the sort who'd do something really *criminal*. The story most folks seemed to believe, at least the one that got around most, was the most horrible. The woman was a dope addict, so this story went, and the husband had brought her up here to help her get rid of the habit. As evidence, the fact of Sallie Wilson's visit was always brought up – Sallie Wilson from the Welcome Wagon. She dropped in on them one afternoon and said later that, no lie, there was something funny about them – the woman, particular. One minute the woman would be sitting and listening to Sallie run on – all ears, it seemed – and the next she'd get up while Sallie was still talking and start to work on her painting as if Sallie wasn't there. Also the way she'd be fondling and kissing the kids, then suddenly start screeching at them for no apparent reason. Well, just the way her *eyes* looked if you came up close to her, Sallie said. But Sallie Wilson has been snooping and prying for years under cover of the Welcome Wagon.

"You don't know," I'd say when someone would bring it up. "Who can say? If he'd just go to work now."

All the same, the way it looked to me was that they had their fair share of trouble down there in San Francisco, whatever was the nature of the trouble, and they decided to get clear away from it. Though why they ever picked Arcata to settle in, it's hard to say, since they surely didn't come looking for work.

The first few weeks there was no mail to speak of, just a few circulars, from Sears and Western Auto and the like. Then a few letters began to come in, maybe one or two a week. Sometimes I'd see one or the other of them out around the house when I came by and sometimes not. But the kids were always there, running in and out of the house or playing in the vacant lot next door. Of course, it wasn't a model home to begin with, but after they'd been there a while the weeds sprouted up and what grass there was yellowed and died. You hate to see something like that. I understand Old Man Jessup came out once or twice to get them to turn the water on, but they claimed they couldn't buy a hose. So he left them a hose. Then I noticed the kids playing with it over in the field, and that was the end of that. Twice I saw a little white sports car in front, a car that hadn't come from around here.

One time only I had anything to do with the woman direct. There was a letter with postage due, and I went up to the door with it. One of the little girls let me in and ran off to fetch her mama. The place was cluttered with odds and ends of old furniture and with clothing tossed just anywhere. But it wasn't what you'd call dirty. Not tidy maybe, but not dirty either. An old couch and chair stood along one wall in the living room. Under the window was a bookcase made out of bricks and boards, crammed full of little paperback books. In the corner there was a stack of paintings with their faces turned away, and to one side another painting stood on an easel covered over with a sheet.

I shifted my mail pouch and stood my ground, but starting to wish I'd paid the difference myself. I eyed the easel as I waited, about to sidle over and raise the sheet when I heard steps.

"What can I do for you?" she said, appearing in the hallway and not at all friendly.

I touched the brim of my cap and said, "A letter here with postage due, if you don't mind."

"Let me see. Who's it from? Why it's from Jer! That kook. Sending us a letter without a stamp. Lee!" she called out. "Here's a letter from Jerry." Marston came in, but he didn't look too happy. I leaned on first one leg, then the other, waiting.

"I'll pay it," she said, "seeing as it's from old Jerry. Here. Now goodbye."

Things went on in this fashion – which is to say no fashion at all. I won't say the people hereabouts got used to them – they weren't the sort you'd ever really get used to. But after a bit no one seemed to pay them much mind any more. People might stare at his beard if they met him pushing the grocery cart in Safeway, but that's about all. You didn't hear any more stories.

Then one day they disappeared. In two different directions. I found out later she'd taken off the week before with somebody – a man – and that after a few days he'd taken the kids to his mother's over to Redding. For six days running, from one Thursday to the following Wednesday, their mail stayed in the box. The shades were all pulled and nobody knew for certain whether or not they'd lit out for good. But that Wednesday I noticed the Ford parked in the yard again, all the shades still down but the mail gone.

Beginning the next day he was out there at the box every day waiting for me to hand over the mail, or else he was sitting on the porch steps smoking a cigarette, waiting, it was plain to see. When he saw me coming, he'd stand up, brush the seat of his trousers, and walk over by the box. If it happened that I had any mail for him, I'd see him start scanning the return addresses even before I could get it handed over. We seldom exchanged a word, just nodded at each other if our eyes happened to meet, which wasn't often. He was suffering, though – anybody could see that – and I wanted to help the boy somehow, if I could. But I didn't know what to say exactly.

It was one morning a week or so after his return that I saw him walking up and down in front of the box with his hands in his back pockets, and I made up my mind to say something. What, I didn't know yet, but I was going to say something, sure. His back was to me as I came up the walk. When I got to him, he suddenly turned on me and there was such a look on his face it froze the words in my mouth. I stopped in my tracks with his article of mail. He took a couple of steps toward me and I handed it over without a peep. He stared at it as if dumbfounded.

"Occupant," he said.

It was a circular from L.A. advertising a hospital-insurance plan. I'd dropped off at least seventy-five that morning. He folded it in two and went back to the house.

Next day he was out there same as always. He had his old look to his face, seemed more in control of himself than the day before. This time I had a hunch I had what it was he'd been waiting for. I'd looked at it down at the station that morning when I was arranging the mail into packets. It was a plain white envelope addressed in a woman's curlicue handwriting that took up most of the space. It had a Portland postmark, and the return address showed the initials JD and a Portland street address.

"Morning," I said, offering the letter.

He took it from me without a word and went absolutely pale. He tottered a minute and then started back for the house, holding the letter up to the light.

I called out, "She's no good, boy. I could tell that the minute I saw her. Why don't you forget her? Why don't you go to work and forget her? What have you got against work? It was work, day and night, work that gave me oblivion when I was in your shoes and there was a war on where I was. . . . "

After that he didn't wait outside for me any more, and he was only there another five days. I'd catch a glimpse of him, though, each day, waiting for me just the same, but standing behind the window and looking out at me through the curtain. He wouldn't come out until I'd gone by, and then I'd hear the screen door. If I looked back, he'd seem to be in no hurry at all to reach the box.

The last time I saw him he was standing at the window and looked calm and rested. The curtains were down, all the shades were raised, and I figured at the time he was getting his things together to leave. But I could tell by the look on his face he wasn't watching for me this time. He was staring past me, over me, you might say, over the rooftops and the trees, south. He just kept staring even after I'd come even with the house and moved on down the sidewalk. I looked back. I could see him still there at the window. The feeling was so strong, I had to turn around and look for myself in the same direction he was. But, as you might guess, I didn't see anything except the same old timber, mountains, sky.

The next day he was gone. He didn't leave any forwarding. Sometimes mail of some kind or other shows up for him or his wife or for the both of them. If it's first-class, we hold it a day, then send it back to where it came from. There isn't much. And I don't mind. It's all work, one way or the other, and I'm always glad to have it.

Mr Sumarsono

Roxana Robinson

Introduction

Roxana Barry was born in Pine Mountain, Kentucky, USA, in 1946. Her mother, Alice Scoville, was from Philadelphia and her father, Stuyvesant Barry, came from New York. Both her grandfathers were lawyers, but her parents turned aside from the privileged world of their families and went to teach at a mountain school in Kentucky. They moved back to Pennsylvania when Stuyvesant Barry, who had become a Quaker, was appointed Principal of Buckingham Friends School, Lahaska, in 1950. Roxana was a pupil there, and later attended her mother's old school, Shipley, in Bryn Mawr. She spent two years at Bennington, the prestigious liberal arts college in Vermont, where one of her teachers was Bernard Malamud. After her first marriage, from which she has one daughter, she took a degree in English Literature at the University of Michigan, but despite the direction of her studies and family leanings (both her parents wrote newspaper columns and her brother is a journalist), she did not immediately pursue a career as a writer. Instead, she worked for several years at Sotheby's in New York, specializing in American painting, and publishing some works of art history. After her divorce and second marriage, to the investor Hamilton Robinson, she began to build her reputation as a fiction-writer.

Robinson's short fiction has appeared, since the 1980s, in numerous American magazines and journals, including the *New Yorker*, *Harper's* and the *Atlantic Monthly*. But it was actually through a British literary periodical, the *Fiction Magazine*, that she established herself, with encouragement to submit a novel to a London publisher. *Summer Light*, which had begun life as a short story, duly appeared in the UK in 1987, then in the USA the following year. She has published two further novels, *This is my Daughter* (1998) and *Sweetwater* (2003), and three collections of short stories, *A Glimpse of Scarlet* (1991), *Asking for Love* (1996), and *A Perfect Stranger* (2005). Her interest in the American short story as a genre can be seen in her Foreword to *The Best Early Stories of F. Scott Fitzgerald* (2005) and her introduction to *The New York Stories of Edith Wharton*, which she compiled in 2007.

Robinson's writing also spans a number of other areas. As a scholar of nineteenth- and early twentieth-century American arts, besides the critical studies she published in the 1970s, she produced in 1989 an acclaimed biography of Georgia O'Keefe, one of the major figures of twentieth-century American art, who had died in 1986. As a journalist Robinson writes frequently on the environment and the natural world in a wide range of magazines and news-papers; she is a book reviewer for the *New York Times* as well as contributing travel articles from time to time. Her creative writing workshops have also taken her to different parts of the USA, including the Universities of Houston and Southern Indiana.

Home for Robinson, though, is in the north-eastern states, principally New York and Maine. Some of her fiction is set in other parts of the USA, or Europe (England or France), but her most characteristic focus is on genteel middle-class communities in and around New York, and because of the nature of her fictional territory, she is sometimes compared with John Cheever. Her finely nuanced observations of family life reveal the complexities of close relationships in all their strangeness, and her short stories often work towards a powerful moment that changes or shifts her characters' perceptions.

'Mr Sumarsono' was first published in the *Atlantic Monthly*, and subsequently appeared in *The Best American Short Stories of 1994*, and in Britain in *The Second Penguin Book of Modern Women's Short Stories*, edited by Susan Hill (1994). It was collected in Robinson's second volume of short stories, *Asking for Love*. Robinson's immersion in the visual arts (which, arguably, leaves traces in most of her fiction) might be discerned here not simply in the story's powerful visual images but also in the idea of portraits and what they reveal.

Mr Sumarsono

Oh, Mr Sumarsono, Mr Sumarsono. We remember you so well. I wonder how you remember us?

The three of us met Mr Sumarsono at the Trenton train station. The platform stretched down the tracks in both directions, long, half-roofed, and dirty. Beyond the tracks on either side were high corrugated-metal sidings, battered and patched. Above the sidings were the tops of weeds and the backs of ramshackle buildings, grimy and desolate. Stretching out above the tracks was an aerial grid of electrical power lines, their knotted, uneven rectangles connecting every city on the Eastern Corridor in a dismal industrial way.

My mother, my sister, Kate, and I stood waiting for Mr Sumarsono at the foot of the escalator, which did not work. The escalator had worked once; I could remember it working, though Kate, who was younger than I, could not. Now the metal staircase towered above the platform, silent and immobile, giving the station a surreal air. If you used it as a staircase, which people often did, as you set your foot on each moveable, motionless step, you had an odd feeling of sensory dislocation, like watching a color movie in black and white. You knew something was wrong, though you couldn't put your finger on it.

Mr Sumarsono got off his train at the other end of the platform from us. He stood still for a moment and looked hesitantly up and down. He didn't know which way to look or who he was looking for. My mother lifted her arm and waved; we knew who he was, though we had never seen him before. It was 1961, and Mr Sumarsono was the only Indonesian to get off the train at Trenton, New Jersey.

Mr Sumarsono was wearing a neat suit and leather shoes, like an American businessman, but he did not look like an American. The suit was brown, not grey, and there was a slight sheen to it. And Mr Sumarsono himself was built in a different way from Americans; he was slight and graceful, with narrow shoulders and an absence of strut. His movements were diffident, and there seemed to be extra curves in them. This was true even of simple movements, like picking up his suitcase and starting down the platform toward the three of us, standing by the escalator that didn't work.

Kate and I stood next to my mother as she waved and smiled. Kate and I did not wave and smile; this was all my mother's idea. Kate was seven and I was ten. We were not entirely sure what a diplomat was, and we were not at all sure that we wanted to be nice to one all weekend. I wondered why he didn't have friends of his own age.

'Hoo-oo,' my mother called, mortifyingly, even though Mr Sumarsono had already seen us and was making his graceful way toward us. His steps were small and his movements modest. He smiled in a non-specific way, to show that he had seen us, but my mother kept on waving and calling. It took a long time, this interlude; encouraging shouts and gestures from my mother, Mr Sumarsono's unhurried approach. I wondered if he too was embarrassed by my mother; once he glanced swiftly around, as though he were looking for an alternative family to spend the weekend with. He had reason to be uneasy; the grimy Trenton platform with its corrugated sidings and aerial grid did not suggest a rural retreat. And when he saw us standing by the stationary escalator, my mother waving and calling, Kate and I sullenly silent, he may have felt that things were off to a poor start.

My mother was short, with big bones and a square face. She had thick, dark hair and a wide mobile mouth. She was a powerful woman. She used to be on the stage, and she still delivered to the back row. When she calls 'Hoo-oo' at a train station, everyone at that station knows it.

'Mr Su*mar*sono,' she called out as he came up to us. The accent is on the second syllable. That's what the people at the UN had told her, and she made us practice, sighing and complaining, until we said it the way she wanted; Su*mar*sono.

Mr Sumarsono gave a formal nod and a small smile. His face was oval, and his eyes were long. His skin was very pale brown, and smooth. His hair was shiny and black, and it was also very smooth. Everything about him seemed polished and smooth.

'Hello!' said my mother, seizing his hand and shaking it. 'I'm Mrs Riordan. And this is Kate, and this is Susan.' Kate and I cautiously put out our hands, and Mr Sumarsono shook them limply, bowing at each of us.

My mother put out her hand again. 'Shall I take your bag?' But Mr Sumarsono defended his suitcase. 'We're just up here,' said my mother, giving up on the bag and leading the way to the escalator.

We all began the climb, but after a few steps my mother looked back.

'This is an escalator,' she said loudly.

Mr Sumarsono gave a short nod.

'It takes you *up*,' my mother called, and pointed to the roof overhead. Mr Sumarsono, holding his suitcase with both hands, looked at the ceiling.

'It doesn't work right now,' my mother said illuminatingly, and turned back to her climb.

'No,' I heard Mr Sumarsono say. He glanced cautiously again at the ceiling.

Exactly parallel to the escalator was a broad concrete staircase, which another group of people was climbing. We were separated only by the handrail, so that for a disorientating second you felt you were looking at a mirror from which you were missing. It intensified the feeling you got from climbing the stopped escalator – dislocation, bewilderment, doubt at your own senses.

A woman on the real staircase looked over at us, and I could tell that my mother gave her a brilliant smile; the woman looked away at once. We were the only people on the escalator.

On the way home Kate and I sat in the back seat and watched our mother keep turning to speak to Mr Sumarsono. She asked him long, complicated, cheerful questions. 'Well, Mr Sumarsono, had you been in this country at all before you came to the UN or is this your first visit? I know you've only been working at the UN for a short time.'

Mr Sumarsono answered everything with a polite unfinished nod. Then he would turn back and look out the window again. I wondered if he was thinking about jumping out of the car. I wondered what Mr Sumarsono was expecting from a weekend in the country. I hoped it was not a walk to the pond; Kate and I had planned one for that afternoon. We were going to watch the mallards nesting, and I hoped we wouldn't have to include a middle-aged Indonesian in leather shoes.

When we got home my mother looked at me meaningfully.

'Susan, will you and Kate show Mr Sumarsono to his room?'

Mr Sumarsono looked politely at us, his head tilted slightly side-ways.

Gracelessly I leaned over to pick up Mr Sumarsono's suitcase, as I had been told. He stopped me by putting his hand out, palm front, in a traffic policeman's gesture.

'No, no,' he said, with a small smile, and he took hold of the suitcase himself. I fell back, pleased not to do as I'd been told, but also I was impressed, almost awed, by Mr Sumarsono.

What struck me was the grace of his gesture. His hand slid easily out of its cuff and exposed a narrow brown wrist, much narrower than my own. When he put his hand up in the *Stop!* that an Amer-ican hand would make, this was a polite, subtle, and yielding signal, quite beautiful and infinitely sophisticated, a gesture that suggested a thousand reasons for doing this, a thousand ways to go about it.

I let him take the suitcase and we climbed the front stairs, me first, Kate next, and then Mr Sumarsono, as though we were playing a game. We marched solemnly, single file, through the second-floor hall and up the back stairs to the third floor. The guest room was small, with a bright hooked rug on the wide old floorboards, white ruffled curtains at the windows, and slanting eaves. There was a spool bed, a table next to it, a straight chair, and a chest of drawers. On the chest of drawers there was a photograph of my great-grandmother, her austere face framed by faded embroidery. On the bedspread was a large tan smudge, where our cat liked to spend the afternoons.

Mr Sumarsono put his suitcase down and looked around the room. I looked around with him, and suddenly the guest room, and in fact our whole house, took on a new aspect. Until that moment, I had thought our house was numbingly ordinary, that it repres-ented the decorating norm; patchwork quilts, steep, narrow stair-cases, slanting ceilings and spool beds. I assumed everyone had faded photographs of Victorian great-grandparents dotted mourn-fully around their rooms. Now it came to me that this was not the case. I wondered what houses were like in Indonesia, or apartments in New York. Somehow I knew; they were low, sleek, modern, all on one floor, with hard gleaming surfaces. They were full of right angles and empty of allusions to the past; they were the exact opposite of

our house. Silently and fiercely I blamed my mother for our environment, which was, I now saw, eccentric, totally abnormal.

Mr Sumarsono looked at me and nodded precisely again.

'Thank you,' he said.

'Don't hit your head,' Kate said.

Mr Sumarsono bowed, closing his eyes.

'On the ceiling,' Kate said, pointing to it.

'The ceiling,' he repeated, looking up at it too.

'Don't hit your head on the ceiling,' she said loudly, and Mr
Sumarsono looked at her and smiled.

'The bathroom's in here,' I said, showing him.

'Thank you,' he said.

'Susan,' my mother called up the stairs, 'tell Mr Sumarsono to
come downstairs when he's ready for lunch.'

'Come-downstairs-when-you're-ready-for-lunch,' I said unneces-
sarily. I pointed graphically into my open mouth and then bolted,
clattering rapidly down both sets of stairs. Kate was right behind me,
our knees banging in our rush to get away.

Mother had set four places for lunch, which was on the screened-
in porch overlooking the lawn. The four places meant a battle.

'Mother,' I said mutinously.

'What is it?' Mother said. 'Would you fill a pitcher of water, Susan.'

'Kate and I are not *having* lunch,' I said, running water into the
blue and white pottery pitcher.

'And get the butter dish. Of course you're having lunch,' said my
mother. She was standing at the old wooden kitchen table, making
a plate of deviled eggs. She was messily filling the rubbery white
hollows with dollops of yolk-and-mayonnaise mixture. The slippery
egg-halves rocked unstably, and the mixture stuck to her spoon.
She scraped it into the little boats with her finger. I watched with
distaste. In a ranch house, I thought, or in New York, this would not
happen. In New York, food would be prepared on polished man-
made surfaces. It would be brought to you on gleaming platters by
silent waiters.

'I told you Kate and I are *not* having lunch,' I said. 'We're taking
a picnic to the pond.' I put the pitcher on the table.

Mother turned to me. 'We have been through this already, Susan.
We have a guest for the weekend, and I want you girls to be polite

to him. He is a stranger in this country, and I expect you to *extend* yourselves. Think how *you* would feel if *you* were in a strange land.'

'Ex*tend* myself,' I said rudely, under my breath, but loud enough so my mother could hear. This was exactly the sort of idiotic thing she said. 'I certainly wouldn't go around hoping people would *extend* themselves.' I thought of people stretched out horribly, their arms yearning in one direction, their feet in another, all for my benefit. 'If I were in a strange country I'd like everyone to leave me alone.'

'Ready for lunch?' my mother said brightly to Mr Sumarsono, who stood diffidently in the doorway. 'We're just about to sit down. Kate, will you bring out the butter?'

'I did already,' I said virtuously, and folded my arms in a hostile manner.

'We're having deviled eggs,' Mother announced as we sat down. She picked up the plate of them and smiled humorously. 'We call them "deviled".'

'De-vil,' Kate said, speaking very loudly and slowly. She pointed at the eggs and then put two forked fingers behind her head, like horns. Mr Sumarsono looked at her horns. He nodded pleasantly.

My mother talked all through lunch, asking Mr Sumarsono mystifying questions and then answering them herself in case he couldn't. Mr Sumarsono kept a polite half-smile on his face, sometimes repeating the last few words of her sentences. Even while he was eating, he seemed to be listening attentively. He ate very neatly, taking small bites, and laying his fork and knife precisely side by side when he was through. Kate and I pointedly said nothing. We were boycotting lunch, though we smiled horribly at Mr Sumarsono if he caught our eyes.

After lunch my mother said she was going to take a nap. As she said this, she laid her head sideways on her folded hands and closed her eyes. Then she pointed upstairs. Mr Sumarsono nodded. He rose from the table, pushed in his chair, and went meekly back to his room, his shoes creaking on the stairs.

Kate and I did the dishes in a slapdash way and took off for the pond. We spent the afternoon on a hill overlooking the marshy end, watching the mallards and arguing over the binoculars. We only had one pair. There had been a second pair once; I could remember this, though Kate could not. Our father had taken the other set with him.

Mother was already downstairs in the kitchen when we got back. She was singing cheerfully, and wearing a pink dress with puffy sleeves and a full skirt. The pink dress was a favorite of Kate's and mine. It irritated me to see that she had put it on as though she were at a party. This was not a party; she had merely gotten hold of a captive guest, a complete stranger who understood nothing she said. This was not a cause for celebration.

She gave us a big smile when we came in.

'Any luck with the mallards?' she asked.

'Not really,' I said coolly. A lie.

Kate and I set the table, and Mother asked Kate to pick some flowers for the centerpiece. We were having dinner in the dining room, my mother said, with the white plates with gold rims from our grandmother. While we were setting the table my mother called in from the kitchen, 'Oh, Susan, put out some wineglasses too, for me and Mr Sumarsono.'

Kate and I looked at each other.

'*Wine*glasses?' Kate mouthed silently.

'Wineglasses?' I called back, my voice sober, for my mother, my face wild, for Kate.

'That's right,' said mother cheerfully. 'We're going to be festive.'

'*Festive!*' I mouthed to Kate, and we doubled over, shaking our heads and rolling our eyes.

We put out the wineglasses, handling them gingerly, as though they gave off dangerous, unpredictable rays. The glasses, standing boldly at the knife tips, altered the landscape of the table. Kate and I felt as though we were in the presence of something powerful and alien. We looked warningly at each other, pointing at the glasses and frowning, nodding our heads meaningfully. We picked them up and mimed drinking from them. We wiped our mouths and began to stagger, crossing our eyes and hiccuping. When Mother appeared in the doorway we froze, and Kate, who was in the process of lurching sideways, turned her movement into a pirouette, her face clear, her eyes uncrossed.

'Be careful with those glasses,' said my mother.

'We are,' said Kate, striking a classical pose, the wineglass held worshipfully aloft, like a chalice.

When dinner was ready mother went to the foot of the stairs and called up, 'Hooo-oo!' several times. There was no answer, and after a pause she called, 'Mr Sumarsono! Dinner. Come down for dinner!' We began to hear noises from overhead as Mr Sumarsono rose obediently from his nap.

When we sat down I noticed that mother was not only in the festive pink dress but that she was bathed and particularly fresh-looking. She had done her hair in a special way, smoothing it back from her forehead. She was smiling a lot. When she had served the plates, my mother picked up the bottle of wine and offered Mr Sumarsono a glass.

'Would you like a little *wine*, Mr Sumarsono?' she asked, leaning forward, her head cocked. We were having the dish she always made for guests; baked chicken pieces in a sauce made of Campbell's cream of mushroom soup.

'Thank you,' Mr Sumarsono nodded and pushed forward his glass. My mother beamed and filled his glass. Kate and I watched her as we cut up our chicken. We watched her as we drank from our milk glasses, our eyes round and unblinking over the rims.

We ate in silence, a silence broken only by my mother. 'Mr Sumarsono,' my mother said, having finished most of her chicken and most of her wine, 'do you have a *wife*? A *family*?'

She gestured first at herself, then at us. Mr Sumarsono looked searchingly across the table at Kate and me. We were chewing and stared solemnly back.

Mr Sumarsono nodded his half-nod, his head stopping at the bottom of the movement, without completing the second half of it.

'A wife?' said my mother, gratified. She pointed again at herself. She is not a wife and hasn't been for five years, but Mr Sumarsono wouldn't know that. I wondered what he did know. I wondered if he wondered where my father was. Perhaps he thought that it was an American custom for the father to live in another house, spending his day apart from his wife and children, eating his dinner alone. Perhaps Mr Sumarsono was expecting my father to arrive ceremoniously after dinner, dressed in silken robes and carrying a carved wooden writing case, ready to entertain his guest with tales of the hill people. What did Mr Sumarsono expect of us? It was unimaginable.

Whatever Mr Sumarsono was expecting, my mother was deter-mined to deliver what she could of it. In the pink dress, full of red wine, she was changing before our very eyes. She was warming up, turning larger and grander, glowing and powerful.

'Mr Sumarsono,' said my mother happily, 'do you have photo-graphs of your family?'

There was a silence. My mother pointed again to her chest, plump and rosy above the pink dress. Then she held up an invisible camera. She closed one eye and clicked loudly at Mr Sumarsono. He watched her carefully.

'Photo of wife?' she said again loudly, and again pointed at herself. Then she pointed at him. Mr Sumarsono gave his truncated nod and stood up. He bowed again and pointed to the ceiling. Then, with a complicated and unfinished look, loaded with meaning, he left the room.

Kate and I looked accusingly at our mother. Dinner would now be prolonged indefinitely, her fault.

'He's gone to get his photographs,' Mother said. 'The poor man, he must miss his wife and children. Don't you feel sorry for him, thousands of miles away from his family? Oh, thousands. He's here for six months, all alone. They told me that at the UN. It's all very uncertain. He doesn't know when he gets leaves, how long after that he'll be here. Think of how his poor wife feels.' She shook her head and took a long sip of her wine. She remembered us and added reprovingly, 'And what about his poor children? Their father is thou-sands of miles away! They don't know when they'll see him!' Her voice was admonitory, suggesting that this was partly our fault.

Kate and I did not comment on Mr Sumarsono's children. We ourselves did not know when we would see our father, and we did not want to discuss that either. What we longed for was for all this to be over, this endless, messy meal, full of incomprehensible exchanges.

Kate sighed discreetly, her mouth slightly open for silence, and she swung her legs under the table. I picked up a chicken thigh with my fingers and began to pick delicately at it with my teeth. This was forbidden, but I thought that the wine and the excite-ment would distract my mother from my behavior. It did. She sighed deeply, shook her head, and picked up her fork. She began eating in a dreamy way.

'Oh, I'm glad we're having rice!' she said suddenly, gratified. 'That must make Mr Sumarsono feel at home.' She looked at me. 'You know that's all they have in Indonesia,' she said in a teacherly sort of way. 'Rice, bamboo, things like lizard.'

Another ridiculous statement. I knew such a place could not exist, but Kate was younger, and I pictured what she must imagine; thin stalks of rice struggling up through a dense and endless bamboo forest. People in brown suits pushing their way among the limber stalks, looking fruitlessly around for houses, telephones, something to eat besides lizard.

Mr Sumarsono appeared again in the doorway. He was holding a large leather camera case. He had already begun to unbuckle and unsnap, to extricate the camera from it. He took out a light meter and held it up. My mother raised her fork at him.

'Rice!' she said enthusiastically. 'That's familiar, isn't it? Does it remind you of *home*?' With her fork she gestured expansively at the dining room. Mr Sumarsono looked obediently round, at the mahogany sideboard with its crystal decanters, the glass-fronted cabinet full of family china, the big, stern portrait of my grandfather in his pink hunting coat, holding his riding crop. Mr Sumarsono looked back at my mother, who was still holding up her fork. He nodded.

'Yes?' my mother said, pleased.

'Yes,' said Mr Sumarsono.

My mother looked down again. Blinking in a satisfied way she said, 'I'm glad I thought of it.' I knew she hadn't thought of it until that moment. She always made rice with the chicken-and-Campbell's-cream-of-mushroom-soup dish. Having an Indonesian turn up to eat it was a lucky chance.

Mr Sumarsono held up his camera. The light meter dangled from a strap, and the flash attachment projected from one corner. He put the camera up to his eye, and his face vanished altogether. My mother was looking down at her plate again, peaceful, absorbed, suffused with red wine and satisfaction.

I could see that my mother's view of all this – the meal, the visit, the weekend – was different from my own. I could see that she was pleased by everything about it. She was pleased by her polite and helpful daughters; she was pleased by her charming farmhouse with its stylish and original touches. She was pleased at her delicious and unusual meal, and most important, she was pleased by her own generosity, by being able to offer this poor stranger her lavish bounty.

She was wrong, she was always wrong, my mother. She was wrong about everything. I was resigned to it; at ten you have no control over your mother. The evening would go on like this, endless, excruciating. My mother would act foolish, Kate and I would be mortified and Mr Sumarsono would be mystified. It was no wonder my father had left; embarrassment.

Mr Sumarsono was now ready and he spoke. 'Please!' he said politely. My mother looked up again and realized this time what he was doing. She shook her head, raising her hands in deprecation.

'No, no,' she said, smiling. 'Not me. Don't take a picture of me. I wanted to see a picture of your wife.' She pointed at Mr Sumarsono. 'Your wife,' she said, 'your children.'

I was embarrassed not only for my mother but for poor Mr Sumarsono. Whatever he had expected from a country weekend in America, it could not have been a cramped attic room, two sullen girls, a voluble and incomprehensible hostess. I felt we had failed him, we had betrayed his unruffled courtesy, by our bewildering commands, our waving forks, our irresponsible talk about lizards. I wanted to save him. I wanted to liberate poor Mr Sumarsono from this aerial grid of misunderstandings. I wanted to cut the power lines, but I couldn't think of a way. I watched him despondently, waiting for him to subside at my mother's next order. Perhaps she would send him upstairs for another nap.

But things had changed. Mr Sumarsono stood gracefully, firm and erect, in charge. Somehow he had performed a coup. He had seized power. The absence of strut did not mean an absence of command, and we now saw how an Indonesian diplomat behaved when he was in charge. Like the *Stop!* gesture, Mr Sumarsono's reign was elegant and sophisticated, entirely convincing. It was suddenly clear that it was no longer possible to tell Mr Sumarsono what to do.

'No,' said Mr Sumarsono clearly. 'You wife.' He bowed firmly at my mother. 'You children.' He bowed at us.

Mr Sumarsono stooped over us, his courtesy exquisite and unyielding. 'Please,' he said, 'now photograph.' He held up the camera. It covered his face entirely, a strange mechanical mask. 'My photograph,' he said in a decisive tone.

He aimed the camera first at me. I produced a taut and artificial smile, and at once he reappeared from behind the camera. 'No smile,' he said firmly, shaking his head. 'No smile.' He himself produced a hideous smile, then shook his head and turned grave. 'Ah!' he said, nodding, and pointed to me. Chastened, I sat solemn and rigid while he disappeared behind the camera again. I didn't move even when he had finished, after the flash and the clicks of lenses and winding sprockets.

Mr Sumarsono turned to Kate, who had learned from me and offered up a smooth and serious face. Mr Sumarsono nodded, but stepped toward her. 'Hand!' he said, motioning toward it, and he made the gesture that he wanted. Kate stared but obediently did as he asked.

When Mr Sumarsono turned to my mother, I worried again that she would stage a last-ditch attempt to take over, that she would insist on mortifying us all.

'Now!' said Mr Sumarsono, bowing peremptorily at her. 'Please.' I looked at her, and to my amazement, relief and delight, my mother did exactly the right thing. She smiled at Mr Sumarsono in a normal and relaxed way, as though they were old friends. She leaned easily back in her chair, graceful – I could suddenly see – and poised. She smoothed her hair back from her forehead.

In Mr Sumarsono's pictures, the images of us that he produced, this is how we look.

I am staring solemnly at the camera, dead serious, head-on. I look mystified, as though I am trying to understand something inexplicable; what the people around me mean when they speak, perhaps. I look as though I am in a foreign country where I do not speak the language.

Kate looks both radiant and ethereal; her eyes are alight. Her mouth is puckered into a mirthful V; she is trying to suppress a smile. The V of her mouth is echoed above her face by her two forked fingers, poised airily behind her head.

But it is the picture of my mother that surprised me the most. Mr Sumarsono's portrait was of someone entirely different from the person I knew, though the face was the same. Looking at it gave me the same feeling that the stopped escalator did; a sense of dislocation, a sudden uncertainty about my own beliefs. In the photograph my mother leans back against her chair like a queen, all her power evident, and at rest. Her face is turned slightly away; she is guarding her privacy. Her nose, her cheeks, her eyes, are bright with wine and excitement, but she is calm and amused. A mother cannot be beautiful, because she is so much more a mother than a woman, but in this picture it struck me, my mother looked, in an odd way, beautiful. I could see for the first time that other people might think she actually was beautiful.

Mr Sumarsono's view of my mother was of a glowing, self-assured, generous woman. And Mr Sumarsono himself was a real person, despite his meekness. I knew that; I had seen him take control. His view meant something; I could not ignore it. And I began to wonder.

We still have the pictures. Mr Sumarsono brought them with him the next time he came out for the weekend.

The Last Mohican

Bernard Malamud

Introduction

Bernard Malamud was born in Brooklyn, New York, in 1914. His parents, Max Malamud and Bertha Fidelman, were Jewish immigrants from Tsarist Russia. His father ran a small grocer's shop in the Gravesend Avenue section of Brooklyn, and one of his uncles was an actor in the Second Avenue Yiddish Theatre. The family spoke Yiddish at home, and the rhythms of Yiddish speech can sometimes be heard in Malamud's writing, although he himself referred to the style of some of his dialogue as simply 'immigrant speech'.

Malamud wrote stories for his high school magazine, then, intending to be an English teacher, he attended New York's City College and later completed his MA at Columbia University. During the Second World War he had a number of temporary jobs, including a brief period working as a clerk in the Bureau of the Census in Washington, DC, before he returned to New York to teach evening high-school English classes in Harlem and Brooklyn, home to many of the city's ethnic minorities. His evening work freed up time in the day for writing, and by then, reflecting on the horrors of the Holocaust, he felt that he had something to say as a writer. But although his work is often seen as part of a Jewish-American literary tradition, one of the distinctive qualities of Jewishness in Malamud's writing is its universality: it is inclusive rather than exclusive, the Jew standing as a metaphor for the human.

In 1949 he took up a teaching post at Oregon State University and remained there until 1961, travelling when he could and writing stories for magazine publication. During this period he spent a year in Rome, on a *Partisan Review* fellowship, with his Italian wife and their two children. He also began to publish novels, using the urban settings of his own New York upbringing in *The Natural* (1952) – one of his few works *not* to feature Jewish characters – and *The Assistant* (1957). He returned to the East Coast to teach for part of each year at Bennington College, Vermont, from 1961 until his death in 1986. By then he had published eight novels and several collections of short stories, and won major awards including a Pulitzer Prize for *The Fixer* (1967).

Short stories constituted a major part of Malamud's literary output throughout his career. He relished the tightness of the form, and his stories are well-packed, sometimes surprising, lyrical, with occasional touches of fantasy. He claims to have been influenced by another American master of the short story form, Ernest Hemingway, and by the films of Charlie Chaplin ('the rhythm and snap of his comedy and his wonderful, wonderful mixture of comedy and sadness'[1]).

'The Last Mohican' was first published in *Partisan Review*, an American literary and political quarterly, in Spring 1958. It then appeared in Malamud's first, acclaimed, collection of short stories, *The Magic Barrel*, the same year, and in a prestigious *Best American Short Stories* anthology[2] the following year. But Malamud had not finished with the story's central character, Arthur Fidelman. 'After I wrote the story in Rome I jotted down ideas for several incidents in the form of a picaresque novel. I was out to loosen up – experiment a little – with narrative structure.'[3] The eventual result was *Pictures of Fidelman: An Exhibition* (1968), composed of six stories, most of them previously published elsewhere, tracing Fidelman's misadventures in Italy, during which he tries without success to attach himself to Christian traditions of art. He finally gives up painting and discovers his identity as a glass-blower in Venice, returning at the end of the final story to America where 'he worked as a craftsman in glass and loved men and women'.[4] The first story's title alludes ironically to James Fenimore Cooper's classic adventure-novel of the American frontier, *The Last of the Mohicans* (1826). In Malamud's story, old and new civilizations meet, with Fidelman, the American innocent, being confronted by Susskind, the European Jew who is an exile from everywhere, and taking his first steps towards acceptance of self and others.

Notes

1. R. Tyler, 'A Talk with the Novelist' (1979), in *Conversations with Bernard Malamud*, ed. L. Lasher (Jackson and London: University Press of Mississippi, 1991), p. 84.
2. M. Foley and D. Burnett (eds), *The Best American Short Stories of 1959* (Boston, MA: Houghton Mifflin, 1959).
3. D. Stern, 'The Art of Fiction: Bernard Malamud' (1975), in *Conversations with Bernard Malamud*, p. 65.
4. B. Malamud, *Pictures of Fidelman* (London: Eyre & Spottiswoode, 1969), p. 179.

The Last Mohican

Fidelman, a self-confessed failure as a painter, came to Italy to prepare a critical study of Giotto, the opening chapter of which he had carried across the ocean in a new pigskin leather brief-case, now gripped in his perspiring hand. Also new were his gum-soled oxblood shoes, a tweed suit he had on despite the late-September sun slanting hot in the Roman sky, although there was a lighter one in his bag; and a dacron shirt and set of cotton-dacron underwear, good for quick and easy washing for the traveller. His suit-case, a bulky, two-strapped affair which embarrassed him slightly, he had borrowed from his sister Bessie. He planned, if he had any money left at the end of the year, to buy a new one in Florence. Although he had been in not much of a mood when he had left the U.S.A., Fidelman picked up in Naples, and at the moment, as he stood in front of the Rome railroad station, after twenty minutes still absorbed in his first sight of the Eternal City, he was conscious of a certain exaltation that devolved on him after he had discovered that directly across the many-vehicled piazza stood the remains of the Baths of Diocletian. Fidelman remembered having read that Michelangelo had had a hand in converting the baths into a church and convent, the latter ultimately changed into the museum that presently was there. 'Imagine,' he muttered. 'Imagine all that history.'

In the midst of his imagining, Fidelman experienced the sensa-tion of suddenly seeing himself as he was, to the pin-point, outside and in, not without bittersweet pleasure; and as the well-known image of his face rose before him he was taken by the depth of pure feeling in his eyes, slightly magnified by glasses, and the sensi-tivity of his elongated nostrils and often tremulous lips, nose divided from lips by a moustache of recent vintage that looked, Fidelman thought, as if it had been sculptured there, adding to his digni-fied appearance although he was a little on the short side. But almost at the same moment, this unexpectedly intense sense of his being – it was more than appearance – faded, exaltation having gone where exaltation goes, and Fidelman became aware that there was an exterior source to the strange, almost tri-dimensional reflection of himself he had felt as well as seen. Behind him, a short distance to the right, he had noticed a stranger – give a skeleton a couple of pounds – loitering near a bronze statue on a stone pedestal of the heavy-dugged Etruscan wolf suckling the infant Romulus and Remus, the man contemplating Fidelman already acquisitively so as to suggest to the traveller that he had been mirrored (lock, stock, barrel) in the other's gaze for some time, perhaps since he had stepped off the train. Casually studying him, though pretending no, Fidelman beheld a person of about his own height, oddly dressed in brown knickers and black, knee-length woollen socks drawn up over slightly bowed, broomstick legs, these grounded in small, porous, pointed shoes. His yellowed shirt was open at the gaunt throat, both sleeves rolled up over skinny, hairy arms. The stranger's high forehead was bronzed, his black hair thick behind small ears, the dark, close-shaven beard tight on the face; his experienced nose was weighted at the tip, and the soft brown eyes, above all, *wanted*. Though his expression suggested humility, he all but licked his lips as he approached the ex-painter.

'Shalom,' he greeted Fidelman.

'Shalom,' the other hesitantly replied, uttering the word – so far as he recalled – for the first time in his life. My God, he thought, a handout for sure. My first hello in Rome and it has to be a schnorrer.

The stranger extended a smiling hand. 'Susskind,' he said, 'Shimon Susskind.'

'Arthur Fidelman.' Transferring his brief-case to under his left arm while standing astride the big suit-case, he shook hands with Susskind. A blue-smocked porter came by, glanced at Fidelman's bag, looked at him, then walked away.

Whether he knew it or not Susskind was rubbing his palms contemplatively together.

'Parla italiano?'

'Not with ease, although I read it fluently. You might say I need the practice.'

'Yiddish?'

'I express myself best in English.'

'Let it be English then.' Susskind spoke with a slight British intonation. 'I knew you were Jewish,' he said, 'the minute my eyes saw you.'

Fidelman chose to ignore the remark. 'Where did you pick up your knowledge of English?'

'In Israel.'

Israel interested Fidelman. 'You live there?'

'Once, not now,' Susskind answered vaguely. He seemed suddenly bored.

'How so?'

Susskind twitched a shoulder. 'Too much heavy labour for a man of my modest health. Also I couldn't stand the suspense.'

Fidelman nodded.

'Furthermore, the desert air makes me constipated. In Rome I am light hearted.'

'A Jewish refugee from Israel, no less,' Fidelman said good humouredly.

'I'm always running,' Susskind answered mirthlessly. If he was light hearted, he had yet to show it.

'Where else from, if I may ask?'

'Where else but Germany, Hungary, Poland? Where not?'

'Ah, that's so long ago.' Fidelman then noticed the grey in the man's hair. 'Well, I'd better be going,' he said. He picked up his bag as two porters hovered uncertainly near by.

But Susskind offered certain services. 'You got a hotel?'

'All picked and reserved.'

'How long are you staying?'

What business is it of his? However, Fidelman courteously replied, 'Two weeks in Rome, the rest of the year in Florence, with a few side trips to Siena, Assisi, Padua and maybe also Venice.'

'You wish a guide in Rome?'

'Are you a guide?'

'Why not?'

'No,' said Fidelman. 'I'll look as I go along to museums, libraries, et cetera.'

This caught Susskind's attention. 'What are you, a professor?'

Fidelman couldn't help blushing. 'Not exactly, really just a student.'

'From which institution?'

He coughed a little. 'By that I mean a professional student, you might say. Call me Trofimov, from Chekov. If there's something to learn I want to learn it.'

'You have some kind of a project?' the other persisted. 'A grant?'

'No grant. My money is hard earned. I worked and saved a long time to take a year in Italy. I made certain sacrifices. As for a project, I'm writing on the painter Giotto. He was one of the most important –'

'You don't have to tell me about Giotto,' Susskind interrupted with a little smile.

'You've studied his work?'

'Who doesn't know Giotto?'

'That's interesting to me,' said Fidelman, secretly irritated. 'How do you happen to know him?'

'How do you?'

'I've given a good deal of time and study to his work.'

'So I know him too.'

I'd better get this over with before it begins to amount up to something, Fidelman thought. He set down his bag and fished with a finger in his leather coin purse. The two porters watched with interest, one taking a sandwich out of his pocket, unwrapping the newspaper and beginning to eat.

'This is for yourself,' Fidelman said.

Susskind hardly glanced at the coin as he let it drop into his pants pocket. The porters then left.

The refugee had an odd way of standing motionless, like a cigar store Indian about to burst into flight. 'In your luggage,' he said vaguely, 'would you maybe have a suit you can't use? I could use a suit.'

At last he comes to the point. Fidelman, though annoyed, controlled himself. 'All I have is a change from the one you now see me wearing. Don't get the wrong idea about me, Mr Susskind. I'm not rich. In fact, I'm poor. Don't let a few new clothes deceive you. I owe my sister money for them.'

Susskind glanced down at his shabby, baggy knickers. 'I haven't had a suit for years. The one I was wearing when I ran away from Germany, fell apart. One day I was walking around naked.'

'Isn't there a welfare organization that could help you out – some group in the Jewish community, interested in refugees?'

'The Jewish organizations wish to give me what they wish, not what I wish,' Susskind replied bitterly. 'The only thing they offer me is a ticket back to Israel.'

'Why don't you take it?'

'I told you already, here I feel free.'

'Freedom is a relative term.'

'Don't tell me about freedom.'

He knows all about that, too, Fidelman thought. 'So you feel free,' he said, 'but how do you live?'

Susskind coughed, a brutal cough.

Fidelman was about to say something more on the subject of freedom but left it unsaid. Jesus, I'll be saddled with him all day if I don't watch out.

'I'd better be getting off to the hotel.' He bent again for his bag.

Susskind touched him on the shoulder and when Fidelman exasperatedly straightened up, the half dollar he had given the man was staring him in the eye.

'On this we both lose money.'

'How do you mean?'

'Today the lira sells six twenty-three on the dollar, but for specie they only give you five hundred.'

'In that case, give it here and I'll let you have a dollar.' From his billfold Fidelman quickly extracted a crisp bill and handed it to the refugee.

'Not more?' Susskind sighed.

'Not more,' the student answered emphatically.

'Maybe you would like to see Diocletian's bath? There are some enjoyable Roman coffins inside. I will guide you for another dollar.'

'No, thanks.' Fidelman said good-bye, and lifting the suit-case, lugged it to the kerb. A porter appeared and the student, after some hesitation, let him carry it towards the line of small dark-green taxis in the piazza. The porter offered to carry the brief-case too, but Fidelman wouldn't part with it. He gave the cab driver the address of the hotel, and the taxi took off with a lurch. Fidelman at last relaxed. Susskind, he noticed, had disappeared. Gone with his breeze, he thought. But on the way to the hotel he had an uneasy feeling that the refugee, crouched low, might be clinging to the little tyre on the back of the cab; however, he didn't look out to see.

Fidelman had reserved a room in an inexpensive hotel not far from the station, with its very convenient bus terminal. Then, as was his habit, he got himself quickly and tightly organized. He was always concerned with not wasting time, as if it were his only wealth – not true, of course, though Fidelman admitted he was an ambitious person – and he soon arranged a schedule that made the most of his working hours. Mornings he usually visited the Italian libraries, searching their catalogues and archives, read in poor light, and made profuse notes. He napped for an hour after lunch, then at four, when the churches and museums were re-opening, hurried off to them with lists of frescoes and paintings he must see. He was anxious to get to Florence, at the same time a little unhappy at all he would not have time to take in in Rome. Fidelman promised himself to return again if he could afford it, perhaps in the spring, and look at anything he pleased.

After dark he managed to unwind himself and relax. He ate as the Romans did, late, enjoyed a half litre of white wine and smoked a cigarette. Afterward he liked to wander – especially in the old sections near the Tiber. He had read that here, under his feet, were the ruins of Ancient Rome. It was an inspiring business, he, Arthur Fidelman, after all, born a Bronx boy, walking around in all this history. History was mysterious, the remembrance of things unknown, in a way burdensome, in a way a sensuous experience. It uplifted and depressed, why he did not know, except that it excited his thoughts more than he thought good for him. This kind of excitement was all right up to a point, perfect maybe for a creative artist, but less so for a critic. A critic, he thought, should live on beans. He walked for miles along the winding river, gazing at the star-strewn skies. Once, after a couple of days in the Vatican Museum, he saw flights of angels – gold, blue, white – intermingled in the sky. 'My God, I got to stop using my eyes so much,' Fidelman said to himself. But back in his room he sometimes wrote till morning.

Late one night, about a week after his arrival in Rome, as Fidelman was writing notes on the Byzantine style mosaics he had seen during the day, there was a knock on the door, and though the student, immersed in his work, was not conscious he had said 'Avanti,' he must have, for the door opened, and instead of an angel, in came Susskind in his shirt and baggy knickers.

Fidelman, who had all but forgotten the refugee, certainly never thought of him, half rose in astonishment. 'Susskind,' he exclaimed, 'how did you get in here?'

Susskind for a moment stood motionless, then answered with a weary smile, 'I'll tell you the truth, I know the desk clerk.'

'But how did you know where I live?'

'I saw you walking in the street so I followed you.'

'You mean you saw me accidentally?'

'How else? Did you leave me your address?'

Fidelman resumed his seat. 'What can I do for you, Susskind?' He spoke grimly.

The refugee cleared his throat. 'Professor, the days are warm but the nights are cold. You see how I go around naked.' He held forth bluish arms, goosefleshed. 'I came to ask you to reconsider about giving away your old suit.'

'And who says it's an old suit?' Despite himself, Fidelman's voice thickened.

'One suit is new, so the other is old.'

'Not precisely. I am afraid I have no suit for you, Susskind. The one I presently have hanging in the closet is a little more than a year old and I can't afford to give it away. Besides, it's gabardine, more like a summer suit.'

'On me it will be for all seasons.'

After a moment's reflection, Fidelman drew out his billfold and counted four single dollars. These he handed to Susskind.

'Buy yourself a warm sweater.'

Susskind also counted the money. 'If four,' he said, 'then why not five?'

Fidelman flushed. The man's warped nerve. 'Because I happen to have four available,' he answered. 'That's twenty-five hundred lire. You should be able to buy a warm sweater and have something left over besides.'

'I need a suit,' Susskind said. 'The days are warm but the nights are cold.' He rubbed his arms. 'What else I need I won't say.'

'At least roll down your sleeves if you're so cold.'

'That won't help me.'

'Listen, Susskind,' Fidelman said gently, 'I would gladly give you the suit if I could afford to, but I can't. I have barely enough money to squeeze out a year for myself here. I've already told you I am indebted to my sister. Why don't you try to get yourself a job somewhere, no matter how menial? I'm sure that in a short while you'll work yourself up into a decent position.'

'A job, he says,' Susskind muttered gloomily. 'Do you know what it means to get a job in Italy? Who will give me a job?'

'Who gives anybody a job? They have to go out and look for it.'

'You don't understand, professor. I am an Israeli citizen and this means I can only work for an Israeli company. How many Israeli companies are there here? – maybe two, El Al and Zim, and even if they had a job, they wouldn't give it to me because I have lost my passport. I would be better off now if I were stateless. A stateless person shows his laissez passer and sometimes he can find a small job.'

'But if you lost your passport why didn't you put in for a duplicate?'

'I did, but did they give it to me?'

'Why not?'

'Why not? They say I sold it.'

'Had they reason to think that?'

'I swear to you somebody stole it from me.'

'Under such circumstances,' Fidelman asked, 'how do you live?'

'How do I live?' He chomped with his teeth. 'I eat air.'

'Seriously?'

'Seriously, on air. I also peddle,' he confessed, 'but to peddle you need a licence, and that the Italians won't give me. When they caught me peddling I was interned for six months in a work camp.'

'Didn't they attempt to deport you?'

'They did, but I sold my mother's old wedding ring that I kept in my pocket so many years. The Italians are a humane people. They took the money and let me go but they told me not to peddle anymore.'

'So what do you do now?'

'I peddle. What should I do, beg? – I peddle. But last spring I got sick and gave my little money away to the doctors. I still have a bad cough.' He coughed fruitily. 'Now I have no capital to buy stock with. Listen, professor, maybe we can go in partnership together? Lend me twenty thousand lire and I will buy ladies' nylon stockings. After I sell them I will return you your money.'

'I have no funds to invest, Susskind.'

'You will get it back, with interest.'

'I honestly am sorry for you,' Fidelman said, 'but why don't you at least do something practical? Why don't you go to the Joint Distribution Committee, for instance, and ask them to assist you? That's their business.'

'I already told you why. They wish me to go back, but I wish to stay here.'

'I still think going back would be the best thing for you.'

'No,' cried Susskind angrily.

'If that's your decision, freely made, then why pick on me? Am I responsible for you then, Susskind?'

'Who else?' Susskind loudly replied.

'Lower your voice, please, people are sleeping around here,' said Fidelman, beginning to perspire. 'Why should I be?'

'You know what responsibility means?'

'I think so.'

'Then you are responsible. Because you are a man. Because you are a Jew, aren't you?'

'Yes, goddamn it, but I'm not the only one in the whole wide world. Without prejudice, I refuse the obligation. I am a single individual and can't take on everybody's personal burden. I have the weight of my own to contend with.'

He reached for his billfold and plucked out another dollar.

'This makes five. It's more than I can afford, but take it and after this please leave me alone. I have made my contribution.'

Susskind stood there, oddly motionless, an impassioned statue, and for a moment Fidelman wondered if he would stay all night, but at last the refugee thrust forth a stiff arm, took the fifth dollar and departed.

Early the next morning Fidelman moved out of the hotel into another, less convenient for him, but far away from Shimon Susskind and his endless demands.

This was Tuesday. On Wednesday, after a busy morning in the library, Fidelman entered a nearby trattoria and ordered a plate of spaghetti with tomato sauce. He was reading his *Messaggero*, anticipating the coming of the food, for he was unusually hungry, when he sensed a presence at the table. He looked up, expecting the waiter, but beheld instead Susskind standing there, alas, unchanged.

Is there no escape from him? thought Fidelman, severely vexed. Is this why I came to Rome?

'Shalom, professor,' Susskind said, keeping his eyes off the table. 'I was passing and saw you sitting here alone, so I came in to say shalom.'

'Susskind,' Fidelman said in anger, 'have you been following me again?'

'How could I follow you?' asked the astonished Susskind. 'Do I know where you live now?'

Though Fidelman blushed a little, he told himself he owed nobody an explanation. So he had found out he had moved – good.

'My feet are tired. Can I sit five minutes?'

'Sit.'

Susskind drew out a chair. The spaghetti arrived, steaming hot. Fidelman sprinkled it with cheese and wound his fork into several tender strands. One of the strings of spaghetti seemed to stretch for miles, so he stopped at a certain point and swallowed the forkful. Having foolishly neglected to cut the long spaghetti string he was left sucking it, seemingly endlessly. This embarrassed him.

Susskind watched with rapt attention.

Fidelman at last reached the end of the long spaghetti, patted his mouth with a napkin, and paused in his eating.

'Would you care for a plateful?'

Susskind, eyes hungry, hesitated. 'Thanks,' he said.

'Thanks yes or thanks no?'

'Thanks no.' The eyes looked away.

Fidelman resumed eating, carefully winding his fork; he had had not too much practice with this sort of thing and was soon involved in the same dilemma with the spaghetti. Seeing Susskind still watching him, he soon became tense.

'We are not Italians, professor,' the refugee said. 'Cut it in small pieces with your knife. Then you will swallow it easier.'

'I'll handle it as I please,' Fidelman responded testily. 'This is my business. You attend to yours.'

'My business,' Susskind sighed, 'don't exist. This morning I had to let a wonderful chance get away from me. I had a chance to buy ladies' stockings at three hundred lire if I had money to buy half a gross. I could easily sell them for five hundred a pair. We would have made a nice profit.'

'The news doesn't interest me.'

'So if not ladies' stockings, I can also get sweaters, scarves, men's socks, also cheap leather goods, ceramics – whatever would interest you.'

'What interests me is what you did with the money I gave you for a sweater.'

'It's getting cold, professor,' Susskind said worriedly. 'Soon comes the November rains, and in winter the tramontana. I thought I ought to save your money to buy a couple of kilos of chestnuts and a bag of charcoal for my burner. If you sit all day on a busy street corner you can sometimes make a thousand lire. Italians like hot chestnuts. But if I do this I will need some warm clothes, maybe a suit.'

'A suit,' Fidelman remarked sarcastically, 'why not an overcoat?'

'I have a coat, poor that it is, but now I need a suit. How can anybody come in company without a suit?'

Fidelman's hand trembled as he laid down his fork. 'To my mind you are utterly irresponsible and I won't be saddled with you. I have the right to choose my own problems and the right to my privacy.'

'Don't get excited, professor, it's bad for your digestion. Eat in peace.' Susskind got up and left the trattoria.

Fidelman hadn't the appetite to finish his spaghetti. He paid the bill, waited ten minutes, then departed, glancing around from time to time to see if he were being followed. He headed down the sloping street to a small piazza where he saw a couple of cabs. Not that he could afford one, but he wanted to make sure Susskind didn't tail him back to his new hotel. He would warn the clerk at the desk never to allow anybody of the refugee's name or description even to make inquiries about him.

Susskind, however, stepped out from behind a plashing fountain at the centre of the little piazza. Modestly addressing the speechless Fidelman, he said, 'I don't wish to take only, professor. If I had something to give you, I would give it to you.'

'Thanks,' snapped Fidelman, 'just give me some peace of mind.'

'That you have to find yourself,' Susskind answered.

In the taxi Fidelman decided to leave for Florence the next day, rather than at the end of the week, and once and for all be done with the pest.

That night, after returning to his room from an unpleasurable walk in the Trastevere – he had a headache from too much wine at supper – Fidelman found his door ajar and at once recalled that he had forgotten to lock it, although he had as usual left the key with the desk clerk. He was at first frightened, but when he tried the armadio in which he kept his clothes and suit-case, it was shut tight. Hastily unlocking it, he was relieved to see his blue gabardine suit – a one-button jacket affair, the trousers a little frayed on the cuffs, but all in good shape and usable for years to come – hanging amid some shirts the maid had pressed for him; and when he examined the contents of the suitcase he found nothing missing, including, thank God, his passport and travellers' cheques. Gazing around the room, Fidelman saw all in place. Satisfied, he picked up a book and read ten pages before he thought of his brief-case. He jumped to his feet and began to search everywhere, remembering distinctly that it had been on the night table as he had laid on the bed that afternoon, re-reading his chapter. He searched under the bed and behind the night table, then again throughout the room, even on top of and behind the armadio. Fidelman hopelessly opened every drawer, no matter how small, but found neither the brief-case, nor, what was worse, the chapter in it.

With a groan he sank down on the bed, insulting himself for not having made a copy of the manuscript, for he had more than once warned himself that something like this might happen to it. But he hadn't because there were some revisions he had contemplated making, and he had planned to retype the entire chapter before beginning the next. He thought now of complaining to the owner of the hotel, who lived on the floor below, but it was already past midnight and he realized nothing could be done until morning. Who could have taken it? The maid or hall porter? It seemed unlikely they would risk their jobs to steal a piece of leather goods that would bring them only a few thousand lire in a pawn shop. Possibly a sneak thief? He would ask tomorrow if other persons on the floor were missing something. He somehow doubted it. If a thief, he would then and there have ditched the chapter and stuffed the brief-case with Fidelman's oxblood shoes, left by the bed, and the fifteen-dollar R. A. Macy sweater that lay in full view of the desk. But if not the maid or porter or a sneak thief, then who? Though Fidelman had not the slightest shred of evidence to support his suspicions he could think of only one person – Susskind. This thought stung him. But if Susskind, why? Out of pique, perhaps, that he had not been given the suit he had coveted, nor was able to pry it out of the armadio? Try as he would, Fidelman could think of no one else and no other reason. Somehow the pedlar had followed him home (he suspected their meeting at the fountain) and had got into his room while he was out to supper.

Fidelman's sleep that night was wretched. He dreamed of pursuing the refugee in the Jewish catacombs under the ancient Appian Way, threatening him a blow on the presumptuous head with a seven-flamed candelabrum he clutched in his hand; while Susskind, clever ghost, who knew the ins and outs of all the crypts and alleys, eluded him at every turn. Then Fidelman's candles all blew out, leaving him sightless and alone in the cemeterial dark; but when the student arose in the morning and wearily drew up the blinds, the yellow Italian sun winked him cheerfully in both bleary eyes.

Fidelman postponed going to Florence. He reported his loss to the Questura, and though the police were polite and eager to help, they could do nothing for him. On the form on which the inspector noted the complaint, he listed the brief-case as worth ten thousand lire, and for 'valor del manuscritto' he drew a line. Fidelman, after giving the matter a good deal of thought, did not report Susskind, first, because he had absolutely no proof, for the desk clerk swore he had seen no stranger around in knickers; second, because he was afraid of the consequences for the refugee if he were written down 'suspected thief' as well as 'unlicensed pedlar' and inveterate refugee. He tried instead to rewrite the chapter, which he felt sure he knew by heart, but when he sat down at the desk, there were important thoughts, whole paragraphs, even pages, that went blank in the mind. He considered sending to America for his notes for the chapter but they were in a barrel in his sister's attic in Levittown, among many notes for other projects. The thought of Bessie, a mother of five, poking around in his things, and the work entailed in sorting the cards, then getting them packaged and mailed to him across the ocean, wearied Fidelman unspeakably; he was certain she would send the wrong ones. He laid down his pen and went into the street, seeking Susskind. He searched for him in neighbourhoods where he had seen him before, and though Fidelman spent hours looking, literally days, Susskind never appeared; or if he perhaps did, the sight of Fidelman caused him to vanish. And when the student inquired about him at the Israeli consulate, the clerk, a new man on the job, said he had no record of such a person or his lost passport; on the other hand, he was known at the Joint Distribution Committee, but by name and address only, an impossibility, Fidelman thought. They gave him a number to go to but the place had long since been torn down to make way for an apartment house.

Time went without work, without accomplishment. To put an end to this appalling waste Fidelman tried to force himself back into his routine of research and picture viewing. He moved out of the hotel, which he now could not stand for the harm it had done him (leaving a telephone number and urging he be called if the slightest clue turned up), and he took a room in a small pensione near the Stazione and here had breakfast and supper rather than go out. He was much concerned with expenditures and carefully recorded them in a notebook he had acquired for the purpose. Nights, instead of wandering in the city, feasting himself upon its beauty and mystery, he kept his eyes glued to paper, sitting steadfastly at his desk in an attempt to recreate his initial chapter, because he was lost without a beginning. He had tried writing the second chapter from notes in his possession but it had come to nothing. Always Fidelman needed something solid behind him before he could advance, some worthwhile accomplishment upon which to build another. He worked late, but his mood, or inspiration, or whatever it was, had deserted him, leaving him with growing anxiety, almost disorientation; of not knowing – it seemed to him for the first time in months – what he must do next, a feeling that was torture. Therefore he again took up his search for the refugee. He thought now that once he had settled it, knew that the man had or hadn't stolen his chapter – whether he recovered it or not seemed at the moment immaterial – just the knowing of it would ease his mind and again he would *feel* like working, the crucial element.

Daily he combed the crowded streets, searching for Susskind wherever people peddled. On successive Sunday mornings he took the long ride to the Porta Portese market and hunted for hours among the piles of second-hand goods and junk lining the back streets, hoping his brief-case would magically appear, though it never did. He visited the open market at Piazza Fontanella Borghese, and observed the ambulant vendors at Piazza Dante. He looked among fruit and vegetable stalls set up in the streets, whenever he chanced upon them, and dawdled on busy street corners after dark, among beggars and fly-by-night pedlars. After the first cold snap at the end of October, when the chestnut sellers appeared throughout the city, huddled over pails of glowing coals, he sought in their faces the missing Susskind. Where in all of modern and ancient Rome was he? The man lived in the open air – he had to appear somewhere. Sometimes when riding in a bus or tram, Fidelman thought he had glimpsed somebody in a crowd, dressed in the refugee's clothes, and he invariably got off to run after whoever it was – once a man standing in front of the Banco di Santo Spirito, gone when Fidelman breathlessly arrived; and another time he overtook a person in knickers, but this one wore a monocle. Sir Ian Susskind?

In November it rained. Fidelman wore a blue beret with his trench coat and a pair of black Italian shoes, smaller, despite their pointed toes, than his burly oxbloods which overheated his feet and whose colour he detested. But instead of visiting museums he frequented movie houses sitting in the cheapest seats and regretting the cost. He was, at odd hours in certain streets, several times accosted by prostitutes, some heart-breakingly pretty, one a slender, unhappy-looking girl with bags under her eyes whom he desired mightily, but Fidelman feared for his health. He had got to know the face of Rome and spoke Italian fairly fluently, but his heart was burdened, and in his blood raged a murderous hatred of the bandy-legged refugee – although there were times when he bethought himself he might be wrong – so Fidelman more than once cursed him to perdition.

One Friday night, as the first star glowed over the Tiber, Fidelman, walking aimlessly along the left riverbank, came upon a synagogue and wandered in among a crowd of Sephardim with Italianate faces. One by one they paused before a sink in an antechamber to dip their hands under a flowing faucet, then in the house of worship touched with loose fingers their brows, mouths, and breasts as they bowed to the Arc, Fidelman doing likewise. Where in the world am I? Three rabbis rose from a bench and the service began, a long prayer, sometimes chanted, sometimes accompanied by invisible organ music, but no Susskind anywhere. Fidelman sat at a desk-like pew in the last row, where he could inspect the congregants yet keep an eye on the door. The synagogue was unheated and the cold rose like an exudation from the marble floor. The student's freezing nose burned like a lit candle. He got up to go, but the beadle, a stout man in a high hat and short caftan, wearing a long thick silver chain around his neck, fixed the student with his powerful left eye.

'From New York?' he inquired, slowly approaching.

Half the congregation turned to see who.

'State, not city,' answered Fidelman, nursing an active guilt for the attention he was attracting. Then, taking advantage of a pause, he whispered, 'Do you happen to know a man named Susskind? He wears knickers.'

'A relative?' The beadle gazed at him sadly.

'Not exactly.'

'My own son – killed in the Ardeatine Caves.' Tears stood forth in his eyes.

'Ah, for that I'm sorry.'

But the beadle had exhausted the subject. He wiped his wet lids with pudgy fingers and the curious Sephardim turned back to their prayer books.

'Which Susskind?' the beadle wanted to know.

'Shimon.'

He scratched his ear. 'Look in the ghetto.'

'I looked.'

'Look again.'

The beadle walked slowly away and Fidelman sneaked out.

The ghetto lay behind the synagogue for several crooked, well-packed blocks, encompassing aristocratic palazzi ruined by age and unbearable numbers, their discoloured façades strung with lines of withered wet wash, the fountains in the piazzas, dirt-laden, dry. And dark stone tenements, built partly on centuries-old ghetto walls, inclined towards one another across narrow, cobblestoned streets. In and among the impoverished houses were the wholesale establishments of wealthy Jews, dark holes ending in jewelled interiors, silks and silver of all colours. In the mazed streets wandered the present-day poor, Fidelman among them, oppressed by history, although, he joked to himself, it added years to his life.

A white moon shone upon the ghetto, lighting it like dark day. Once he thought he saw a ghost he knew by sight, and hastily followed him through a thick stone passage to a blank wall where shone in white letters under a tiny electric bulb: VIETATO URINARE. Here was a smell but no Susskind.

For thirty lire the student bought a dwarfed, blackened banana from a street vendor (not S) on a bicycle, and stopped to eat. A crowd of ragazzi gathered to watch.

'Anybody here know Susskind, a refugee wearing knickers?' Fidelman announced, stooping to point with the banana where the pants went beneath the knees. He also made his legs a trifle bowed but nobody noticed.

There was no response until he had finished his fruit, then a thin-faced boy with brown liquescent eyes out of Murillo, piped: 'He sometimes works in the Cimitero Verano, the Jewish section.'

There too? thought Fidelman. 'Works in the cemetery?' he inquired. 'With a shovel?'

'He prays for the dead,' the boy answered, 'for a small fee.'

Fidelman bought him a quick banana and the others dispersed.

In the cemetery, deserted on the Sabbath – he should have come Sunday – Fidelman went among the graves, reading legends carved on tombstones, many topped with small brass candelabra, whilst withered yellow chrysanthemums lay on the stone tablets of other graves, dropped stealthily, Fidelman imagined, on All Souls Day – a festival in another part of the cemetery – by renegade sons and daughters unable to bear the sight of their dead bereft of flowers, while the crypts of the goyim were lit and in bloom. Many were burial places, he read on the stained stones, of those who, for one reason or another, had died in the late large war, including an empty place, it said under a six-pointed star engraved upon a marble slab that lay on the ground, for 'My beloved father / Betrayed by the damned Fascists / Murdered at Auschwitz by the barbarous Nazis / *O Crime Orribile.*' But no Susskind.

Three months had gone by since Fidelman's arrival in Rome. Should he, he many times asked himself, leave the city and this foolish search? Why not off to Florence, and there, amid the art splendours of the world, be inspired to resume his work? But the loss of his first chapter was like a spell cast over him. There were times he scorned it as a man-made thing, like all such, replaceable; other times he feared it was not the chapter per se, but that his volatile curiosity had become somehow entangled with Susskind's strange personality – Had he repaid generosity by stealing a man's life work? Was he so distorted? To satisfy himself, to know man, Fidelman had to know, though at what a cost in precious time and effort. Sometimes he smiled wryly at all this; ridiculous, the chapter grieved him for itself only – the precious thing he had created then lost – especially when he got to thinking of the long diligent labour, how painstakingly he had built each idea, how cleverly mastered problems of order, form, how impressive the finished product, Giotto reborn! It broke the heart. What else, if after months he was here, still seeking?

And Fidelman was unchangingly convinced that Susskind had taken it, or why would he still be hiding? He sighed much and gained weight. Mulling over his frustrated career, on the backs of envelopes containing unanswered letters from his sister Bessie he aimlessly sketched little angels flying. Once, studying his minuscule drawings, it occurred to him that he might someday return to painting, but the thought was more painful than Fidelman could bear.

One bright morning in mid-December, after a good night's sleep, his first in weeks, he vowed he would have another look at the Navicella and then be off to Florence. Shortly before noon he visited the porch of St Peter's, trying, from his remembrance of Giotto's sketch, to see the mosaic as it had been before its many restorations. He hazarded a note or two in shaky handwriting, then left the church and was walking down the sweeping flight of stairs, when he beheld at the bottom – his heart misgave him, was he still seeing pictures, a sneaky apostle added to the overloaded boatful? – ecco, Susskind! The refugee, in beret and long green G.I. raincoat, from under whose skirts showed his black-stockinged, rooster's ankles – indicating knickers going on above though hidden – was selling black and white rosaries to all who would buy. He held several strands of beads in one hand, while in the palm of the other a few gilded medallions glinted in the winter sun. Despite his outer clothing, Susskind looked, it must be said, unchanged, not a pound more of meat or muscle, the face though aged, ageless. Gazing at him, the student ground his teeth in remembrance. He was tempted quickly to hide, and unobserved observe the thief; but his impatience, after the long unhappy search, was too much for him. With controlled trepidation he approached Susskind on his left as the refugee was busily engaged on the right, urging a sale of beads upon a woman drenched in black.

'Beads, rosaries, say your prayers with holy beads.'

'Greetings, Susskind,' Fidelman said, coming shakily down the stairs, dissembling the Unified Man, all peace and contentment. 'One looks for you everywhere and finds you here. Wie gehts?'

Susskind, though his eyes flickered, showed no surprise to speak of. For a moment his expression seemed to say he had no idea who was this, had forgotten Fidelman's existence, but then at last remembered – somebody long ago from another country, whom you smiled on, then forgot.

'Still here?' he perhaps ironically joked.

'Still,' Fidelman was embarrassed at his voice slipping.

'Rome holds you?'

'Rome,' faltered Fidelman, '– the air.' He breathed deep and exhaled with emotion.

Noticing the refugee was not truly attentive, his eyes roving upon potential customers, Fidelman, girding himself, remarked, 'By the way, Susskind, you didn't happen to notice – did you? – the brief-case I was carrying with me around the time we met in September?'

'Brief-case – what kind?' This he said absently, his eyes on the church doors.

'Pigskin. I had in it –' Here Fidelman's voice could be heard cracking, '– a chapter of a critical work on Giotto I was writing. You know, I'm sure, the Trecento painter?'

'Who doesn't know Giotto?'

'Do you happen to recall whether you saw, if, that is –'. He stopped, at a loss for words other than accusatory.

'Excuse me – business.' Susskind broke away and bounced up the steps two at a time. A man he approached shied away. He had beads, didn't need others.

Fidelman had followed the refugee. 'Reward,' he muttered up close to his ear. 'Fifteen thousand for the chapter, and who has it can keep the brand new brief-case. That's his business, no questions asked. Fair enough?'

Susskind spied a lady tourist, including camera and guide book. 'Beads – holy beads.' He held up both hands, but she was just a Lutheran, passing through.

'Slow today,' Susskind complained as they walked down the stairs, 'but maybe it's the items. Everybody has the same. If I had some big ceramics of the Holy Mother, they go like hot cakes – a good investment for somebody with a little cash.'

'Use the reward for that,' Fidelman cagily whispered, 'buy Holy Mothers.'

If he heard, Susskind gave no sign. At the sight of a family of nine emerging from the main portal above, the refugee, calling addio over his shoulder, fairly flew up the steps. But Fidelman uttered no response. I'll get the rat yet. He went off to hide behind a high fountain in the square. But the flying spume raised by the wind wet him, so he retreated behind a massive column and peeked out at short intervals to keep the pedlar in sight.

At two o'clock, when St Peter's closed to visitors, Susskind dumped his goods into his raincoat pockets and locked up shop. Fidelman followed him all the way home, indeed the ghetto, although along a street he had not consciously been on before, which led into an alley where the refugee pulled open a left-handed door, and without transition, was 'home'. Fidelman, sneaking up close, caught a dim glimpse of an overgrown closet containing bed and table. He found no address on wall or door, nor, to his surprise, any door lock. This for a moment depressed him. It meant Susskind had nothing worth stealing. Of his own, that is. The student promised himself to return tomorrow, when the occupant was elsewhere.

Return he did, in the morning, while the entrepreneur was out selling religious articles, glanced around once and was quickly inside. He shivered – a pitch black freezing cave. Fidelman scratched up a thick match and confirmed bed and table, also a rickety chair, but no heat or light except a drippy candle stub in a saucer on the table. He lit the yellow candle and searched all over the place. In the table drawer a few eating implements plus safety razor, though where he shaved was a mystery, probably a public toilet. On a shelf above the thin-blanketed bed stood half a flask of red wine, part of a package of spaghetti, and a hard panino. Also an unexpected little fish bowl with a bony gold fish swimming around in Arctic seas. The fish, reflecting the candle flame, gulped repeatedly, threshing its frigid tail as Fidelman watched. He loves pets, thought the student. Under the bed he found a chamber pot, but nowhere a brief-case with a fine critical chapter in it. The place was not more than an ice-box someone probably had lent the refugee to come in out of the rain. Alas, Fidelman sighed. Back in the pensione, it took a hot water bottle two hours to thaw him out; but from the visit he never fully recovered.

In this latest dream of Fidelman's he was spending the day in a cemetery all crowded with tombstones, when up out of an empty grave rose this long-nosed brown shade, Virgilio Susskind, beckoning.

Fidelman hurried over.

'Have you read Tolstoy?'

'Sparingly.'

'Why is art?' asked the shade, drifting off.

Fidelman, willy nilly, followed, and the ghost, as it vanished, led him up steps going through the ghetto and into a marble synagogue.

The student, left alone, for no reason he could think of lay down upon the stone floor, his shoulders keeping strangely warm as he stared at the sunlit vault above. The fresco therein revealed this saint in fading blue, the sky flowing from his head, handing an old knight in a thin red robe his gold cloak. Nearby stood a humble horse and two stone hills.

Giotto. San Francesco dona le vesti al cavaliere povero.

Fidelman awoke running. He stuffed his blue gabardine into a paper bag, caught a bus, and knocked early on Susskind's heavy portal.

'Avanti.' The refugee, already garbed in beret and raincoat (probably his pyjamas), was standing at the table, lighting the candle with a flaming sheet of paper. To Fidelman the paper looked the underside of a typewritten page. Despite himself, the student recalled in letters of fire his entire chapter.

'Here, Susskind,' he said in a trembling voice, offering the bundle, 'I bring you my suit. Wear it in good health.'

The refugee glanced at it without expression. 'What do you wish for it?'

'Nothing at all.' Fidelman laid the bag on the table, called goodbye and left.

He soon heard footsteps clattering after him across the cobblestones.

'Excuse me, I kept this under my mattress for you.' Susskind thrust at him the pigskin brief-case.

Fidelman savagely opened it, searching frenziedly in each compartment, but the bag was empty. The refugee was already in flight. With a bellow the student started after him. 'You bastard, you burned my chapter!'

'Have mercy,' cried Susskind, 'I did you a favour.'

'I'll do you one and cut your throat.'

The words were there but the spirit was missing.

In a towering rage, Fidelman forced a burst of speed, but the refugee, light as the wind in his marvellous knickers, his green coat-tails flying, rapidly gained ground.

The ghetto Jews, framed in amazement in their medieval

windows, stared at the wild pursuit. But in the middle of it, Fidelman, stout and short of breath, moved by all he had lately learned, had a triumphant insight.

'Susskind, come back,' he shouted, half sobbing. 'The suit is yours. All is forgiven.'

He came to a dead halt but the refugee ran on. When last seen he was still running.

The End of the World

Mavis Gallant

Introduction

Mavis de Trafford Young was born in 1922, in Montreal, the largest city of French-speaking Quebec province in eastern Canada. Her mother was a Canadian, though raised in the USA, who spoke German as well as French, and through her Mavis became well read in European literature. Her father, Stewart Young, was of English and Scots parentage; he was a painter but also a 'remittance man', an emigrant assisted by money from 'home', living a drifting life of exile – a condition that his daughter explores extensively in her fiction. He died while she was still young, having already disappeared from her life, and her mother remarried, moving to Toronto and then New York. Mavis spent most of her childhood, unhappily, in a succession of boarding schools in Canada (sometimes as the only English-speaking Canadian) and the USA, and as a teenager lived for a while in New York with a psychiatrist and his wife.

In 1941 she returned to Montreal, on her own, and worked at a variety of jobs before becoming a journalist on the Montreal *Standard* in 1944. In 1943 she had married Johnny Gallant, a nightclub pianist from Winnipeg, but they were divorced in 1946. By then she was writing short stories, and found it was easy to get them published in Canada. However, after six years at the *Standard* she decided to leave, sent some of her stories to the *New Yorker*, and on the strength of their acceptance set off for Europe, where she has lived ever since, though she retains her Canadian citizenship. She has travelled widely in Europe, and her writing is often marked, both thematically and in its detail, by awareness of contemporary politics and history.

Most of Gallant's short stories – and since 1951 that amounts to well over a hundred – have made their first appearance in the *New Yorker*. Although her literary reputation rests on the short stories, of which there are numerous collections, she has also published novels (*Green Water, Green Sky* in 1959 and *A Fairly Good Time* in 1970) and her play *What is to Be Done?* was staged in Toronto in 1982. In 1983–4 she returned to Canada as writer-in-residence at the University of Toronto, but Paris is her adopted home, and she still lives there. Her *Paris Notebooks* (1986) include pieces on the student uprisings of 1968 (the 'days of rage'), as well as other essays and reviews.

Her reputation as a writer having been established after she moved to Europe, Gallant's work was initially much better known in the USA and Britain than it was in Canada. Her novels and first three collections of stories were published in the USA and England, but in 1974 *The End of the World and Other Stories* was published in Toronto, in a series called the *New Canadian Library*.

From then on, critical commentaries and literary awards brought Gallant more widespread recognition in Canada. Her 1981 collection, *Home Truths: Selected Canadian Stories*, which includes an impressive semi-autobiographical sequence of stories about a nineteen-year-old called Linnet Muir returning from the USA to her native Montreal, won the Governor General's Award for Fiction. More recently, in 2006, Gallant was awarded the Prix Athanase-David by the provincial government of Quebec, an extraordinary honour for a writer working in English.

'The End of the World' was first published in the *New Yorker* in 1967. In it we find some of the characteristic dislocations – between Europe and Canada, between parents and children – that so often feature in Gallant's stories. Another characteristic element is the use of first-person narration: as her friend Mordecai Richler comments in the Afterword to another of the collections of Gallant's stories, she is able to assume many diverse identities in her stories, 'getting the social nuances and inner-life details exactly right, settling for nothing less than a character's tap-root'.[1] Not surprisingly, her stories have often been compared with those of Anton Chekhov, a writer for whom she has professed particular admiration.

Note

1. Mavis Gallant, *The Moslem Wife and Other Stories* (Toronto: McLelland & Stewart, 1994), p. 249.

The End of the World

I never like to leave Canada, because I'm disappointed every time. I've felt disappointed about places I haven't even seen. My wife went to Florida with her mother once. When they arrived there, they met some neighbors from home who told them about a sign saying "No Canadians." They never saw this sign anywhere, but they kept hearing about others who did, or whose friends had seen it, always in different places, and it spoiled their trip for them. Many people, like them, have never come across it but have heard about it, so it must be there somewhere. Another time I had to go and look after my brother Kenny in Buffalo. He had stolen a credit card and was being deported on that account. I went down to vouch for him and pay up for him and bring him home. Neither of us cared for Buffalo.

"What have they got here that's so marvellous?" I said.

"Proust," said Kenny.

"What?"

"Memorabilia," he said. He was reading it off a piece of paper.

"Why does a guy with your education do a dumb thing like swiping a credit card?" I said.

"Does Mother know?" said Kenny.

"Mum knows, and Lou knows, and I know, and Beryl knows. It was in the papers, 'Kenneth Apostolesco, of this city . . . '"

"I'd better stay away," my brother said.

"No, you'd better not, for Mum's sake. We've only got one mother."

"Thank God," he said. "Only one of each. One mother and one father. If I had more than one of each, I think I'd still be running."

It was our father who ran, actually. He deserted us during the last war. He joined the Queen's Own Rifles, which wasn't a Montreal regiment – he couldn't do anything like other people, couldn't even join up like anyone else – and after the war he just chose to go his own way. I saw him downtown in Montreal one time after the war. I was around twelve, delivering prescriptions for a drugstore. I knew him before he knew me. He looked the way he had always managed to look, as if he had all the time in the world. His mouth was drawn in, like an old woman's, but he still had his coal black hair. I wish we had his looks. I leaned my bike with one foot on the curb and he came down and stood by me, rocking on his feet, like a dancer, and looking off over my head. He said he was night watchman at a bank and that he was waiting for the Army to fix him up with some teeth. He'd had all his teeth out, though there wasn't anything wrong with them. He was eligible for new ones provided he put in a claim that year, so he thought he might as well. He was a bartender by profession, but he wasn't applying for anything till he'd got his new teeth. "I've told them to hurry it up," he said. "I can't go round to good places all gummy." He didn't ask how anyone was at home.

I had to leave Canada to be with my father when he died. I was the person they sent for, though I was the youngest. My name was on the back page of his passport: "In case of accident or death notify WILLIAM APOSTOLESCO. Relationship: Son." I was the one he picked. He'd been barman on a ship for years by then, earning good money, but he had nothing put by. I guess he never expected his life would be finished. He collapsed with a lung hemorrhage, as far as I could make out, and they put him off at a port in France. I went there. That was where I saw him. This town had been shelled twenty years ago and a lot of it looked bare and new. I wouldn't say I hated it exactly, but I would never have come here of my own accord. It was worse than Buffalo in some ways. I didn't like the food or the coffee, and they never gave you anything you needed in the hotels – I had to go out and buy some decent towels. It didn't matter, because I had to buy everything for my father anyway – soap and towels and Kleenex. The hospital didn't provide a thing except the bedsheets, and when a pair of those was put on the bed it seemed to be put there once and for all. I was there twenty-three days and I think I saw the sheets changed once. Our grandfathers had been glad to get out of Europe. It took my father to go back. The hospital he was in was an old convent or monastery. The beds were so close together you could hardly get a chair between them. Women patients were always wandering around the men's wards, and although I wouldn't swear to it, I think some of them had their beds there, at the far end. The patients were given crocks of tepid water to wash in, not by their beds but on a long table in the middle of the ward. Anyone too sick to get up was just out of luck unless, like my father, he had someone to look after him. I saw beetles and cockroaches, and I said to myself, This is what a person gets for leaving home.

My father accepted my presence as if it were his right – as if he hadn't lost his claim to any consideration years ago. So as not to scare him, I pretended my wife's father had sent me here on business, but he hardly listened, so I didn't insist.

"Didn't you drive a cab one time or other?" he said. "What else have you done?"

I wanted to answer, "You know what I've been doing? I've been supporting your wife and educating your other children, practically singlehanded, since I was twelve."

I had expected to get here in time for his last words, which ought to have been "I'm sorry." I thought he would tell me where he wanted to be buried, how much money he owed, how many bastards he was leaving behind, and who was looking out for them. I imagined them in ports like this, with no-good mothers. *Somebody* should have been told – telling me didn't mean telling the whole world. One of the advantages of having an Old Country in the family is you can always say the relations that give you trouble have gone there. You just say, "He went back to the Old Country," and nobody asks any questions. So he could have told me the truth, and I'd have known and still not let the family down. But my father never confided anything. The trouble was he didn't know he was dying – he'd been told, in fact, he was getting better – so he didn't act like a dying man. He used what breath he had to say things like "I always liked old Lou," and you would have thought she was someone else's daughter, a girl he had hardly known. Another time he said, "Did Kenny do well for himself? I heard he went to college."

"Don't talk," I said.

"No, I mean it. I'd like to know how Kenny made out."

He couldn't speak above a whisper some days, and he was careful how he pronounced words. It wasn't a snobbish or an English accent – nothing that would make you grit your teeth. He just sounded like a stranger. When I was sent for, my mother said, "He's dying a pauper, after all his ideas. I hope he's satisfied." I didn't answer, but I said to myself, This isn't a question of satisfaction. I wanted to ask her, "Since you didn't get along with him and he didn't get along with you, what did you go and have three children for?" But those are the questions you keep to yourself.

"What's your wife like?" my father croaked. His eyes were interested. I hadn't been prepared for this, for how long the mind stayed alive and how frivolous it went on being. I thought he should be more serious. "*Wife*," my father insisted. "What about her?"

"Obedient" came into my head, I don't know why; it isn't important. "Older than me," I said, quite easily, at last. "Better educated. She was a kindergarten teacher. She knows a lot about art." Now, why that, of all the side issues? She doesn't like a bare wall, that's all. "She prefers the Old Masters," I said. I was thinking about the Scotch landscape we've got over the mantelpiece.

"Good, good. Name?"

"You know – *Beryl*. We sent you an announcement, to that place in Mexico where you were then."

"That's right. Beryl." "Burrull" was what he actually said.

I felt reassured, because my father until now had sounded like a strange person. To have "Beryl" pronounced as I was used to hearing it made up for being alone here and the smell of the ward and the coffee made of iodine. I remembered what the Old Master had cost – one hundred and eighty dollars in 1962. It must be worth more now. Beryl said it would be an investment. Her family paid for half. She said once, about my father, "One day he'll be sick; we'll have to look after him." "We can sell the painting," I said. "I guess I can take care of my own father."

It happened – I was here, taking care of him; but he spoiled it now by saying, "You look like you'd done pretty well. That's not a bad suit you've got on."

"Actually," I said, "I had to borrow from Beryl's father so as to get here."

I thought he would say, "Oh, I'm sorry," and I had my next answer ready about not begrudging a cent of it. But my father closed his eyes, smiling, saving up more breath to talk about nothing.

"I liked old Lou," he said distinctly. I was afraid he would ask, "Why doesn't she write to me?" and I would have to say, "Because she never forgave you," and he was perfectly capable of saying then, "Never forgave me for what?" But instead of that he laughed, which was the worst of the choking and wheezing noises he made now, and when he had recovered he said, "Took her to Eaton's to choose a toy village. Had this shipment in, last one in before the war. Summer

'39. The old man saw the ad, wanted to get one for the kid. Old man came – each of us had her by the hand. Lou looked round, but every village had something the matter, as far as Her Royal Highness was concerned. The old man said, 'Come on, Princess, hurry it up,' but no, she'd of seen a scratch, or a bad paint job, or a chimney too big for a collage. The old man said, 'Can't this kid make up her mind about anything? She's going to do a lot more crying than laughing,' he said, 'and that goes for you, too.' He was wrong about me. Don't know about Lou. But she was smart that time – not to want something that wasn't perfect."

He shut his eyes again and breathed desperately through his mouth. The old man in the story was his father, my grandfather.

"Nothing is perfect," I said. I felt like standing up so everyone could hear. It wasn't sourness but just the way I felt like reacting to my father's optimism.

Some days he seemed to be getting better. After two weeks I was starting to wonder if they hadn't brought me all this way for nothing. I couldn't go home and come back later, it had to be now; but I couldn't stay on and on. I had already moved to a cheaper hotel room. I dreamed I asked him, "How much longer?" but luckily the dream was in a foreign language – so foreign I don't think it was French, even. It was a language no one on earth had ever heard of. I wouldn't have wanted him to understand it, even in a dream. The nurses couldn't say anything. Sometimes I wondered if they knew who he was – if they could tell one patient from another. It was a big place, and poor. These nurses didn't seem to have much equipment. When they needed sterile water for anything, they had to boil it in an old saucepan. I got to the doctor one day, but he didn't like it. He had told my father he was fine, and that I could go back to Canada any time – the old boy must have been starting to wonder why I was staying so long. The doctor just said to me, "Family business is of no interest to me. You look after your duty and I'll look after mine." I was afraid that my dream showed on my face and that was what made them all so indifferent. I didn't know how much time there was. I wanted to ask my father why he thought everything had to be perfect, and if he still stood by it as a way of living. Whenever he was reproached about something – by my mother, for instance – he just said, "Don't make my life dark for me." What could you do?

He certainly made her life dark for her. One year when we had a summer cottage, he took a girl from the village, the village tramp, out to an island in the middle of the lake. They got caught in a storm coming back, and around fifty people stood on shore waiting to see the canoe capsize and the sinners drown. My mother had told us to stay in the house, but when Kenny said, to scare me, "I guess the way things are, Mum's gone down there to drown herself," I ran after her. She didn't say anything to me, but took her raincoat off and draped it over my head. It would have been fine if my father had died then – if lightning had struck him, or the canoe gone down like a stone. But no, he waded ashore – the slut, too – and someone even gave her a blanket. It was my mother that was blamed, in a funny way. "Can't you keep your husband home?" this girl's father said. I remember that same summer some other woman saying to her, "You'd better keep your husband away from my daughter. I'm telling you for your own good, because my husband's got a gun in the house." Someone did say, "Oh, poor Mrs. Apostolesco!" but my mother only answered, "If you think that, then I'm poor for life." That was only one of the things he did to her. I'm not sure if it was even the worst.

It was hard to say how long he had been looking at me. His lips were trying to form a word. I bent close and heard, "Sponge."

"Did you say 'sponge'? Is 'sponge' what you said?"

"Sponge," he agreed. He made an effort: "Bad night last night. Awful. Wiped everything with my sponge – blood, spit. Need new sponge."

There wasn't a bed table, just a plastic bag that hung on the bedrail with his personal things in it. I got out the sponge. It needed to be thrown away, all right. I said, "What color?"

"Eh?"

"This," I said, and held it up in front of him. "The new one. Any special color?"

"Blue." His voice broke out of a whisper all at once. His eyes were mocking me, like a kid seeing how far he can go. I thought he would thank me now, but then I said to myself, You can't expect anything; he's a sick man, and he was always like this.

"Most people think it was pretty good of me to have come here," I wanted to explain – not to boast or anything, but just for the sake of

conversation. I was lonely there, and I had so much trouble understanding what anybody was saying.

"Bad night," my father whispered. "Need sedation."

"I know. I tried to tell the doctor. I guess he doesn't understand
my French."

He moved his head. "Tip the nurses."

"You don't mean it!"

"Don't make me talk." He seemed to be using a reserve of breath.
"At least twenty dollars. The ward girls less."

I said, "Jesus God!" because this was new to me and I felt out of my
depth. "They don't bother much with you," I said, talking myself
into doing it. "Maybe you're right. If I gave them a present, they'd
look after you more. Wash you. Maybe they'd put a screen around
you – you'd be more private then."

"No, thanks," my father said. "No screen. Thanks all the same."

We had one more conversation after that. I've already said there
were always women slopping around in the ward, in felt slippers,
and bathrobes stained with medicine and tea. I came in and found
one – quite young, this one was – combing my father's hair. He could
hardly lift his head from the pillow, and still she thought he was
interesting. I thought, Kenny should see this.

"She's been telling me," my father gasped when the woman had
left. "About herself. Three children by different men. Met a North
African. He adopts the children, all three. Gives them his name.
She has two more by him, boys. But he won't put up with a sick
woman. One day he just doesn't come. She's been a month in
another place; now they've brought her here. Man's gone. Left the
children. They've been put in all different homes, she doesn't know
where. Five kids. Imagine."

I thought, You left *us*. He had forgotten; he had just simply
forgotten that he'd left his own.

"Well, we can't do anything about her, can we?" I said. "She'll
collect them when she gets out of here."

"If she gets out."

"That's no way to talk," I said. "Look at the way she was talking
and walking around . . . " I could not bring myself to say, "and

combing your hair." "Look at how *you* are," I said. "You've just told me this long story."

"She'll seem better, but she'll get worse," my father said. "She's like me, getting worse. Do you think I don't know what kind of ward I'm in? Every time they put the screen around a patient, it's because he's dying. If I had t.b., like they tried to make me believe, I'd be in a t.b. hospital."

"That just isn't true," I said.

"Can you swear I've got t.b.? You can't."

I said without hesitating, "You've got a violent kind of t.b. They had no place else to put you except here. The ward might be crummy, but the medicine . . . the medical care . . . " He closed his eyes. "I'm looking you straight in the face," I said, "and I swear you have this unusual kind of t.b., and you're almost cured." I watched, without minding it now, a new kind of bug crawling along the base of the wall.

"Thanks, Billy," said my father.

I really was scared. I had been waiting for something without knowing what it would mean. I can tell you how it was: it was like the end of the world. "I didn't realize you were worried," I said. "You should of asked me right away."

"I knew you wouldn't lie to me," my father said. "That's why I wanted you, not the others."

That was all. Not long after that he couldn't talk. He had deserted the whole family once, but I was the one he abandoned twice. When he died, a nurse said to me, "I am sorry." It had no meaning, from her, yet only a few days before it was all I thought I wanted to hear.

The Distant Past

William Trevor

Introduction

William Trevor Cox was born in Mitchelstown, County Cork, in what was then the Irish Free State, in 1928. His parents were both Protestant, though the family did not enjoy the kind of settled and privileged lives usually associated with the Anglo-Irish. His father, William Cox, was a bank manager who, because of his work, was continually moving from place to place. His son was educated at 13 different schools, some of them Catholic, though the final phase of his schooling, at St Columba's College, Dublin, lasted from 1942 to 1946. He took his BA at Trinity College, Dublin, and then became a teacher of history in Armagh, Northern Ireland.

In 1953 he moved to England, for economic reasons, and took up another teaching post (art, this time) in Rugby. A few years later he moved to Somerset, and worked as a sculptor, with some success, having exhibitions in both Dublin and London under the name Trevor Cox. He also had a job as an advertising copywriter for several years whilst trying to establish a career as a writer. He published his first novel, *A Standard of Behaviour*, in 1958, under the name William Trevor.

For the last half-century, Trevor has gone on publishing novels and collections of short stories, prolifically, as well as writing plays for stage, radio and television. His work has brought him numerous awards and honours in both Britain and Ireland. He has won the Whitbread Prize three times, for example, with *The Children of Dynmouth* (1968), *Fools of Fortune* (1983) and *Felicia's Journey* (1994); in 1999 he was awarded the prestigious David Cohen British Literature Prize by the English Arts Council. Irish literary prizes include the *Irish Times* Irish Literature Prize for Fiction (for his short story collection *The Hill Bachelors*, in 2001), and he is a member of the Irish Academy of Letters. Although he is often described as Ireland's greatest living novelist, he has continued to live in England, and he and his wife now have their home in Devon.

In his fiction Trevor draws on both English and Irish material, and sometimes, as in 'The Distant Past', the relationship between the two countries forms part of the subject matter. The disabling weight of history is a recurring theme, and sometimes, along with history, violence surfaces. More generally, the world in Trevor's fiction often seems to be divided along the lines of prey and predator, but even amongst his more sombre imaginings there is often an ironic edge to his spare, precise style. He is especially adept at rendering the tensions and confusions that can arise in small communities, be they English or Irish.

Trevor's interest in the short story as a literary form has been in evidence throughout his career as a writer, and he is widely regarded as one of the masters of the genre. Many of his stories have been published in the USA, notably in the *New Yorker*, as well as in Britain and Ireland. He edited the *Oxford Book of Irish Short Stories* (1989), and although Irish story-telling has not been the only influence on his short fiction, he acknowledges James Joyce, in particular, as an important predecessor. His style and wit recall Joyce, without any suggestion of imitation. Like Joyce, he is sometimes a chronicler of stagnation and disappointment, and many of his keenly observed stories set in isolated Irish communities strike a note of understated melancholy, one of the best known being 'The Ballroom of Romance' (the title story of his 1972 collection of short stories).

'The Distant Past' appeared in Trevor's third volume of short stories, *Angels at the Ritz and Other Stories*, published in London in 1975. A few years later it featured as the title story in a collection published in Dublin, *The Distant Past, and Other Stories* (1979). The story is set in the kind of rural community about which Trevor writes so well, and spans the two periods of Ireland's 'Troubles'. The escalating violence in Northern Ireland from 1969 onwards, against which the events in the present-day of the story take place, also recalls the earlier Troubles, just after the First World War, when Ireland was fighting for independence from Britain (and then descended into civil war). Here we see Trevor, as the critic Patricia Craig puts it, 'making it his business to tackle the whole murky business of bygone social arrangements in the country, and their political implications',[1] a business he would pursue further in his later novels *Fools of Fortune* and *The Silence in the Garden* (1988).

Note

1. P. Craig, 'Ireland', in *The Oxford Guide to Contemporary Writing*, ed. John Sturrock (Oxford: Oxford University Press, 1996), p. 225.

The Distant Past

In the town and beyond it they were regarded as harmlessly peculiar. Odd, people said, and in time this reference took on a burnish of affection.

They had always been thin, silent with one another, and similar in appearance: a brother and sister who shared a family face. It was a bony countenance, with pale blue eyes and a sharp, well-shaped nose and high cheekbones. Their father had had it too, but unlike them their father had been an irresponsible and careless man, with red flecks in his cheeks that they didn't have at all. The Middletons of Carraveagh the family had once been known as, but now the brother and sister were just the Middletons, for Carraveagh didn't count any more, except to them.

They owned four Herefords, a number of hens, and the house itself, three miles outside the town. It was a large house, built in the reign of George II, a monument that reflected in its glory and later decay the fortunes of a family. As the brother and sister aged, its roof increasingly ceased to afford protection, rust ate at its gutters, grass thrived in two thick channels all along its avenue. Their father had mortgaged his inherited estate, so local rumour claimed, in order to keep a Catholic Dublin woman in brandy and jewels. When he died, in 1924, his two children discovered that they possessed only a dozen acres. It was locally said also that this adversity hardened their will and that, because of it, they came to love the remains of Carraveagh more than they could ever have loved a husband or a wife. They blamed for their ill-fortune the Catholic Dublin woman whom they'd never met and they blamed as well the new national regime, contriving in their eccentric way to relate the two. In the days of the Union Jack such women would have known their place: wasn't it all part and parcel?

Twice a week, on Fridays and Sundays, the Middletons journeyed into the town, first of all in a trap and later in a Ford Anglia car. In the shops and elsewhere they made, quite gently, no secret of their continuing loyalty to the past. They attended on Sundays St Patrick's Protestant Church, a place that matched their mood, for prayers were still said there for the King whose sovereignty their country had denied. The revolutionary regime would not last, they quietly informed the Reverend Packham: what sense was there in green-painted pillar-boxes and a language that nobody understood?

On Fridays, when they took seven or eight dozen eggs to the town, they dressed in pressed tweeds and were accompanied over the years by a series of red setters, the breed there had always been at Carraveagh. They sold the eggs in Gerrity's grocery and then had a drink with Mrs Gerrity in the part of her shop that was devoted to the consumption of refreshment. Mr Middleton had whiskey and his sister Tio Pepe. They enjoyed the occasion, for they liked Mrs Gerrity and were liked by her in return. Afterwards they shopped, chatting to the shopkeepers about whatever news there was, and then they went to Healy's Hotel for a few more drinks before driving home.

Drink was their pleasure and it was through it that they built up, in spite of their loyalty to the past, such convivial relationships with the people of the town. Fat Cranley, who kept the butcher's shop, used even to joke about the past when he stood with them in Healy's Hotel or stood behind his own counter cutting their slender chops or thinly slicing their liver. 'Will you ever forget it, Mr Middleton? I'd ha' run like a rabbit if you'd lifted a finger at me.' Fat Cranley would laugh then, rocking back on his heels with a glass of stout in his hand or banging their meat on to his weighing-scales. Mr Middleton would smile. 'There was alarm in your eyes, Mr Cranley,' Miss Middleton would murmur, smiling also at the memory of the distant occasion.

Fat Cranley, with a farmer called Maguire and another called Breen, had stood in the hall of Carraveagh, each of them in charge of a shot-gun. The Middletons, children then, had been locked with their mother and father and an aunt into an upstairs room. Nothing else had happened: the expected British soldiers had not, after all, arrived and the men in the hall had eventually relaxed their vigil. 'A massacre they wanted,' the Middletons' father said after they'd gone. 'Damn bloody ruffians.'

The Second World War took place. Two Germans, a man and his wife called Winkelmann who ran a glove factory in the town, were suspected by the Middletons of being spies for the Third Reich. People laughed, for they knew the Winkelmanns well and could lend no credence to the Middletons' latest fantasy: typical of them, they explained to the Winkelmanns, who had been worried. Soon after the War the Reverend Packham died and was replaced by the Reverend Bradshaw, a younger man who laughed also and regarded the Middletons as an anachronism. They protested when prayers were no longer said for the Royal Family in St Patrick's, but the Reverend Bradshaw considered that their protests were as absurd as the prayers themselves had been. Why pray for the monarchy of a neighbouring island when their own island had its chosen President now? The Middletons didn't reply to that argument. In the Reverend Bradshaw's presence they rose to their feet when the BBC played 'God Save the King', and on the day of the coronation of Queen Elizabeth II they drove into the town with a small Union Jack propped up in the back window of their Ford Anglia. 'Bedad, you're a holy terror, Mr Middleton!' Fat Cranley laughingly exclaimed, noticing the flag as he lifted a tray of pork steaks from his display shelf. The Middletons smiled. It was a great day for the Commonwealth of Nations, they replied, a remark which further amused Fat Cranley and which he later repeated in Phelan's public house. 'Her Britannic Majesty,' guffawed his friend Mr Breen.

Situated in a valley that was noted for its beauty and with convenient access to rich rivers and bogs over which game-birds flew, the town benefited from post-war tourism. Healy's Hotel changed its title and became, overnight, the New Ormonde. Shopkeepers had their shop-fronts painted and Mr Healy organized an annual Salmon Festival. Even Canon Cotter, who had at first commented severely on the habits of the tourists, and in particular on the summertime dress of the women, was in the end obliged to confess that the morals of his flock remained unaffected. 'God and good sense', he proclaimed, meaning God and his own teaching. In time he even derived pride from the fact that people with other values came briefly to the town and that the values esteemed by his parishioners were in no way diminished.

The town's grocers now stocked foreign cheeses, brie and camembert and Port Salut, and wines were available to go with them. The plush Cocktail Room of the New Ormonde set a standard: the wife of a solicitor, a Mrs Duggan, began to give six o'clock parties once or twice a year, obliging her husband to mix gin and Martini in glass jugs and herself handing round a selection of nuts and small

Japanese crackers. Canon Cotter looked in as a rule and satisfied himself that all was above board. He rejected, though, the mixture in the jugs, retaining his taste for a glass of John Jameson.

From the windows of their convent the Loreto nuns observed the long, sleek cars with GB plates; English and American accents drifted on the breeze to them. Mothers cleaned up their children and sent them to the Golf Club to seek employment as caddies. Sweet-shops sold holiday mementoes. The brown, soda and currant breads of Murphy-Flood's bakery were declared to be delicious. Mr Healy doubled the number of local girls who served as waitresses in his dining-room, and in the winter of 1961 he had the builders in again, working on an extension for which the Munster and Leinster Bank had lent him twenty-two thousand pounds.

But as the town increased its prosperity Carraveagh continued its decline. The Middletons were in their middle-sixties now and were reconciled to a life that became more uncomfortable with every passing year. Together they roved the vast lofts of their house, placing old paint tins and flower-pot saucers beneath the drips from the roof. At night they sat over their thin chops in a dining-room that had once been gracious and which in a way was gracious still, except for the faded appearance of furniture that was dry from lack of polish and of a wallpaper that time had rendered colourless. In the hall their father gazed down at them, framed in ebony and gilt, in the uniform of the Irish Guards. He had conversed with Queen Victoria, and even in their middle-sixties they could still hear him saying that God and Empire and Queen formed a trinity unique in any worthy soldier's heart. In the hall hung the family crest, and on ancient Irish linen the Cross of St George.

The dog that accompanied the Middletons now was called Turloch, an animal whose death they dreaded for they felt they couldn't manage the antics of another pup. Turloch, being thirteen, moved slowly and was blind and a little deaf. He was a reminder to them of their own advancing years and of the effort it had become to tend the Herefords and collect the weekly eggs. More and more they looked forward to Fridays, to the warm companionship of Mrs Gerrity and Mr Healy's chatter in the hotel. They stayed longer now with Mrs Gerrity and in the hotel, and idled longer in the shops, and drove home more slowly. Dimly, but with no less loyalty, they still recalled the distant past and were listened to without ill-feeling when they spoke of it and of Carraveagh as it had been, and of the Queen whose company their careless father had known.

The visitors who came to the town heard about the Middletons and were impressed. It was a pleasant wonder, more than one of them remarked, that old wounds could heal so completely, that the Middletons continued in their loyalty to the past and that, in spite of it, they were respected in the town. When Miss Middleton had been ill with a form of pneumonia in 1958 Canon Cotter had driven out to Carraveagh twice a week with pullets and young ducks that his housekeeper had dressed. 'An upright couple,' was the Canon's public opinion of the Middletons, and he had been known to add that eccentric views would hurt you less than malice. 'We can disagree without guns in this town,' Mr Healy pronounced in his Cocktail Room, and his visitors usually replied that as far as they could see this was the result of living in a Christian country. That the Middletons bought their meat from a man who had once locked them into an upstairs room and had then waited to shoot soldiers in their hall was a fact that amazed the seasonal visitors. You lived and learned, they remarked to Mr Healy.

The Middletons, privately, often considered that they led a strange life. Alone in their two beds at night they now and again wondered why they hadn't just sold Carraveagh forty-eight years ago when their father died: why had the tie been so strong and why had they in perversity encouraged it? They didn't fully know, nor did they attempt to discuss the matter in any way. Instinctively they had remained at Carraveagh, instinctively feeling that it would have been cowardly to go. Yet often it seemed to them now to be no more than a game they played, this worship of the distant past. And at other times it seemed as real and as important as the remaining acres of land, and the house itself.

'Isn't that shocking?' Mr Healy said one day in 1968. 'Did you hear about that, Mr Middleton, blowing up them post offices in Belfast?'

Mr Healy, red-faced and short-haired, spoke casually in his Cocktail Room, making midday conversation. He had commented in much the same way at breakfast-time, looking up from the *Irish*

Independent. Everyone in the town had said it too: that the blowing up of sub-post offices in Belfast was a shocking matter.

'A bad business,' Fat Cranley remarked, wrapping the Middletons' meat. 'We don't want that old stuff all over again.'

'We didn't want it in the first place,' Miss Middleton remined him. He laughed, and she laughed, and so did her brother. Yes, it was a game, she thought: how could any of it be as real or as important as the afflictions and problems of the old butcher himself, his rheumatism and his reluctance to retire? Did her brother, she wondered, privately think so too?

'Come on, old Turloch,' he said, stroking the flank of the red setter with the point of his shoe, and she reflected that you could never tell what he was thinking. Certainly it wasn't the kind of thing you wanted to talk about.

'I've put him in a bit of mince,' Fat Cranley said, which was something he often did these days, pretending the mince would otherwise be thrown away. There'd been a red setter about the place that night when he waited in the hall for the soldiers: Breen and Maguire had pushed it down into a cellar, frightened of it.

'There's a heart of gold in you, Mr Cranley,' Miss Middleton murmured, nodding and smiling at him. He was the same age as she was, sixty-six: he should have shut up shop years ago. He would have, he'd once told them, if there'd been a son to leave the business to. As it was, he'd have to sell it and when it came to the point he found it hard to make the necessary arrangements. 'Like us and Carraveagh,' she'd said, even though on the face of it it didn't seem the same at all.

Every evening they sat in the big old kitchen, hearing the news. It was only in Belfast and Derry, the wireless said; outside Belfast and Derry you wouldn't know anything was happening at all. On Fridays they listened to the talk in Mrs Gerrity's bar and in the hotel. 'Well, thank God it has nothing to do with the South,' Mr Healy said often, usually repeating the statement.

The first British soldiers landed in the North of Ireland, and soon people didn't so often say that outside Belfast and Derry you wouldn't know anything was happening. There were incidents in Fermanagh and Armagh, in Border villages and towns. One Prime

Minister resigned and then another one. The troops were unpopular, the newspapers said; internment became part of the machinery of government. In the town, in St Patrick's Protestant Church and in the Church of the Holy Assumption, prayers for peace were offered, but no peace came.

'We're hit, Mr Middleton,' Mr Healy said one Friday morning. 'If there's a dozen visitors this summer it'll be God's own stroke of luck for us.'

'Luck?'

'Sure, who wants to come to a country with all that malarkey in it?'

'But it's only in the North.'

'Tell that to your tourists, Mr Middleton.'

The town's prosperity ebbed. The Border was more than sixty miles away, but over that distance had spread some wisps of the fog of war. As anger rose in the town at the loss of fortune so there rose also the kind of talk there had been in the distant past. There was talk of atrocities and counter-atrocities, and of guns and gelignite and the rights of people. There was bitterness suddenly in Mrs Gerrity's bar because of the lack of trade, and in the empty hotel there was bitterness also.

On Fridays, only sometimes at first, there was a silence when the Middletons appeared. It was as though, going back nearly twenty years, people remembered the Union Jack in the window of their car and saw it now in a different light. It wasn't something to laugh at any more, nor were certain words that the Middletons had gently spoken, nor were they themselves just an old, peculiar couple. Slowly the change crept about, all around them in the town, until Fat Cranley didn't wish it to be remembered that he had ever given them mince for their dog. He had stood with a gun in the enemy's house, waiting for soldiers so that soldiers might be killed: it was better that people should remember that.

One day Canon Cotter looked the other way when he saw the Middletons' car coming and they noticed this movement of his head, although he hadn't wished them to. And on another day Mrs Duggan, who had always been keen to talk to them in the hotel, didn't reply when they addressed her.

The Middletons naturally didn't discuss these rebuffs, but they each of them privately knew that there was no conversation they could have at this time with the people of the town. The stand they had taken and kept to for so many years no longer seemed ridiculous in the town. Had they driven with a Union Jack now they might, astoundingly, have been shot.

'It will never cease.' He spoke disconsolately one night, standing by the dresser where the wireless was.

She washed the dishes they'd eaten from, and the cutlery. 'Not in our time,' she said.

'It is worse than before.'

'Yes, it is worse than before.'

They took from the walls of the hall the portrait of their father in the uniform of the Irish Guards because it seemed wrong to them that at this time it should hang there. They took down also the crest of their family and the Cross of St George, and from a vase on the drawing-room mantelpiece they removed the small Union Jack that had been there since the Coronation of Queen Elizabeth II. They did not remove these articles in fear, but in mourning for the *modus vivendi* that had existed for so long between them and the people of the town. They had given their custom to a butcher who had planned to shoot down soldiers in their hall and he, in turn, had given them mince for their dog. For fifty years they had experienced, after suspicion had seeped away, a tolerance that never again in the years that were left to them would they know.

One November night their dog died and he said to her after he had buried it that they must not be depressed by all that was happening. They would die themselves and the house would become a ruin because there was no one to inherit it, and the distant past would be set to rest. But she disagreed: the *modus vivendi* had been easy for them, she pointed out, because they hadn't really minded the dwindling of their fortunes while the town prospered. It had given them a life, and a kind of dignity: you could take a pride out of living in peace.

He did not say anything and then, because of the emotion that both of them felt over the death of their dog, he said in a rushing way that they could no longer at their age hope to make a living out of the remains of Carraveagh. They must sell the hens and the four Herefords. As he spoke, he watched her nodding, agreeing with the sense of it. Now and again, he thought, he would drive slowly into the town, to buy groceries and meat with the money they had saved, and to face the silence that would sourly thicken as their own two deaths came closer and death increased in another part of their island. She felt him thinking that and she knew that he was right. Because of the distant past they would die friendless. It was worse than being murdered in their beds.

American Dreams

Peter Carey

Introduction

Peter Carey, a third-generation Australian of English descent, was born in 1943 in the small town of Bacchus Marsh, Victoria. His parents, Percival Stanley and Helen Jean Carey, owned and ran a garage and car dealership called Carey's Motors. Peter was educated at first at a local primary school and then at the prestigious Geelong Grammar School; he went on to study chemistry and zoology at Monash University, near Melbourne. At this period in his life his literary interests were, he claims, non-existent.[1] He left his science course at Monash after the first year, and began working at an advertising agency in Melbourne. Here he met people who were enthusiastic readers, and lent him books, as well as being writers. Before long, he began to write more than advertising copy himself, producing several (unpublished) novels and short stories over the next few years.

Troubled by Australia's involvement in the war in Vietnam, Carey left Australia in 1967 and travelled extensively in Europe. He settled for a while in London, again working as an advertising copywriter, before returning to Australia in 1970. It was then that he began writing the stories, including 'American Dreams', that would appear in his first collection, *The Fat Man in History* (1974). In 1976 he went to live in a commune in Queensland, continuing his work in advertising in Sydney for one week a month, and writing the rest of the time. His second collection of short stories, *War Crimes*, was published in 1979. These two collections, a partial amalgam of which was published in Britain as *Exotic Pleasures* (1981), established his reputation as a fresh and exciting writer of short fiction.

In 1980 Carey set up his own advertising agency, in which he worked part-time. He published his first novel, *Bliss*, in 1981, and literary awards began to flow his way. He has now published nine novels, and has twice won the Booker Prize, with *Oscar and Lucinda* in 1988 and *The True History of the Kelly Gang* in 2001. He has also been involved in a number of theatre and film projects, most notably writing the screenplay for Wim Wenders' *Until the End of the World* (1991).

Since 1989 Carey and his family have lived in New York, and he has taught Creative Writing, part-time, at New York and Princeton Universities. Although resident in the USA, he is regarded as Australia's foremost fiction writer, and is a fellow of the Australian Academy of Humanities (as well as of the American Academy of Arts and Science, and Britain's Royal Society of Literature). His explorations of Australian history in his epic-sized novels are formally innovative, often blending naturalistic and fantastic elements. It is sometimes claimed that the influence of South American writers such as Jorge Luis Borges and Gabriel García Márquez can be discerned in Carey's fiction.

Certainly in his short stories from the 1970s Carey breaks away decisively from the strong Australian tradition of realism. His interests in the bizarre, the nightmarish, and aspects of science fiction sit alongside a keen concern for the plight of ordinary, average people in a post-colonial world dominated by the demands of international capitalism. 'American Dreams' is one of the most famous of these stories, set in a quiet 1950s provincial town resembling, probably, the Bacchus Marsh of Carey's boyhood. In deceptively matter-of-fact style, the story explores the dangers of cultural dependency as well as the relationship between art and reality.

Note

1. See Bruce Woodcock, *Peter Carey* (Manchester and New York: Manchester University Press, 1996), p. 2.

American Dreams

No one can, to this day, remember what it was we did to offend him. Dyer the butcher remembers a day when he gave him the wrong meat and another day when he served someone else first by mistake. Often when Dyer gets drunk he recalls this day and curses himself for his foolishness. But no one seriously believes that it was Dyer who offended him.

But one of us did something. We slighted him terribly in some way, this small meek man with the rimless glasses and neat suit who used to smile so nicely at us all. We thought, I suppose, he was a bit of a fool and sometimes he was so quiet and grey that we ignored him, forgetting he was there at all.

When I was a boy I often stole apples from the trees at his house up in Mason's Lane. He often saw me. No, that's not correct. Let me say I often sensed that he saw me. I sensed him peering out from behind the lace curtains of his house. And I was not the only one. Many of us came to take his apples, alone and in groups, and it is possible that he chose to exact payment for all these apples in his own peculiar way.

Yet I am sure it wasn't the apples.

What has happened is that we all, all eight hundred of us, have come to remember small transgressions against Mr Gleason, who once lived amongst us.

My father, who has never borne malice against a single living creature, still believes that Gleason meant to do us well, that he loved the town more than any of us. My father says we have treated the town badly in our minds. We have used it, this little valley, as nothing more than a stopping place. Somewhere on the way to somewhere else. Even those of us who have been here many years have never taken the town seriously. Oh yes, the place is pretty. The hills are green and the woods thick. The stream is full of fish. But it is not where we would rather be.

For years we have watched the films at the Roxy and dreamed, if not of America, then at least of our capital city. For our own town, my father says, we have nothing but contempt. We have treated it badly, like a whore. We have cut down the giant shady trees in the main street to make doors for the school house and seats for the football pavilion. We have left big holes all over the countryside from which we have taken brown coal and given back nothing.

The commercial travellers who buy fish and chips at George the Greek's care for us more than we do, because we all have dreams of the big city, of wealth, of modern houses, of big motor cars: American dreams, my father has called them.

Although my father ran a petrol station he was also an inventor. He sat in his office all day drawing strange pieces of equipment on the back of delivery dockets. Every spare piece of paper in the house was covered with these little drawings and my mother would always be very careful about throwing away any piece of paper no matter how small. She would look on both sides of any piece of paper very carefully and always preserved any that had so much as a pencil mark.

I think it was because of this that my father felt that he understood Gleason. He never said as much, but he inferred that he understood Gleason because he, too, was concerned with similar problems. My father was working on plans for a giant gravel crusher, but occasionally he would become distracted and become interested in something else.

There was, for instance, the time when Dyer the butcher bought a new bicycle with gears, and for a while my father talked of nothing else but the gears. Often I would see him across the road squatting down beside Dyer's bicycle as if he were talking to it.

We all rode bicycles because we didn't have the money for anything better. My father did have an old Chev truck, but he rarely used it and it occurs to me now that it might have had some mechanical problem that was impossible to solve, or perhaps it was just that he was saving it, not wishing to wear it out all at once. Normally, he went everywhere on his bicycle and, when I was younger, he carried me on the crossbar, both of us dismounting to trudge up the hills that led into and out of the main street. It was a common sight in our town to see people pushing bicycles. They were as much a burden as a means of transport.

Gleason also had his bicycle and every lunchtime he pushed and pedalled it home from the shire offices to his little weatherboard house out at Mason's Lane. It was a three-mile ride and people said that he went home for lunch because he was fussy and wouldn't eat either his wife's sandwiches or the hot meal available at Mrs Lessing's café.

But while Gleason pedalled and pushed his bicycle to and from the shire offices everything in our town proceeded as normal. It was only when he retired that things began to go wrong.

Because it was then that Mr Gleason started supervising the building of the wall around the two-acre plot up on Bald Hill. He paid too much for this land. He bought it from Johnny Weeks, who now, I am sure, believes the whole episode was his fault, firstly for cheating Gleason, secondly for selling him the land at all. But Gleason hired some Chinese and set to work to build his wall. It was then that we knew that we'd offended him. My father rode all the way out to Bald Hill and tried to talk Mr Gleason out of his wall. He said there was no need for us to build walls. That no one wished to spy on Mr Gleason or whatever he wished to do on Bald Hill. He said no one was in the least bit interested in Mr Gleason. Mr Gleason, neat in a new sports-coat, polished his glasses and smiled vaguely at his feet. Bicycling back, my father thought that he had gone too far. Of course we had an interest in Mr Gleason. He pedalled back and asked him to attend a dance that was to be held on the next Friday, but Mr Gleason said he didn't dance.

"Oh well," my father said, "any time, just drop over."

Mr Gleason went back to supervising his family of Chinese labourers on his wall.

Bald Hill towered high above the town and from my father's small filling station you could sit and watch the wall going up. It was an interesting sight. I watched it for two years, while I waited for customers who rarely came. After school and on Saturdays I had all the time in the world to watch the agonizing progress of Mr Gleason's wall. It was as painful as a clock. Sometimes I could see the Chinese labourers running at a jog-trot carrying bricks on long wooden planks. The hill was bare, and on this bareness Mr Gleason was, for some reason, building a wall.

In the beginning people thought it peculiar that someone would build such a big wall on Bald Hill. The only thing to recommend Bald Hill was the view of the town, and Mr Gleason was building a wall that denied that view. The top soil was thin and bare clay showed through in places. Nothing would ever grow there. Everyone assumed that Gleason had simply gone mad and after the initial interest they accepted his madness as they accepted his wall and as they accepted Bald Hill itself.

Occasionally someone would pull in for petrol at my father's filling station and ask about the wall and my father would shrug and I would see, once more, the strangeness of it.

"A house?" the stranger would ask. "Up on that hill?"

"No," my father would say, "chap named Gleason is building a wall."

And the strangers would want to know why, and my father would shrug and look up at Bald Hill once more. "Damned if I know," he'd say.

Gleason still lived in his old house at Mason's Lane. It was a plain weatherboard house, with a rose garden at the front, a vegetable garden down the side, and an orchard at the back.

At night we kids would sometimes ride out to Bald Hill on our bicycles. It was an agonizing, muscle-twitching ride, the worst part of which was a steep, unmade road up which we finally pushed our bikes, our lungs rasping in the night air. When we arrived we found nothing but walls. Once we broke down some of the brickwork and another time we threw stones at the tents where the Chinese labourers slept. Thus we expressed our frustration at this inexplicable thing.

The wall must have been finished on the day before my twelfth birthday. I remember going on a picnic birthday party up to Eleven Mile Creek and we lit a fire and cooked chops at a bend in the river from where it was possible to see the walls on Bald Hill. I remember standing with a hot chop in my hand and someone saying, "Look, they're leaving!"

We stood on the creek bed and watched the Chinese labourers walking their bicycles slowly down the hill. Someone said they were going to build a chimney up at the mine at A.1 and certainly there is a large brick chimney there now, so I suppose they built it.

When the word spread that the walls were finished most of the town went up to look. They walked around the four walls which were as interesting as any other brick walls. They stood in front of the big wooden gates and tried to peer through, but all they could see was a small blind wall that had obviously been constructed for this special purpose. The walls themselves were ten feet high and topped with broken glass and barbed wire. When it became obvious that we were not going to discover the contents of the enclosure, we all gave up and went home.

Mr Gleason had long since stopped coming into town. His wife came instead, wheeling a pram down from Mason's Lane to Main Street and filling it with groceries and meat (they never bought vegetables, they grew their own) and wheeling it back to Mason's Lane. Sometimes you would see her standing with the pram halfway up the Gell Street hill. Just standing there, catching her breath. No one asked her about the wall. They knew she wasn't responsible for the wall and they felt sorry for her, having to bear the burden of the pram and her husband's madness. Even when she began to visit Dixon's hardware and buy plaster of Paris and tins of paint and waterproofing compound, no one asked her what these things were for. She had a way of averting her eyes that indicated her terror of questions. Old Dixon carried the plaster of Paris and the tins of paint out to her pram for her and watched her push them away. "Poor woman," he said, "poor bloody woman."

From the filling station where I sat dreaming in the sun, or from the enclosed office where I gazed mournfully at the rain, I would see, occasionally, Gleason entering or leaving his walled compound, a tiny figure way up on Bald Hill. And I'd think "Gleason," but not much more.

Occasionally strangers drove up there to see what was going on, often egged on by locals who told them it was a Chinese temple or some other silly thing. Once a group of Italians had a picnic outside the walls and took photographs of each other standing in front of the closed door. God knows what they thought it was.

But for five years between my twelfth and seventeenth birthdays there was nothing to interest me in Gleason's walls. Those years seem lost to me now and I can remember very little of them. I developed a crush on Susy Markin and followed her back from the swimming pool on my bicycle. I sat behind her in the pictures and wandered past her house. Then her parents moved to another town and I sat in the sun and waited for them to come back.

We became very keen on modernization. When coloured paints became available the whole town went berserk and brightly coloured houses blossomed overnight. But the paints were not of good quality and quickly faded and peeled, so that the town looked like a garden of dead flowers. Thinking of those years, the only real thing I recall is the soft hiss of bicycle tyres on the main street. When I think of it now it seems very peaceful, but I remember then that the sound induced in me a feeling of melancholy, a feeling somehow mixed with the early afternoons when the sun went down behind Bald Hill and the town felt as sad as an empty dance hall on a Sunday afternoon.

And then, during my seventeenth year, Mr Gleason died. We found out when we saw Mrs Gleason's pram parked out in front of Phonsey Joy's Funeral Parlour. It looked very sad, that pram, standing by itself in the windswept street. We came and looked at the pram and felt sad for Mrs Gleason. She hadn't had much of a life.

Phonsey Joy carried old Mr Gleason out to the cemetery by the Parwan Railway Station and Mrs Gleason rode behind in a taxi. People watched the old hearse go by and thought, "Gleason," but not much else.

And then, less than a month after Gleason had been buried out at the lonely cemetery by the Parwan Railway Station, the Chinese labourers came back. We saw them push their bicycles up the hill. I stood with my father and Phonsey Joy and wondered what was going on.

And then I saw Mrs Gleason trudging up the hill. I nearly didn't recognize her, because she didn't have her pram. She carried a black umbrella and walked slowly up Bald Hill and it wasn't until she stopped for breath and leant forward that I recognized her.

"It's Mrs Gleason," I said, "with the Chinese."

But it wasn't until the next morning that it became obvious what was happening. People lined the main street in the way they do for a big funeral but, instead of gazing towards the Grant Street corner, they all looked up at Bald Hill.

All that day and all the next people gathered to watch the destruction of the walls. They saw the Chinese labourers darting to and fro, but it wasn't until they knocked down a large section of the wall facing the town that we realized there really was something inside.

It was impossible to see what it was, but there was something there. People stood and wondered and pointed out Mrs Gleason to each other as she went to and fro supervising the work.

And finally, in ones and twos, on bicycles and on foot, the whole town moved up to Bald Hill. Mr Dyer closed up his butcher shop and my father got out the old Chev truck and we finally arrived up at Bald Hill with twenty people on board. They crowded into the back tray and hung onto the running boards and my father grimly steered his way through the crowds of bicycles and parked just where the dirt track gets really steep. We trudged up this last steep track, never for a moment suspecting what we would find at the top.

It was very quiet up there. The Chinese labourers worked diligently, removing the third and fourth walls and cleaning the bricks which they stacked neatly in big piles. Mrs Gleason said nothing either. She stood in the only remaining corner of the walls and looked defiantly at the townspeople, who stood open-mouthed where another corner had been.

And between us and Mrs Gleason was the most incredibly beautiful thing I had ever seen in my life. For one moment I didn't recognize it. I stood open-mouthed, and breathed the surprising beauty of it. And then I realized it was our town. The buildings were two feet high and they were a little rough but very correct. I saw Mr Dyer nudge my father and whisper that Gleason had got the faded U in the BUTCHER sign of his shop.

I think at that moment everyone was overcome with a feeling of simple joy. I can't remember ever having felt so uplifted and happy. It was perhaps a childish emotion but I looked up at my father and saw a smile of such warmth spread across his face that I knew he felt just as I did. Later he told me that he thought Gleason had built the model of our town just for this moment, to let us see the beauty of our town, to make us proud of ourselves and to stop the American Dreams we were so prone to. For the rest, my father said, was not Gleason's plan and he could not have foreseen the things that happened afterwards.

I have come to think that this view of my father's is a little sentimental and also, perhaps, insulting to Gleason. I personally believe that he knew everything that would happen. One day the proof of my theory may be discovered. Certainly there are in existence some personal papers, and I firmly believe that these papers will show that Gleason knew exactly what would happen.

We had been so overcome by the model of the town that we hadn't noticed what was the most remarkable thing of all. Not only had Gleason built the houses and the shops of our town, he had also peopled it. As we tiptoed into the town we suddenly found ourselves. "Look," I said to Mr Dyer, "there you are."

And there he was, standing in front of his shop in his apron. As I bent down to examine the tiny figure I was staggered by the look on its face. The modelling was crude, the paintwork was sloppy, and the face a little too white, but the expression was absolutely perfect: those pursed, quizzical lips, and the eyebrows lifted high. It was Mr Dyer and no one else on earth.

And there beside Mr Dyer was my father, squatting on the foot-path and gazing lovingly at Mr Dyer's bicycle gears, his face marked with grease and hope.

And there was I, back at the filling station, leaning against a petrol pump in an American pose and talking to Brian Sparrow, who was amusing me with his clownish antics.

Phonsey Joy standing beside his hearse. Mr Dixon sitting inside his hardware store. Everyone I knew was there in that tiny town. If they were not in the streets or in their backyards they were inside their houses, and it didn't take very long to discover that you could lift off the roofs and peer inside.

We tiptoed around the streets, peeping into each other's windows, lifting off each other's roofs, admiring each other's gardens, and while we did it, Mrs Gleason slipped silently away down the hill towards Mason's Lane. She spoke to nobody and nobody spoke to her.

I confess that I was the one who took the roof from Cavanagh's house. So I was the one who found Mrs Cavanagh in bed with young Craigie Evans.

I stood there for a long time, hardly knowing what I was seeing. I stared at the pair of them for a long, long time. And when I finally knew what I was seeing I felt such an incredible mixture of jealousy and guilt and wonder that I didn't know what to do with the roof.

Eventually it was Phonsey Joy who took the roof from my hands and placed it carefully back on the house, much, I imagine, as he would have placed the lid on a coffin. By then other people had seen what I had seen and the word passed around very quickly.

And then we all stood around in little groups and regarded the model town with what could only have been fear. If Gleason knew about Mrs Cavanagh and Craigie Evans (and no one else had), what other things might he know? Those who hadn't seen themselves yet in the town began to look a little nervous and were unsure of whether to look for themselves or not. We gazed silently at the roofs and felt mistrustful and guilty.

We all walked down the hill then, very quietly, the way people walk away from a funeral, listening only to the crunch of the gravel under our feet while the women had trouble with their high-heeled shoes.

The next day a special meeting of the shire council passed a motion calling on Mrs Gleason to destroy the model town on the grounds that it contravened building regulations.

It is unfortunate that this order wasn't carried out before the city newspapers found out. Before another day had gone by the government had stepped in.

The model town and its model occupants were to be preserved. The minister for tourism came in a large black car and made a speech to us in the football pavilion. We sat on the high, tiered seats eating potato chips while he stood against the fence and talked to us. We couldn't hear him very well, but we heard enough. He called the model town a work of art and we stared at him grimly. He said it would be an invaluable tourist attraction. He said tourists would come from everywhere to see the model town. We would be famous. Our businesses would flourish. There would be work for guides and interpreters and caretakers and taxi drivers and people selling soft drinks and ice creams.

The Americans would come, he said. They would visit our town in buses and in cars and on the train. They would take photographs and bring wallets bulging with dollars. American dollars.

We looked at the minister mistrustfully, wondering if he knew about Mrs Cavanagh, and he must have seen the look because he said that certain controversial items would be removed, had already been removed. We shifted in our seats, like you do when a particularly tense part of a film has come to its climax, and then we relaxed and listened to what the minister had to say. And we all began, once more, to dream our American dreams.

We saw our big smooth cars cruising through cities with bright lights. We entered expensive nightclubs and danced till dawn. We made love to women like Kim Novak and men like Rock Hudson. We drank cocktails. We gazed lazily into refrigerators filled with food and prepared ourselves lavish midnight snacks which we ate while we watched huge television sets on which we would be able to see American movies free of charge and for ever.

The minister, like someone from our American dreams, re-entered his large black car and cruised slowly from our humble sportsground, and the newspaper men arrived and swarmed over the pavilion with their cameras and notebooks. They took photographs of us and photographs of the models up on Bald Hill. And the next day we were all over the newspapers. The photographs of the model people side by side with photographs of the real people. And our names and ages and what we did were all printed there in black and white.

They interviewed Mrs Gleason but she said nothing of interest. She said the model town had been her husband's hobby.

We all felt good now. It was very pleasant to have your photograph in the paper. And, once more, we changed our opinion of Gleason. The shire council held another meeting and named the dirt track up Bald Hill "Gleason Avenue". Then we all went home and waited for the Americans we had been promised.

It didn't take long for them to come, although at the time it seemed an eternity, and we spent six long months doing nothing more with our lives than waiting for the Americans.

Well, they did come. And let me tell you how it has all worked out for us.

The Americans arrive every day in buses and cars and sometimes the younger ones come on the train. There is now a small airstrip out near the Parwan cemetery and they also arrive there, in small aeroplanes. Phonsey Joy drives them to the cemetery where they look at Gleason's grave and then up to Bald Hill and then down to the town. He is doing very well from it all. It is good to see someone doing well from it. Phonsey is becoming a big man in town and is on the shire council.

On Bald Hill there are half a dozen telescopes through which the Americans can spy on the town and reassure themselves that it is the same down there as it is on Bald Hill. Herb Gravney sells them ice creams and soft drinks and extra film for their cameras. He is another one who is doing well. He bought the whole model from Mrs Gleason and charges five American dollars' admission. Herb is on the council now too. He's doing very well for himself. He sells them the film so they can take photographs of the houses and the model people and so they can come down to the town with their special maps and hunt out the real people.

To tell the truth most of us are pretty sick of the game. They come looking for my father and ask him to stare at the gears of Dyer's bicycle. I watch my father cross the street slowly, his head hung low. He doesn't greet the Americans any more. He doesn't ask them questions about colour television or Washington, D.C. He kneels on the footpath in front of Dyer's bike. They stand around him. Often they remember the model incorrectly and try to get my father to pose in the wrong way. Originally he argued with them, but now he argues no more. He does what they ask. They push him this way and that and worry about the expression on his face which is no longer what it was.

Then I know they will come to find me. I am next on the map. I am very popular for some reason. They come in search of me and my petrol pump as they have done for four years now. I do not await them eagerly because I know, before they reach me, that they will be disappointed.

"But this is not the boy."

"Yes," says Phonsey, "this is him all right." And he gets me to show them my certificate.

They examine the certificate suspiciously, feeling the paper as if it might be a clever forgery. "No," they declare. (Americans are so confident.) "No," they shake their heads, "this is not the real boy. The real boy is younger."

"He's older now. He used to be younger." Phonsey looks weary when he tells them. He can afford to look weary.

The Americans peer at my face closely. "It's a different boy."

But finally they get their cameras out. I stand sullenly and try to look amused as I did once. Gleason saw me looking amused but I can no longer remember how it felt. I was looking at Brian Sparrow. But Brian is also tired. He finds it difficult to do his clownish antics and to the Americans his little act isn't funny. They prefer the model. I watch him sadly, sorry that he must perform for such an unsympathetic audience.

The Americans pay one dollar for the right to take our photographs. Having paid the money they are worried about being cheated. They spend their time being disappointed and I spend my time feeling guilty, that I have somehow let them down by growing older and sadder.

Bella Makes Life

Lorna Goodison

Introduction

Lorna Gaye Goodison was born in Kingston, Jamaica, in 1947, one of nine siblings. Her parents, Vivian Marcus Goodison, a car mechanic and chauffeur, and Doris Louise Harvey, a seamstress, met and married in north-east Jamaica. Doris Harvey's English grandfather, William Harvey, had settled in Jamaica in the 1830s; with his brother John he established a home in the island's north-ernmost parish, Hanover, to which they gave the name Harvey River. After the death of his English wife, William married a young black woman, Frances Duhaney, and their family grew up in Harvey River. A generation later, Doris was also born there, and she and Marcus lived nearby after their marriage. On the outbreak of war in 1939, and the failure of Marcus's garage business, they moved to the distant and very different world of Kingston.

Lorna Goodison was educated at an Anglican High School, and studied at the Jamaica School of Art before going in 1968 to the School of the Art Students' League, New York. She is well known as a painter – she has exhibited her paintings internationally and illustrates her own books – but her major reputa-tion rests on her writing, and especially her poetry. She began writing poetry as a teenager, and published some poems anonymously in the *Jamaica Gleaner* (where her older sister Barbara was establishing a career in journalism), then under her own name in the influential *Jamaica Journal*. As one of a number of Caribbean women writers beginning to make their voices heard from the 1970s onwards, Goodison won considerable acclaim in Jamaica with the publication of her first poetry collection, *Tamarind Season*, in 1980. However, it was her second volume, *I Am Becoming My Mother* (1986), that brought her international recognition and won her the Commonwealth Writers Prize (Americas region).

As the title of this second collection indicates, Goodison's own mother is a significant figure in her writing, but alongside the 'womanist' concerns of her poetry there is also a deeply felt sense of history. Her 'Nanny', for example, is the legendary 'Nanny of the Maroons', an African-born resistance leader of eighteenth-century Jamaican runaway slaves: 'I was sent, tell that to history', says the speaker of Goodison's poem.[1] Another poem celebrates Rosa Parks, the African-American civil rights activist whose quiet resistance sparked the 1955 bus boycott in Montgomery, Alabama, a 'time of walking' that is linked in the poem to the slave-trade, when people walked 'in yoked formations down to Calabar / into the belly of close-ribbed whales'.[2] Her later poetry widens in scope to incorporate Third World experiences of the 'Favela and dungle dwellers, children of nothing new' who inhabit cities of waste.[3]

Although she has lived most of her life in Jamaica, Goodison has also spent some time in the USA and Canada, with writing residencies and part-time teaching posts at a number of universities, including Harvard, Toronto and Michigan. She has published eleven collections of poems, two volumes of short stories, and a memoir of her mother's family, *From Harvey River*. Her work, which has won her numerous literary awards, has been translated into German, French, Italian, Spanish and Chinese.

'Bella Makes Life' first appeared in the African Diaspora literary journal *Callaloo* in the summer of 1989 (no. 40), and then in Goodison's first short story collection, *Baby Mother and the King of Swords* (1990). The story has subsequently been anthologized, most notably alongside stories by Alice Walker, Maya Angelou and Olive Senior in Longman's *Quartet of Stories*, edited by Liz Gerschel (1993). Although the language of Goodison's poetry is often lyrical and uses a wide range of linguistic registers, what we hear in 'Bella Makes Life' is the kind of 'Jamaica talk' that became increasingly prominent in writing and performance of stories and poems from the island around the time Goodison was born, after the Second World War.

Notes

1. Lorna Goodison, 'Nanny', in *I Am Becoming My Mother* (London and Port of Spain: Beacon Books, 1986), p. 45.
2. Lorna Goodison, 'For Rosa Parks', in *I Am Becoming My Mother*, p. 41.
3. Lorna Goodison, 'To the Heirs of Low Bequests ... ', in *Travelling Mercies* (Toronto: McClelland & Stewart, 2001), p. 28.

Bella Makes Life

He was embarrassed when he saw her coming toward him. He wished he could have just disappeared into the crowd and kept going as far away from Norman Manley Airport as was possible. Bella returning. Bella come back from New York after a whole year. Bella dressed in some clothes which make her look like a checker cab. What in God's name was a big forty-odd-year-old woman who was fat when she leave Jamaica, and get worse fat since she go to America, what was this woman doing dressed like this? Bella was wearing a stretch-to-fit black pants, over that she had on a big yellow and black checked blouse, on her feet was a pair of yellow booties, in her hand was a big yellow handbag and she had on a pair of yellow-framed glasses. See ya Jesus! Bella no done yet, she had dyed her hair with red oxide and Jherri curls it till it shine like it grease and spray. Oh Bella what happen to you? Joseph never ever bother take in her anklet and her big bracelets and her gold chain with a pendant, big as a name plate on a lawyer's office, marked 'Material Girl'.

Joseph could sense the change in Bella through her letters. When she just went to New York, she used to write him DV every week.

Dear Joe Joe,

How keeping my darling? I hope fine. I miss you and the children so till I think I want to die. Down in Brooklyn here where I'm living, I see a lot of Jamaicans, but I don't mix up with them. The lady who sponsor me say that a lot of the Jamaicans up here is doing wrongs and I don't want to mix up with those things as you can imagine. You know that I am only here to work some dollars to help you and me to make life when I come home. Please don't have any other woman while I'm gone. I know that a man is different from a woman, but please do try and keep yourself to yourself till we meet and I'm saving all my love for you.

Your sweet, sweet,

Bella

That was one of the first letters that Bella write Joseph, here one of the last letters.

Dear Joseph,

What you saying? I really sorry that my letter take so long to reach you and that the Post Office seem to be robbing people money left, right and centre. Man, Jamaica is something else again. I don't write as often as I used to because I working two jobs. My night job is doing waitressing in a night club on Nostrand Avenue, the work is hard but tips is good. I make friends with a girl on the job named Yvonne and sometimes she and I go with some other friends on a picnic or so up to Bear Mountain. I guess that's where Peaches says she saw me. I figure I might as well enjoy myself while I not so old yet.

Your baby,

Bella

Enjoy herself? This time Joseph was working so hard to send the two children to school clean and neat, Joseph become mother and father for them, even learn to plait the little girl hair. Enjoy himself? Joseph friend them start to laugh after him because is like him done with woman.

Joseph really try to keep himself to himself. Although the nice, nice woman who live at the corner of the next road. Nice woman you know, always talking so pleasant to him. Joseph make sure that the two of them just remain social friends . . . and Bella up in New York about she gone a Bear Mountain, make blabbamouth Peaches come back from New York and tell everybody in the yard how she buck up Bella a picnic and how Bella really into the Yankee life fully.

It was Norman, Joseph's brother, who said that Bella looked like a checker cab. Norman had driven Joseph and the children to the airport in his van to meet Bella, because she write to say she was coming with a lot of things. When the children saw her they jumped up and down yelling mama come, mama come . . . When Norman saw her (he was famous for his wit), he said, 'Blerd Naught, a Bella dat, whatta way she favour a checker cab.' When Bella finally cleared her many and huge bags from Customs and come outside, Joseph was very quiet, he didn't know quite how to greet the new Bella. Mark you Bella was always 'nuff' but she really was never as wild as this. She ran up to Joseph and put her arms around him. Part of him felt a great sense of relief that she was home, that Joseph and Bella and their two children were a family once more.

Bella was talking a little too loudly, 'Man, I tell you those customs people really give me a warm time, oh it's so great to be home though, it was so cold in New York!' As she said this she handed her winter coat with its mock fur collar to her daughter who staggered under the weight of it. Norman, who was still chuckling to himself over his checker cab joke, said, 'Bwoy, Bella a you broader than Broadway.' Bella said, 'Tell me about it . . . '

They all went home. Joseph kind of kept quiet all the way home and allowed the children to be united with their mother . . . she was still Mama Bella though, asking them about school, if they had received certain parcels she had sent and raising an alarm how she had sent a pair of the latest high-top sneakers for the boy and that they had obviously stolen them at the Post Office.

Every now and again she leaned across and kissed Joseph. He was a little embarrassed but pleased. One time she whispered in his ear, 'I hope you remember I've been saving all my love for you.' This was a new Bella though, the boldness and the forwardness was not the old Bella who used to save all her love for when they were alone together with the bolt on the door.

She would not encourage too much display of affection before the children. That change in Bella pleased Joseph. There were some other changes in Bella that did not please him so much though. Like he thought that all the things in the many suitcases were for their family. No sir! While Bella brought quite a few things for them, she had also brought a lot of things to sell and many evenings when Joe Joe come home from work just wanting a little peace and quiet, to eat his dinner, watch a little TV and go to him bed and hug up his woman, his woman (Bella) was out selling clothes and 'things'. She would go to different offices and apartment buildings and she was always talking about which big important brown girl owed her money . . . Joseph never loved that. He liked the idea of having extra money, they now had a number of things they could not afford before, but he missed the old Bella who he could just sit down and reason with and talk about certain little things that a one have store up in a one heart . . . Bella said, America teach her that if you want it, you have to go for it. Joe Joe nearly ask her if she want what? The truth is that Joe Joe felt that they were doing quite all right. He owned a taxi which usually did quite well, they lived in a Government Scheme which gave you the shell of a house on a little piece of land under a scheme called 'Start to build up your own home' . . . and they had built up quite a comfortable little two-bedroom house with a nice living-room, kitchen, bathroom and verandah. What did Bella mean when she said, 'You have to make it'? As far as Joe Joe was concerned, he had made it. And him was not going to go and kill himself to get to live upon Beverley Hills because anyhow the people up there see all him taxi friend them drive up that way to visit him, them would call police and set guard dog on them . . . Joe Joe was fairly contented . . . is what happen to Bella?

'Come ya little Bella, siddown, make me ask you something. You no think say that you could just park the buying and selling little make me and you reason bout somethings?'

'Joe Joe, you live well yah. I have three girls from the bank coming to fit some dresses and if them buy them then is good breads that.'

After a while, Joe Joe stopped trying to reclaim their friendship. After a month, Bella said she wanted to go back to New York. Joe Joe asked her if she was serious.

'You know that nobody can't love you like me, Joe Joe.'

Joe Joe wondered about that. Sometimes he looked at the lady at the corner of the next road, their social friendship had been severely curtailed since Bella returned home, but sometimes he found himself missing the little talks they used to have about life and things in general.

She was a very simple woman. He liked her style, she was not fussy. Sometimes he noticed a man coming to her, the man drive a Lada, look like him could work with the Government, but him look married too. You know how some man just look married? Well this man here look like a man who wear a plaid bermuda shorts with slippers when him relax on a Sunday evening, and that is a married man uniform.

When Joe Joe begun to think of life without Bella, the lady at the corner of the next road began to look better and better to him.

'So Bella really gone back a New York?'

'Yes mi dear, she say she got to make it while she can.'

'Make what?'

'It!'

'A wha it so?'

'You know . . . Oh forget it.'

And that is what Joe Joe decided to do. The lady, whose name was Miss Blossom, started to send over dinner for Joe Joe not long after Bella went back to New York.

'Be careful of them stew peas and rice you a eat from that lady they you know, mine she want tie you.' Joe Joe said, 'True?' and continued eating the dinner that Miss Blossom had sent over for him. He didn't care what Peaches said, her mouth was too big anyway. He just wanted to enjoy eating the 'woman food'. Somehow, food taste different, taste more nourishing when a woman cook it.

Bella write to say that she was doing fine.

Dear Joe Joe,

I know you're mad with me because you didn't want me to come back to the Stales, but darling, I'm just trying to make it so that you and me and the children can live a better life and slop having to box feeding outta hog mouth.

Now that really hurt Joe Joe. He would never describe their life together as that . . . True, sometimes things had been tight but they always had enough to eat and wear. Box feeding outta hog mouth . . . that was the lowest level of human existence and all these years he thought they were doing fine, that is how Bella saw their life together . . . well sir. Joe Joe was so vex that him never even bother to reply to that letter.

Joe Joe started to take Miss Blossom to pictures and little by little the line of demarcation between social friends and sweetheart just blurred. Joe Joe tell her that the married man better stop come to her and Miss Blossom say him was only a social friend and Joe Joe say 'Yes', just like how him and her was social friend . . . and she told him he was too jealous and him say yes he was, 'But I don't want to see the man in here again,' and she said, 'Lord, Joe Joe.'

Little by little Miss Blossom started to look after the children and look after Joe Joe clothes and meals, is like they choose to forget Bella altogether. Then one Christmas time Bella phone over the grocery shop and tell Mr Lee to tell Joe Joe that she was coming home for Christmas.

Well to tell the truth, Joe Joe never want to hear anything like that. Although Miss Blossom couldn't compare to Bella because Bella was the first woman Joe Joe ever really love . . . Joe Joe was feeling quite contented and he was a simple man, him never really want to take on Bella and her excitement and her 'got to make it'. Anyway, him tell Miss Blossom say Bella coming home and she say to him, 'Well Joe, I think you should tell her that anything stay too long will serve two masters, or two mistresses as the case might be.'

Joe Joe say, 'Mmmmm . . . but remember say Bella is mi baby mother you know and no matter what is the situation, respect is due.'

Miss Blossom said that, 'When Bella take up herself and gone to New York and leave him, she should know that respect was due to him too.' Joe Joe say, 'Yes', but him is a man who believe that all things must be done decently and in good order, so if him was going to put away Bella him would have to do it in the right and proper way. Miss Blossom say she hope that when Bella gone again him don't bother ask her fi nuttin. Joe Joe became very depressed.

If Bella looked like a checker cab the first time, she looked like Miami Vice this time, inna a pants suit that look like it have in every colour flowers in the world and the colour them loud! And Bella broader than ever . . . Oh man. Norman said, 'Bees mus take up Bella inna that clothes dey. Any how she pass Hope Gardens them must water her.'

Bella seemed to be oblivious to the fact that Joe Joe was under great strain. She greeted him as if they had parted yesterday, 'Joe Joe what you saying sweet pea.' Joe Joe just looked at her and shook his head and said, 'Wha happen Bella?' They went home but Joe Joe felt like he and the children went to meet a stranger at the airport. Bella had become even stranger than before to Joe Joe. He began to wonder exactly what she was doing in America, if she really was just waitressing at that club. Bella told him that he should come forward, because this was the age of women's liberation, and Joe Joe told her that maybe she should liberate her backside outta him life because he couldn't take her.

Bella cried and said how much she loved him. Then things became really intense and it was like a movie and they had to turn up the radio really high to prevent the children from hearing them.

Joe Joe decided to just bite him tongue while Bella was home. He took to coming home very late all through the Christmas season because the house was usually full of Bella's posse including the 'Yvonne' of Bear Mountain Fame, and when they came to visit the house was just full up of loud laughing and talking and all kinds of references that Joe Joe didn't understand. The truth was that he was really dying for Bella to leave. He really didn't much like the woman she had become. First of all everything she gave to him or the children, she tell them how much it cost ... 'Devon, beg you don't bother to take that Walkman outside, is Twenty-Nine Ninety-Nine, I pay for it at Crazy Eddies,' or, 'Ann-Marie, just take time with that jagging suit, I pay Twenty-Three Dollars for it in May's Department Store. Oh Lord.'

Bella also came armed with two junior Jherri curls kits and one day Joe Joe come home and find him son and him daughter heads well Jherri curls off.

Joe Joe nearly went mad. 'So you want Devon fi tun pimp or what?'

'Joe, you really so behind time, you should see all the kids on my block.'

'On your block, well me ago black up you eye if you don't find some way fi take that nastiness outta my youth man hair, him look like a cocaine seller. Bella what the hell do you, you make America turn you inna idiot? Why you don't just gwan up there and stay then, me tired a you foolishness ... '

Bella couldn't believe that Joe Joe was saying this to her ... then she told him that he was a worthless good-for-nuttin and that him never have no ambition, him just want to stay right inna the little two by four (their house) and no want no better and that she was really looking for a better way and that he clearly did not fit into her plans.

Joe Joe say him glad she talk what was in her mind because now him realize say that she was really just a use him fi convenience through nobody a New York no want her. Bella said ... then he said ... Oh, they said some things to each other!

One thing though, Bella catch her fraid and try wash out the Jherri curls outta Devon hair. No amount of washing could bring it round. The barber had was to nearly bald the little boy head and he spent the worse Christmas of his life.

All his friends 'smashed' him as they passed by. As New Year done so, Bella pack up herself and went back to New York.

Joe Joe make a two weeks pass before him make a check by Miss Blossom. The whole Christmas gone him never see her. He figured that she had gone to spend the holidays in the country with her family. When he asked in the yard where she was, they told him they had no idea where she was gone, and that her room was empty. Joe Joe felt like a beaten man. He went home and decided to just look after him two children and just rest within himself. About a month later he was driving home when he saw somebody looking like Miss Blossom standing at the corner of the road. It look like Miss Blossom, but no, it couldn't be, this woman was dressed like a punk . . . in full black, she had on a black socks with a lace frothing over the top of her black leather ankle boots. A big woman. He slowed the cab down and said, 'Blossom . . . where you was?' . . . and then he thought quickly, 'No, don't bother answer me . . . you go to New York, right?'

'No,' said Blossom, 'I was in Fort Lawdadale. You seem to think only Bella one can go to America.'

Joe Joe never even bother ask her if she want a drive, him just draw a gear and move off down the road, then him go inside him house and slam the door.

Before him drop asleep, it come to him that maybe what him should do was to find an American woman who wanted to live a simple life in Jamaica. Him know a rasta man who have a nice yankee woman like that . . .

Martha, Martha

Zadie Smith

Introduction

Sadie Smith was born in north-west London in 1975, to a Jamaican mother, Yvonne McLean, who had emigrated from the Caribbean in 1969, and an English father, Harvey Smith. She was educated at Malorees Junior School and Hampstead Comprehensive, and at fourteen she cannily changed her first name to 'Zadie'; her main interests at this stage were in singing and dancing. She went to Cambridge University to study English, and her first short stories were published in the University's *May Anthologies*; they attracted immediate attention, opening the way for Smith's extraordinary debut as a novelist.

Her first novel, *White Teeth*, was completed while she was still a student at Cambridge, and the massive marketing hype that surrounded it included frequent mention of a fabulously large publisher's advance as well as considerable emphasis on the multicultural credentials of both author and book. *White Teeth* is set in contemporary London (the Willesden of Smith's own childhood) and its broad scope, as it traces the fortunes of three families and engages with the ethics of science, prompted comparisons with the work of Salman Rushdie when it was finally published in 2000. The novel was an immediate critical as well as commercial success, winning several 'first book' awards whilst climbing to the top of the bestseller lists. It has subsequently been widely translated and was adapted for TV in 2002.

Since then Smith has published two more novels, *The Autograph Man* (2002), about a Jewish/Chinese Londoner, which won the *Jewish Quarterly* Literary Prize for Fiction, and *On Beauty* (2005), a campus novel exploring the politics of race and gender, which also acknowledges E. M. Forster's 1910 novel *Howards End* as an influence. This third novel was short-listed for the Booker Prize, and subsequently won the Orange Prize for Fiction. She has also published a number of short stories, both in Britain and in the USA, and essays on a wide range of subjects.

Soon after the publication of *White Teeth*, Smith spent some time at London's Institute of Contemporary Arts as writer-in-residence, then made a transatlantic move, spending 2002–3 as Fellow in Creative Arts at the Radcliffe Institute, Harvard University. While at Harvard she worked on a book of essays about twentieth-century writers and moral philosophy, which was published after her return to Britain under the title *Fail Better: The Morality of the Novel* (2006). She now lives in Kilburn, north London, and has recently edited a volume about the fictional concept of character, *The Book of Other People* (2007).

Her Harvard winter provided Smith with the setting for the short story 'Martha, Martha', published in *Granta's Best of Young British Writers, 2003*. 'Young', in *Granta's* ten-yearly lists, means under the age of 40, a definition that in 2003 easily admitted Zadie Smith. In the introduction to the collection, the editor, Ian Jack, remarks that if the test for selection was producing a 'state-of-England' novel, then in the opening years of the twenty-first century Smith's *White Teeth* is 'probably the closest England can come to that'.[1] However, she is represented in the *Granta* volume not by an extract from a novel, but by this new short story that was later paired with 'Hanwell in Hell', another story that appeared in *The New Yorker* in 2004, published under the title *Martha and Hanwell* (2005). 'Martha, Martha' is set in the winter after the terrorist attacks of 11 September 2001, events that were still especially vivid in the minds of Americans. Running through the brief episode of a Massachusetts real estate agent's encounter with the mysterious Martha are suggestions of restlessness and uncertainty that, despite the entertaining surface of the characters' dialogue, produce an effect of inescapable edginess.

Note

1. Ian Jack, *Granta*, 81 (Spring 2003), p. 12.

Martha, Martha

Though the telephone is a perfectly useless indicator of most human qualities, it's pretty precise about age. From her tiny office on the third floor, Pam Roberts looked through a window and correctly identified the Martha Penk she was waiting for, a shrimpish girl pushing twenty-two, lost down there. She had on a red overcoat and cream snow boots, putting her weight on their edges like an ice skater; she seemed to waver between two doorways. Pam opened her mouth to call out 'Miss Penk!' but never got to make the curious sound – abruptly the girl turned the corner and headed back down Apple towards the river. Pam went to her own door, opened it, worried her chapped lips with a finger, closed it again. The cold was just too extreme; today the first snows were due, opening performance of a show that would last a dreary, relentless four months. Besides, she had her slippers on. Miss Martha Penk, who appeared to believe that two bedrooms and a garden could be had for a thousand dollars a month, would figure out her second mistake soon enough, come back, discover the bell. The confusion was common; it arose from the higgledy-piggledy arrangement of the ground floor – a busy bookshop and a swing-doored optician obscured the sign that told you of the dentist, the insurers, the accountant and Pam's own dinky realty business at the top of the building; also the antique elevator that would take you to them. Pam tapped her door with a knuckle, warning it she would return, and crossed the room to the filing cabinet. On tiptoes she slid open the top drawer and began flicking through files, her Mozart swelling behind her. She sang along with that section of the *Requiem* that sounds so very like 'OH I SEE YOU WILL GO *DOWN*! AND I SEE YOU WILL GO ALSO!', although it could not be this for the words are Latin. As she sang she ground one of her Chinese slippers rhythmically into the carpet and pressed herself into the metal drawer to reach for something at the very back: 'OH I SEE YOU WILL GO DOWN, OH! I SEE YOU WILL GO DOWN! ALSO! ALSO!'

Pam found what she wanted, closed the cabinet suddenly with an elbow and sat down in a fat armchair opposite a lithograph of Venice. She put a foot in her hand and said 'Phee-yoo! Now, *there* you go,' pressing relief into a sore instep. She started picking out every third sheet or so from the listings and laying them on the floor before her in a small pile. At the opening of the 'Lacrimosa' she removed her slipper entirely, but then hearing someone gallop up the stairs, replaced it and quickly rose to greet a large, dark, bearded man in a sheepskin overcoat, who stood bent at the knees like a shortstop, trying to recover his breath in the hallway. He took a step towards her, looked up and frowned. He paused where he was, supporting himself with a hand on the door frame. Pam knew exactly why he had come and the two spoke at the same time.

'This temping agency?' he asked, a heavy accent, quickly identified by Pam as Middle-Easterny. A Middle-Easterny scarf, too, and a hat.

'No dear, *no*,' said Pam, and let her glasses fall to her chest from their chain, 'It's above the *other* Milliner's Books, right? There's two Milliner's Books – you need the one on the corner of Apple and Wallace – this is the wrong Milliner's, this is above the *children's* Milliner's – I don't know why they just don't say that to people –'

The man groaned pleasantly and hit his temple with the hub of his palm.

'I make mistake. Sorry, please.'

'No, they just didn't say, they never *do*. It's not *you*, dear, it's them – people always come here by mistake, it's not *you*. It's two minutes from here. Now, you go back down, turn left, then immediately right, you can see it from there. I've got somebody who just did the *exact* same, but *exactly* – only vice versa – she's gone to . . . '

A further thundering on the stairs and three more men, younger, also bearded. They stood bent like their friend, panting, one man crying the involuntary tears of a Massachusetts winter. They stared at Pam who stared frankly back at them, with her hands on her makeshift hips, up there where her black linen trousers began, high under the breasts. A black T-shirt and cardigan finished the thing off. Pam was a recognized doodlenut when it came to clothes, buying the same things over and over, black and loose, like a fat Zen monk. She didn't mind. Her moustache was moist and visible – oh, so let 'em *stare* was how Pam felt about it. Young men did not register with Pam any more.

'My friends,' explained the man, and with his friends began the descent, emptying out a demotic mystery language into the stairwell.

Miss Penk must have passed them on the bend. A moment later she was in the room apologizing for her lateness.

'Sorry I'm late, I'm sorry,' she said, but did not look sorry. Her face, very black, could not blush, and her accent, to Pam's ears very English, could not apologize. She stood in the centre of the room, clumsily divesting herself of the loud red coat. She was short, but more muscular, more solid than she had appeared from three floors up. A cheap-looking grey trouser suit and some fake pearls were conspiring to make her older than she was. The buttons on the jacket looked like rusty spare change.

'No, I saw *you*, you see,' began Pam warmly, coming forward to catch what was falling, a scarf, a woolly hat, 'There's *two* Milliner's – did you see those men? On the stairs? They did the exact same thing – and I saw you down –'

'The lift's broken, it don't work,' said Martha, and now lifted her head and reached out a hand. Pam felt faintly interrupted, but took the hand and gave it a double-handed shake.

'Pam Roberts, we spoke on the phone. It's so good to *meet* you!'

'I'm Martha,' she replied and quickly freed herself. She passed a smoothing hand over her own short ironed hair, cut in a flapper's style, a helmet brilliant with some kind of polish. A concrete kiss curl had been plastered on to her left cheek. Pam had never seen anything quite like it in her office before.

'Well. Now, did you come from far? Are you nearby?' Pam asked, a question that had a little business in it.

'Near, yeah,' said the girl, firmly. She stood oddly, hands by her sides, feet together, 'A hotel, it's called The Charles? It's just like by the river – it's just if you go down by –'

'Oh, I know where it is – it's *very* nice.'

'It costs too much, man,' said Martha, tutting loudly, removing a pair of childish mittens, 'But I came right from London and I didn't have any place arranged – I just arksed the taxi to take me to the nearest hotel – I been there a week, but I can't afford it for much longer, you know?'

Usually Pam would use these minutes in the office to ascertain something about likely wealth, class, all very gently – what kind of house, what kind of taste, what kind of price – but she had been wrong about English accents before, not knowing which were high class, which not. Or whether high class meant money at *all* – if you watched PBS as Pam did you soon found out that in England it could, often did, mean the exact opposite.

'It *is* such a nice place, The Charles. They really do things properly there, don't they? They really make the best of that location, I think. I stayed there once for a realty conference, and I really appreciated the standard of the breakfasts. People talk about pool this, steam-room that, but in actual fact it's the little things, like a *breakfast*. A good hot *breakfast*. But my *God* the price isn't any fun – Martha, we'll have you out of there in no time, I promise, especially if we find something empty –'

'Yes,' said Martha, but rather too quick, too desperate, 'How long would it be before I could move in somewhere?'

Pam felt herself immediately on surer ground and slipped down a gear into patter, 'Well, as I'm saying, dear, it depends on whether the place has people in it at the *moment* – but even then, we can turn it around very *very* quickly. It just needs to happen so that everybody wants to make it work, that's all. Don't worry, we'll find something that works. And if it doesn't work, we'll cut it loose and go on to the next,' she said loudly, clapping her hands and glancing at a clock on the wall, 'Now, I've got about two hours free – it's really very dry at the moment so there's *plenty* to show.' She bent down to scoop the remembered listings from the floor, 'I think I understand what you're looking for, Martha, I received your letter, I have it right here – Wait –' Pam reached over to her stereo like a woman with one foot each in two drifting boats; she punched at a couple of buttons to no avail, 'Sometimes it gets a little loud. Funny little machine. It's completely wireless! It's like a single unit stereo for single people, very liberating. You can't really adjust it without the remote, though, which is a little frustrating. And I find it gets louder sometimes, do you know? Sort of when you don't expect it?'

'Classical,' said Martha, and looked at Pam and the surrounding office with determined reverence, 'I want to listen to more classical music. I want to know more about it. It's on my list.'

And this she said in such a way that Pam had no doubt that there was such a list, and that renting an apartment *today* was somewhere on it. The girl had a manner that was all itinerary, charmless and determined, and Pam, a Midwesterner by birth, had the shameful idea that she might go far, this Martha Penk, here on the East Coast.

'Oh! Well, I don't know what there is to *know*, really. I mean, I don't know anything at *all*. It's the violins that do it for me, I guess, the way they sound like somebody's crying? The "Lacrimosa" means crying, I'm pretty sure. Lachrymose – that's from the eye, isn't it? But are you at the university?'

'No!' said Martha but her face at last released a flood of undisguised pleasure, as when a girl is told she could be a model or an actress or do whatever she does amateurishly, professionally, 'I wish! Maybe one day. I'm looking for that next level – qualifications, getting forward, raising myself, my consciousness. But that's like a dream, yeah, for me at this stage?'

She looked serious again, began enlisting her hands in her speech, drawing out these 'levels' in the air, 'It's about stepping a bit further, I mean, for me, I really want to improve myself while I'm here, go up a bit, like listening to different music, like that.'

'*Well*,' said Pam brightly, and sounded her desk with her hand, 'We'll just have to find you the right place where you can do that. Hmm?' But Miss Penk had returned her attention to the CD case, and Pam found herself nodding into the silence, and talking to fill it, 'Oh, I just like all kinds of music, really. I am just the *biggest* fan of music. Cuban, classical, hillbilly – or whatever you call that sort of close harmony singing? A lot of jazz . . . don't know a thing about it, though! Oh *my*. Maybe I can't be improved. Too old to be any better than I am,' said Pam in a saccharine sing-song, as if it were a proverb.

'Yeah,' said Martha, the sort of absent yes that a silly proverb probably deserves. She took the sleeve notes out of the case and opened them up.

'Now,' said Pam, struggling a little, 'From your letter I understood you were thinking around the thousand mark – but that's really a little *low* – I mean, I'll *show* you those places, Martha, but I can't guarantee you're going to *like* them. I mean, they're not there to be *liked*,' Pam said patiently, and gathered up her car keys from her desk, 'But we'll find something that works – we just need to get a handle on it. I'd like to show you a big place that's going for two thousand, maybe – maybe lower – it's negotiable with the present owner. In more vibrant times, it's worth at least three. It'll give us some idea anyway. I'm here to make it work for you, so, I'm going to be led by you . . . '

Outside a plane roared low like some prehistoric bird, Pam shuddered; Martha did not move. Pam tried jostling her keys expectantly in her hand; Martha put down the CD case leaving the notes unfolded and walked over to the window. From behind she was an even more neatly made girl than from the front, everything tight and defined, fighting slightly against the banal restraint of polyester.

'We'll take my car, if that's all right,' tried Pam, anxious that Martha should not open a window but unwilling to ask her not to. It *was* hot in the room, but it was that time of year: you either fried or you froze. But Martha had already tugged on the sash, in a second her head was out there in the open air. Pam winced. She hated to see people lean all the way out of a window like that.

'Do you get a lot of university people? Students?'

'Oh, *yes*. At the beginning of a semester, certainly. Students around here have some money to spare, if you know what I mean.'

Martha took her plastic pearls in her hand and twisted them.

'They must be amazing. Focused people.'

'Oh! Well, yes, I suppose. Certainly, they're *bright*. There's just no denying that. But I'm afraid,' said Pam in her own, overused, comic whisper, 'They can be pretty *obnoxious* as well.'

'There aren't any black students,' Martha said in a tone somewhere between statement and question. Pam, who was in the middle of forcing her arm though a recalcitrant coat sleeve, stopped in her position like a scarecrow, 'Well, of *course* there are students of colour, dear! I see them all the time – I mean, even before the affirmative action and all of that – I mean, there's *always* been the basketball scholarships and the rest – though it's much, much better now of course. They're *completely* here on their own steam *now*. Lots of Chinese young people too, and Indian, many. Many! Oh, there's plenty, *plenty* of people of colour here, you'll see,' said Pam and switched off her desk lamp. 'But have you been to America before?'

'Only Florida when I was twelve. I didn't like it – it's quite vulgar?' said Martha, and the word was most definitely borrowed in her mouth. Pam, who also occasionally borrowed words, recognized the habit and tried to look kindly upon it.

'Florida and Nigeria are the only places I've been, really, out of England,' continued Martha, leaning yet further out, gazing across the square, 'And now here.'

'Oh, are you Nigerian?' Pam asked, kicked off her slippers and began to replace them with treasured walking boots. When people remarked that Pam had become 'so *hard*' recently or suggested that she'd turned into a doodlenut since her divorce, they often meant these boots and nothing more than these boots.

'My parents.'

'Penk, it's very unusual, isn't it?' said Pam to Martha's back, 'Is that a Nigerian name?'

'No.'

Nothing further came. Discovering her remote control behind a coffee cup, Pam stopped the CD and then approached, reaching briskly around Martha to close the window. Clearly, the girl blew hot and cold; in the end Pam just needed her name on a contract, nothing more. Even that was not essential – plenty of people take up your whole afternoon and never call again; Pam called them her one-day stands.

'Look at that sky. It's gonna snow any minute. You know, we should try to get going before it really starts to come down . . . '

With a simple, businesslike nod Pam indicated the coat that Martha had left draped over the photocopier.

About a half-hour later the two of them were completing their tour of Professor Herrin's house, climbing back down the stairs into his open-plan ground-floor lounge. The place was big, but in some disrepair. The carpets felt springy, damp. Mould was the overarching theme. Martha was stepping over an empty cat-food can, and Pam's voice was taking on the fluidity of a woman who feels she is moving down the home straight of her anecdote, 'He's just a very, very impressive man. Not only is he a Professor of Chinese, he holds a law degree – can you imagine – he's on all *kinds* of boards, I'm sure he plays that piano – When the *President of the United States* wants advice on China, the *President*, mind you, he calls up Professor Herrin. It's such a pleasure talking with that man about *Taoism* or, I don't know, *science* or health matters . . . So many men, they just don't achieve anything at *all* – they don't *expect* to – beyond *business* or a little bit of *golf*, maybe. But there's no attention to the spiritual side, not at all. I mean, his wife, well, actually his wife's a little peculiar – but the mind just boggles to think about living with a man like Professor Herrin, I mean, the attempt to satisfy him, *mentally* . . . and it's *such* a beautiful house, a little fusty; but – have you seen this? He carved it, he really did. He's a Zen Buddhist, death for him is just an *idea*. He *made* the bookshelf – and of course that would all stay here – he would just want to know from you how many of his books he'll have to store, I mean how much shelving you would need, and so on. He's already in New York, and he's intending to be there until at *least* next February. He's a sort of an *expert* on relations between the races,' whispered Pam, 'so he feels it's important to be in New York right now. In its hour of *need*, you know.'

'I don't have any books,' said Martha, opening the screen door and stepping into a small walled garden, 'I'm going to get books, though, prob'ly, I'll – Oh, it's snowing – it must've started when we were in there. It's on the ground, look.'

Pam turned to look and already the ebony sheen of Martha's hair was speckled white, like dusting on a chocolate cake.

'This house feels sad, man,' said Martha, and lifted one foot off the ground. She reached behind herself and grabbed the ankle, pressing the foot into her buttocks. First one leg, then the other.

'Does it?' asked Pam, as if the idea had never occurred to her, but her passion for gossip was stronger then her instinct for business, 'Well, actually his wife is very peculiar, a terrible thing happened to her. Terrible. It's partly why they're moving again – she can't stand to be in one place, she *broods*. Now, aren't you *cold* out there?'

Martha shrugged, crouched, and tried sweeping a half-inch of snow into her hands, began packing it. Pam sat on the piano stool and stretched her legs out in front of her.

'His wife, Professor Herrin's wife – it's such an awful story – she was in *China*, about twenty-five years ago, and this young man stole her bag. Well, *naturally* she reported it – and what do you think? Two months later when she got back to America, she heard he'd been executed, can you imagine? What that would *do* to a person, it's just terrible. It's a terrible weight to bear.'

'She shouldn't have said nothing,' said Martha, and appeared to think no more about it.

'Well,' considered Pam, pushing her glasses up her nose, 'I think it's quite a difficult marriage – I think he's quite eager to leave this place, so I imagine he'd be flexible vis-á-vis the rent, Martha. Martha?'

'Yeah? Sorry, what?'

'Now, Martha, let's talk now. What are you thinking – are you at all . . . ?'

Martha took her half-packed snowball and threw it limply at the wall.

'I can't afford it. It's too much. Loads too much. Why does it smell weird out here?'

'*Okay* . . . well, now I wanted to ask about money,' said Pam slowly, coming to the opening and hugging herself against the chill, 'I mean, are we talking about savings? You're very young. Or will you be working? Just so I have some *idea* of how much space we have to manoeuvre.'

Martha stayed where she was in the garden but put both hands out in front of her, awaiting whatever came. The flakes were massive, consistent and quick, as if the snow was not merely falling but being delivered, like manna, because people needed it.

'I've been left some,' said Martha quietly, 'In a will. My uncle passed. Basically, it's enough for a year. A thousand a month, two bedrooms and a garden, yeah? Maybe a bit more, maybe. I need space for people. To come.' She paused. 'If they want.' Suddenly she seemed agitated, even panicked; she attacked her bottom lip with her teeth and looked up and over into the next garden, 'People who might visit, you get me? But this is too too big, I can't afford it. I can't. Don't you have anything I can *afford*?'

It looked for a moment that the girl was about to cry – out of instinct Pam hurried towards her – but by the time she stepped outside Martha had already recovered herself, turning to peer now over the back wall towards the piercing towers and stark white crosses of the university. She seemed calmly framed by them and remote, a figure in a plastic snowstorm.

'Something a bit further out, maybe,' offered Pam a minute later as they climbed back into the car.

'If I had all that education,' said Martha, fastening her seat belt, 'Believe me, I wouldn't live somewhere like *that*.'

'Oh no?'

'I'd live somewhere *new*.'

'I see,' said Pam tersely, starting the car and welcoming the automatic resuscitation of the stereo, Mozart and his death song as background filler. 'Well, each to their own, I suppose, Martha, that's what this business is about, of course. Actually, I used to live on this street, at the top end, at this end, in the more modern architecture, and I must say I found it very pleasant for a long time. Though I also enjoy – I have a sort of apartment now, downtown, and that's also very nice, in a different way.'

'You used to live in one of these big houses?' Martha asked, with unseemly incredulity, and as she spoke they drove past the very house. For the first time in months Pam resisted the urge to inspect the curtains, the lawn, the little things he'd changed for somebody else.

'Why'd you go?'

'Circumstances. My circumstances changed. I guess you could say that.'

'How?'

'My *gosh*, you *are* a nosy parker. I'll guess I'll have to tell you my dress size next.'

'I'm just arksing, you don't have to answer.'

'You should be a lawyer or something, it's like being cross-*examined*.'

'So why'd you go?'

Pam sighed, but in fact she had, some time ago, designed a speech to answer the question, whoever it came from, 'Well, I suppose at my age, Martha, and especially in the light of the events of last September, I just think you have to make things work for you, work for you *personally*, because life is really too short, and if they don't work, you just have to go ahead and cut them loose, and that's basically –'

'I'd love to be a lawyer,' interrupted Martha, 'My friend is a lawyer. She has a house like that. Big-up house. We used to get the bus together to school. Now she's a big lawyer. That's like the best thing you can be.'

'You know what?' said Pam, drumming the steering wheel and preparing to lie, 'I like what I do. I don't think I'd change it to be a lawyer for all the tea in China. I really don't. I guess that's just me.'

Martha pulled down the passenger mirror, licked her finger and began to reshape her kiss curl.

'She's my role model, Kara – she definitely took it to the next level – as a young black woman, you know? She didn't get caught up in a lot of the things you can get caught up in – kids and that. She took it forward. That's where I'm aiming for – if you don't aim high, there's no point, really.'

Martha wound down the window that Pam had just closed and Pam felt she might just scream if the girl kept letting the outside in everywhere they went.

'Now, *good* for her! And good for you, too. God knows, when I was your age, all I did was have children, oh *my*. I've *three* girls. But it's such a different world. I wouldn't even want to bring up children in this world now. My *gosh*, it's really snowing. That's a couple of inches since we left the office.'

They drove twenty minutes and then parked a street from the one they wanted so Martha would have an opportunity to see a bit of this new neighbourhood by foot. It was cold beyond cold. Everything laid out like a promise, delayed for summer; bleached porches, dead gardens, naked trees, a sky-blue clapboard house, its rose-pink neighbour. Part of the East Coast realtor's skill is to explain what places will look like when the sun finally comes.

'And this just goes the most *incredible* orange when the fall comes. It's like the whole city is on fire. Just life, life, life *everywhere*. Now: the couple we're about to see,' said Pam, walking briskly ahead, 'They are just darling. Yousef and Amelia. He's Moroccan and *so* handsome and she's American, just American, and they have such a beautiful daughter, Lily.'

'Where they going to go, then, if I move in?'

'They're moving to Morocco. It's just what we were saying, they don't really want to bring up children in this country, I'm afraid. And frankly, I can understand that. They're *artists* too, so, they're a little bit flaky. But *very* sophisticated. So witty, and they make you feel comfortable right away, you know? Now, Martha, I've shown so many people this house, but it's a little too small for a family and a little too big for a single person, so it's awkward – but it's *perfect* for you – now, what *is* that –'

There had been a babbling noise the past minute or so, excited foreign voices, and as they turned the corner Martha saw some snow come flying and guessed at children, but the next second revealed the depth of the voices – these were bearded men, with dark, ashen skins – and the argument was over design, a snowman. It was incompetently begun, a tall upturned cone upon which a future head would never sit. And now work had stopped entirely; at the sight of the two women, the men froze and looked at their gloved hands and seemed to find themselves ridiculous.

'But those are the men!' cried Pam when they were not five yards out of hearing range, 'From my office. They just came just before you. But isn't that *weird*? They're making a snowman!'

'Is that what they were doing?' asked Martha, and dug into her pocket for a mint she had quietly lifted from the bowl of same in Pam's office.

'Well, what *else* were they doing. You know, Martha, they've probably never seen snow. Isn't that amazing – what a thing to see!'

'Grown men playing in the snow,' said Martha, but Pam could not be dissuaded from the romance of it, and it was the first anecdote she told as they walked through the door of 28 Linnaean, a canary-yellow first-floor apartment with two porches, front and back, nestled behind a nineteenth-century police station. Yousef was handsome as promised, curly-haired and with eyes many shades lighter brown than his skin; he was frying something with a great deal of chilli in it and offered his elbow for Martha to shake. Amelia was very skinny and freckled, with an angular hip and a toddler perched on it. She had the kindly, detached air of a young mother, the world outside the screen door having grown distant and surreal, brought to her only in tiresome reports from other people. But she good-humouredly let Pam hustle her to a window at the front of the house and followed the direction of her finger.

'Over there, can you see? They're making a *snow*man! Egyptian or Iranian or *something*. They were so *sheepish* about it. They were so embarrassed. I don't think they've ever seen snow before! And I saw these men, an *hour* ago in my *office*. It's the same men. But the *exact* same. Martha doesn't think anything of it, but I think it's darling.'

'That *is* sweet,' conceded Amelia, and hitched Lily up over her shoulder.

'Amelia –' said Pam, suddenly, taking a step back from her and appraising a small bulge around her middle, 'Now, are you pregnant again?'

'NO,' called Yousef from the other room, laughing, 'She's just a fat girl now! I feed her too much!'

'Four months,' said Amelia, shaking her head, 'And I'm going to have it in Morocco, God help me. Hey there, Martha. Do you think you'll take this place off our hands? *Please* won't you, please? We're totally desperate!'

'I don't know yet, do I?' said Martha very fiercely and made the odd, contemptuous noise with her teeth again. Lily reached out a doughy pink hand for Martha's face; she flinched from it.

'Oh,' said Amelia, reddening, and battling Lily's tiny kicking legs, 'I didn't mean to –'

Pam almost blew up right there – she just *could not* understand what kind of a girl this was, where she came from, what kind of conversation was normal for her. She drummed her fingers on the patch of wall behind her – as close an expression of suppressed fury as Pam ever managed.

'Martha, I'm sure Amelia only meant –'

'I was really joking, I didn't –' said Amelia, putting an incautious hand on Martha's shoulder, feeling a taut, inflexible muscle. She soon retracted it, but Martha continued to look and speak to the spot where the hand had been, 'I didn't mean that, I mean I meant I think I want to be nearer the university, nearer all of that, yeah? It's very alone up here, if you're alone, isn't it?'

'Well, you know, there's a very convenient bus –' said Amelia, looking over Martha to Pam who was performing a minimal mime with her thumbs to the effect that she did not know the girl well nor could she explain her.

'I'll look around,' said Martha, and walked away from them both, down the hall.

'Look everywhere,' said Amelia feelingly. She let Lily loose from her struggle, laying her on the floor. 'Please, feel absolutely at liberty.'

'Oh, she will,' said Pam rather tartly, but Amelia did not smile and Pam was mortified to see that she had thought the comment cruel. Without any skill, Pam turned the conversation to the problem of noisy plumbing.

At the other end of the apartment, Martha's walk changed; she was alone. She moved through the two big bedrooms, loose and alert, examining the strange foreign things in them: Arabic writing, meaningless paintings, and all those touches that rich people seem to use to look poor: wood floors, threadbare rugs, no duvets, all blankets, nothing matching. Old leather instead of new, fireplaces instead of central heating, everything wrong. Only the bathroom was impressive; very clean, white tiled. It had a mirror with a movie star's bald light bulbs circling it. Martha locked herself in here, ran both of the taps full blast, and sat on the closed toilet seat. She took a worn-looking, folded photograph from her coat pocket and wept. She was crying even before she had unfolded it, but flattening it out now against her knee made it almost impossible for her to breathe. In the picture a grinning, long-lashed boy, about eighteen months old, with a head like a polished ackee nut, sat on the lap of a handsome black man. Neither the picture nor their mutual beauty was in any way marred by the fact that both of them had sellotaped their noses to their foreheads to give the impression of pigs' snouts. Martha turned over the photograph and read what was written there.

> Martha, Martha, I love U
> And I'm trying 2 tell U true
> For this New Year 2002
> I am going to be there for U
> I know that U have many dreams
> And life is not always how it seems
> But I want U 2 put me 2 the test
> And I will do all the rest
> Together we will get so much higher
> Through my love and our desire
> Don't give up on what we've got
> Cos Ben and Jamal love U a lot!

It took another five minutes to recover herself. She rinsed her face in the sink and flushed the toilet. She came close up to the mirror and gave thanks to God for her secretive skin that told nobody anything; no flush, no puffiness. She could hear a great deal of laughter the other side of the door and wondered what they were saying about her; especially *him*, who was probably the worst, because he'd married like that and those ones that marry white always feel even more superior. She hadn't expected this. She didn't know what she'd expected.

'Martha!' cried Pam as she appeared again in the kitchen-lounge, 'I thought you'd been eaten by something. Eaten by a bear.'

'Just looking around. It's nice.'

Pam sat on a high kitchen stool beaming at Yousef, but he was busy pulling a giggling Lily out from under the sofa by her ankles.

'So you've had a good look around – she's had a good look around, Yousef, so that's something. Now,' said Pam, reaching down to the floor to get her bag, 'I don't want to hurry anybody. It always helps to get to know each other a little bit, I think. How can we make this work, for everybody?'

'But I don't know if I – I can't –'

'Martha, *dear*,' said Pam, returning a pen and pad she was holding back to her bag, 'There's no hurry whatsoever, that's not the way this works at all.'

'You know what?' replied Martha. With trembling fingers, she undid and then retied the waistband of her coat, 'I've got to go.'

'Well –' said Pam, completely astonished, and shook her head, 'But – if you'll give me – just wait a *minute*, I'll –'

'I'll walk. I want to walk – I need some air.'

Pam put down her coffee cup, and smiled awkwardly between Yousef and Amelia on the one hand and Martha on the other, increasing, as only Pam knew how, the awkwardness on both sides.

'I think I want a one bedroom thing,' mumbled Martha, her hand already on the doorknob, 'One bedroom would be more . . . ' she said but could not finish. 'I'm sorry,' she said, and again Pam could not tell if she meant it. You can't tell anything about a one-day stand. They aren't there to be known. Pam shunted herself off the stool and put her hands out as if for something falling but Martha had already backed on to the porch. She struggled down the snowy steps, felt the same panic that rightly belongs to a fire escape. She could hear the clamour of snowman builders, speaking in tongues, laughing about something.

Pit Strike

Alan Sillitoe

Introduction

Alan Sillitoe was born in Nottingham, England, in 1928. His paternal grandfather was an upholsterer, originally from Wolverhampton, and his mother's father was a blacksmith who worked at Wollaton Pit, just outside Nottingham, shoeing ponies underground. His father, Christopher, missed a lot of schooling because of illness, never learned to read or write, and worked as a labourer, though the depression of the 1930s meant that he was frequently out of work. Christopher and his wife Sylvia brought up their five children in a succession of rented houses in Nottingham, dependent on the dole and a 'dinner centre' that would provide hot meals for the children.

Like many of his relations, Sillitoe left school at fourteen and went to work in the Raleigh bicycle factory in Nottingham. When he was eighteen he joined the Royal Air Force as a wireless operator, and was posted to Malaya. After two years he returned home with tuberculosis, and spent eighteen months in an RAF hospital. This was a turning-point in his life, because during his enforced inactivity he began to write. In 1951, he met the young American poet Ruth Fainlight, and supported by Sillitoe's RAF pension they travelled around Europe together for several years, living in France, Italy and Spain. The poet Robert Graves, whom they met in Majorca, offered Sillitoe encouragement, and in 1957 he published his first volume of poetry, *Without Bread or Beer*. Ted Hughes was another source of encouragement, and he collaborated with Sillitoe and Fainlight in *Poems* (1971).

Although Sillitoe is a prolific poet (his *Collected Poems* was published in 1993) he is best known for his prose fiction, and for two works in particular. His first published novel, *Saturday Night and Sunday Morning* (1958), with its rebellious working-class hero, Arthur Seaton, quickly achieved classic status, especially after Karel Reisz's film of 1960. His 1959 novella *The Loneliness of the Long-Distance Runner*, about a young borstal boy, confirmed Sillitoe's reputation as a social realist, and this too became a landmark film, directed by Tony Richardson.

Sillitoe now lives in London, although Nottinghamshire continues to be the setting for some of his work. Since the labels 'regional' and 'working-class' writer often carry patronizing undertones, it is hardly surprising that Sillitoe rejects them, along with assertions that he is the literary 'descendant' of Nottingham's most controversial writer, D. H. Lawrence. But in a symposium on Lawrence in 1972 Sillitoe emphasized the importance of place, for Lawrence, and perhaps implicitly for himself: 'If Lawrence hadn't been born in Nottinghamshire he would not have been the same writer. Like all other nations, perhaps,

England is full of little countries, for better or worse, dozens of little class, race and geographical divisions which fortunately defy analysis or sociology. It still pertains more than is generally admitted, and only writers are properly equipped to chart a way between them to the more fundamental issues that lie beyond.'[1]

The 'little countries' within England are clearly depicted in 'Pit Strike'. The journey made by a group of Nottinghamshire miners from the Midlands to south London, as they go to support fellow-miners from the Kent coalfield, might as well be a journey between different countries, so marked are the cultural differences between north and south. The story's title refers to a national strike that took place early in 1972, as members of the National Union of Mineworkers throughout the country demanded higher wages. Coal stocks were high, and stopping production was not likely to have any immediate impact, so the Union organized groups of 'flying pickets' to block the movement of coal at power stations and docks. As intended, this led to major power cuts and the Conservative government led by Edward Heath declared a state of emergency. The strike ended on 27 February 1972, with victory, on this occasion, for the miners. 'Pit Strike' appeared in Sillitoe's fourth book of short stories, *Men Women and Children* (1973). He later adapted the story for television, and it was broadcast on 22 September 1977, to considerable acclaim.

Note

1. A. Sillitoe, 'Lawrence and District' (1972), in *Mountains and Caverns* (London: W. H. Allen, 1975), p. 140.

Pit Strike

As the long line of bodies bunched up at the centre and collided with the police a cry went out: 'Get your false teeth into his knackers, Joshua!'

It was a Welsh voice whose owner may not have seen Wales even as a child, having inherited the accent from the haven of his family. Many such militants at Aylesham had gone to the Kent coalmines when they had first opened forty years ago. Some had been black-listed in Wales after the strike of 1926, and denied work in the place they belonged, while others went to Aylesham hoping for better rates and conditions.

The voice and its foul words enraged Joshua, who had come down from Nottinghamshire to help with picketing, but such was the force of men at his back that he was unable to turn round and get at it, there being nothing he could do with his anger except vent it on the red-faced policeman in front.

Perhaps the miners were beginning to get Joshua's number at last, by goading him in this way, for as he kicked and punched – keeping his hands low enough to be fairly hidden – he became calmer at realizing it was only a mark of solidarity after all. He was almost glad of the copper's kick aimed at his shins, though it was the policeman who shouted at the concrete his shoes seemed to meet.

He'd never had much to do with the police in the Nottingham-shire village where he lived. They existed at a distance, as it were, and Joshua's life hadn't led him closer than that. By accident his actions had been law-abiding. In a strike, however, you could only do as the union advised and your own mates willed, and if it meant pushing up against the coppers then there was nothing else to do but do it.

When suddenly confronted with such ranks of police, he felt, perhaps because numerical superiority was on his side, that they had no right to stand in his way. The atmosphere was so heady that all fear went – that apprehension of danger and readiness to run that he'd often experienced down the pit when a prop was about to go.

Joshua carried a copy of the Bible in the back pocket of his trousers. It was a small black book that went to all places except the pit-face, for he left it with his fags and matches in the locker up top – nothing inflammatory being allowed down below.

Though fifty years of age he had long thought he looked younger than that. He could run faster than might have been expected, lift greater weights than many men of his age who had already been stricken with a hernia, and often work longer hours than were called for.

He played football in the pit team. In fact he did not appear younger than his years, but the confidence he gained by thinking he did gave more life to his face and more authority to his voice. His three sons had married and 'left home', so maybe it was the sudden emptiness of the house that made him feel younger. When grand-children began to turn up he expected to have the years put back on him ten-fold.

A big man of six-foot-four, he had worked at the pit since he was fourteen, even during the war, so that he'd never been in the army or worn any uniform. Such 'false raiment' was the only thing foreign to his back. All he needed, he said, were sweat-rags on the face when, after going two miles on wide conveyor-belts through darkened neatly hewn tunnels that looked safe but were by no means reliable, and jumping on for a ride with the rest of them when they weren't supposed to, he'd walk awhile and then go on hands and knees to a seam that, being only three or four feet and held apart by a few brace of Doughty props, was 'bloody murder' to work. There were seams so narrow that no machines could be slotted in, though men had to crawl in and rip out the coal nonetheless.

He laboured with the gang, nothing on but Wellingtons up to the knees when there was water about, lay on his side and swung a pick at the grey-black shine of the fuel, the mellow beam of his head-lamp giving vague illumination through the falling dust.

With half the shift gone they'd knock off, and he'd open his snap-tin to see what Jessie had packed the night before. Whether it was ham or cheese, or a bit of meat and an apple, it made no difference but was turned by a mighty appetite into grub that went into his mouth with any grit picked up on the way. Tea washed it down, and that was the best intake of the lot.

As a child Joshua had never worn shoes, but put on plimsolls to school in summer, and clogs in winter. Later it was either boots or welloes. For best he got a pair of good boots which he polished shinier than any fancy slippers, not too heavy though or hobnailed, but boots of good leather, top and bottom, which held the feet firm and supported the ankles.

'If you aren't well shod,' he said, 'you're nothing. It was all right for the Israelites to go in sandals, but they'd not lived in Nottinghamshire.'

He put on boots when he went to the Welfare Club for a drink in the evening, and wore a high-necked pullover under his jacket to keep out the wind that leapt up the escarpment on which the pit village stood. The houses, built in the twenties, were thought of as new by those who lived in them and saw the black and damp-walled state of other settlements.

Joshua's three-bedroomed house was as comfortable a place as almost thirty years of married life could make it. He'd bought much of his furniture after the war when wages were good, but lately the colliers' 'living standard' had been going downhill fast, and nobody knew it more than he did.

Ever since they'd married he and Jessie had accounted for every penny. Not that they marked each item in a little red cashbook, but nothing was spent that wasn't talked about and remembered – at least till the next wage-packet came in. They'd never had the pleasure of spending without thought, but at the same time the shared thrift had been enjoyed in that it was one of many factors which had kept them close together.

Being a 'Bible man' Joshua was often the butt of other blokes at the Welfare, and one or two communists who saw his worth thought it a pity he wouldn't join them. Good for an argument, Joshua usually revelled in it, a fact which ought to have told them there was never any hope of converting him to their way of looking at things.

He had his pride, though that didn't keep him from accepting their views. It was just that he liked reading his Bible, obstinately so, and they hadn't such a book, as far as he could see, to put in its place. Those parsons who kept an eye open for him sooner or later found out that it wasn't Christianity which kept his back upright and his face in fettle.

It wasn't that he went to church or chapel even. When Joshua argued about the existence of God with his friends at the club it was more to please himself than to convince them. It was also more to please himself than to please God, for it was the Book he took to, and all the bits in it that highlighted his own existence. They often did, dramatically, and not always in a way he liked.

The New Testament didn't interest him. He'd long since given that up because he couldn't reconcile himself to the 'turning the other cheek' part, being more in tune to the 'eye for an eye' reality of the Old Testament. And as for paying Caesar what was Caesar's, and giving to God what was God's – all right, but what had Caesar ever given him? Nothing. With God it was another matter. Sometimes He gave and sometimes He didn't. In any case, had Caesar ever been down the pit? Not likely – but he didn't doubt that God had been there from time to time. He engendered hope, and gave cause for despair. He gave back life, and He created abysmal misery.

Joshua was popular because he was a good worker who could be relied on. He wouldn't let anybody down, and his friends felt it, not doubting that he was one of them. He never questioned it, though he'd question everything else. His Bible-mania set him apart, but no more so than his inordinate height. Being separate in several ways merely emphasized his unity with the others, which became even more of a closeness when he was included in it.

The ballot papers came and he voted for the strike. Caesar had to be taken on, even if it meant the destruction of Rome itself.

He dug his garden over the first day, though there wasn't much point with such a frost. In the evening he switched on the television, but could only stand it for an hour because every word spoken and picture shown seemed to be coming straight out of Caesar's tent, never mind his camp. He was filled with bitter loathing when news announcers said that the miners were 'idle' instead of 'on strike'. He switched the set off and picked up his tin of tobacco to roll a cigarette.

'It's going to be a long do,' he said. 'They don't want to know. The truth means nothing to them.'

Since it was wickedness to be still, Jessie knitted pullovers, went at the rate of two a year, and had a drawer full upstairs. She was a tall woman, but thin. 'We'll have to manage.'

He made two cigarettes, and put one back into the tin. 'There's plenty more besides us. The young blokes'll feel it most.'

'They say the country don't need coal any more.'

'They say a lot o' things. Time'll tell.'

'It'll be a long while, though.'

He stood up. 'Nobody denies that. They think they've got us where they want us, forcing us into a strike so's they can finish us off. It's the last thing I wanted.'

'It's early days yet, Josh.'

'It's tragic, though,' he said. 'It's going to be a whole waste of time, and time's the most valuable thing in the world. There's none of us got that much as we can throw it away.'

'Ne' mind. Cheer up, love. We've had worse bouts. I'll put the kettle on. I know you allus get thirsty when you get depressed.'

He smiled at her concern for him. He would have laughed with pleasure, but stopped himself because the reason for his smile was too serious. He thought there was no greater mark of a person's love than when they tried to get you out of a low mood, especially when a woman did it, who had a rough life anyway.

It was unnatural having nothing to do. It made the world empty and took all its meaning away. Coming home from work the trees and buildings were clear because he knew what they were for, but wandering along to the shop at midday without the ache of work in his muscles he felt that even he himself was unreal, right down to the marrow, as if the slightest breath of wind would blow him away.

When a man went to work every day at set hours the aches and pains he might feel if he didn't were crushed out of him. A whole new world opened up when you didn't go to work, and though the first few days had been interesting Joshua didn't want it at all for a permanent set-up. There wasn't much to do, and that was a fact. Few pickets were needed at their own pit, and there were more than enough to sew up all those in the region good and tight.

Squads were sent out to starve the Trent Valley power stations of coal, without which they couldn't work. A new urgency came into the fight, and the union called for volunteers to go south and help the Kent miners, whose coalfield was much smaller than theirs in the Midlands.

Bill Marriot persuaded Joshua: 'Caesar's bloody strong down there, Josh, and our lads in Kent could do with a few reinforcements.'

'When do we start, then?' he asked, the half pint looking no more than a thimble in his hand.

'Five in't morning. There'll be six of us in my owd banger. We're going to Greenwich so's we can block the Thames power stations. We'll never get anywhere till we strangle them. Heath'll be playin' his organ by candlelight before we've done.'

Marriot said they wouldn't bother with the motorway because grub was too dear at the service stations. He knew a few good transport caffs on the old North Road.

Joshua's travels and mystery trips had gone no further than Skegness and Bridlington, Blackpool and Matlock. The further south he got the more dispirited he became. Though he'd seen it on television the landscape looked unreal and soft, and didn't have the pinkish hue of frost or mist that made the Trent Valley so remote and mysterious when the hills on the northern bank merged into the remnants of Sherwood Forest.

To him Notts was a place that stood on its own, too low for the Pennines, too high for the Fens. Neither north nor south, east or west, field or forest, and in some areas neither town nor country, it could hold its own for beauty, obstinacy, and homeliness with any other spot on earth. Joshua realized he only felt that way because he was born there, and he was leaving it now for just as long as it would take them to get enough money to live more comfortably in it.

Even the houses going south were different, less raw and stony and purely useful than the ones where he lived. But the others in the car enjoyed the sights, and laughed when Marriot said they were at last taking the war into the enemy's territory.

Joshua sat in the back hardly able to move, as if their gaiety and confidence was an ungodly force set on kidnapping his true heart and spirit, which should have stayed at home. Pushed into the upholstery so as to give the others more room, he felt the padding and sharp edges of the Bible in his back pocket, and for some reason wished he's left that behind also.

Each two men shared a suitcase for their kit, so that three were roped on to the luggage rack overhead. Room might have been found in one for Joshua's bible, but he didn't trust it to be anywhere except in his pocket.

North of London they needed petrol, and pulled into a filling-station forecourt. All six eased out to get life back into their thighs and ankles, and strolled around in the raw air while Marriot asked for six gallons.

The pump man was the owner as well, and when he saw the notice in their back window saying SUPPORT THE MINERS he turned a different shade of clay-pink: 'I'm not serving you.'

'You what?' Marriot was stunned.

'What does he mean?' Joshua asked. 'Hasn't he got none left?'

'Not a drop,' the man called, slotting his hose back into place. He was a young-looking energetic person in his forties. 'You can try some other place.'

They stood around him by the garage door. 'How far is the next one?' Joshua said, not fully understanding.

'That's your problem. You ought to be driven back to work. I do eighty hours a week and don't get the wages you lot make. By God, I started work at fourteen and I've never stopped going since, night or day. There's no set hours for me.'

'And no set wages, either,' said Marriot. 'You've made your pile all right, I expect. You've never been more than a stone's throw from daylight, either. I'd like to see you do eight hours a week down the pit, ne' mind eighty.'

'If it were my job, I'd do it,' the man said courageously. 'I wouldn't whine and strike about it.'

Because it had taken him longest to understand what was happening Joshua lost his temper sooner than the others when he did catch on. He was not normally a slow man, was known in fact for his picturesque wit and speed of argument, but two hours cramped in the car, and his brooding doubts about coming to this alien part of the realm, had caused him to retreat into himself as a means of self-preservation.

In this mood he did not loom as tall and bulky as he actually was but, seeing an injustice about to be perpetrated on his mates and himself, he held himself fully erect and lifted his fist as he approached the petrol-pump attendant.

'Nay, lad,' he said with false kindliness when he drew back with an offended sneer, 'I'll not touch a hair o' thy Philistine head – even though I am four cubits high.'

The man clearly thought him a maniac on the loose from Rampton, for after this opening Joshua reached into his back pocket and pulled out the flexible fully-fledged Bible and waved it at him (as if it were a lump of coal, Marriot said later) the others looking on, either dumbfounded or cracking with amusement.

'Pharaoh is pursuing us, and we are in dire need of victuals for our chariot. And Moses said unto the people, "Remember this day, in which ye came out of Egypt, out of the house of bondage; for by strength of hand the Lord brought you out from this place." So my advice to you, dear son of a glutton and king of all the idolaters, is to help us to get on our way or we'll verily call the seven plagues to pestificate your inheritance and lay the place as waste as the Desert of Sin.'

Wind drove flecks of rain against Joshua's face so that it looked as if he were weeping with emotion at the godliness of his advice.

'You tell the bastard, Josh,' said Marriot, who saw they might after all be getting somewhere by his harangue. 'And if he wain't listen, throw the bleddy book at him!'

'You won't be served here,' said the proprietor, though plainly worried.

Joshua was more interested in Marriot's advice that he should throw the *bloody* book at him. He reminded him that the Book wasn't to be used like that, nor so wantonly insulted. The Book was God's word and all His works were in it. There was no other Book so blessed by God's advice, and there never would be, and what's more he'd never *throw* it at anyone lest it land in the mud of iniquity or be trodden underfoot by slothful worshippers of the graven image.

He seemed more threatening to Marriot than he had been to the proprietor, who now saw an internecine punch-up as something worse than an assault on himself by this religious bigot who had somehow got entangled in the coal strike. Or it may have been that the proprietor used this swing against Marriot as an opportunity to get out of a dangerous and tricky situation without losing too much face, for he took the hose-nozzle from its bracket, switched the peg on to six gallons, and began sending it into their almost empty tank.

'You can have your petrol,' he said, 'and then go away. I don't want you on my premises.'

Joshua turned from sermonizing Marriot, an ecstatic look on his fully fleshed but pale face: 'Milk and honey,' he said, 'milk and shining honey, lads. Let's pay him and get on to them power stations. He'll be pumping it in by hand next week, and counting his shekels out by candlelight!'

Going through the streets of east London, thumbs-up signs were frequent. At a pub in Hackney a group of bus drivers wouldn't let them pay for their beer.

Marriot took them over the Thames by Tower Bridge, so that Joshua could have a look at it, and see something else he might only have looked at before on television. Joshua was not impressed. Only the river took his gaze, and he thought that maybe he was crossing the Jordan instead of the Thames, and wondered how long it would be before he went back over it.

He felt like removing his Wellingtons before entering the living room. In any case it all opened into one with the kitchen so that you didn't know which was special and which was not, so he narrowed his eyes and decided his boots were good enough for any carpet.

He followed Pam Seymour who, like her husband Jack was a university lecturer, and towered over her as she said with a smile that he was to make himself comfortable while in their house. Marriot had gone scooting off up the road in his car, so there wasn't much else he could do except try.

A dark-haired girl showed him to the spare room with his luggage. He looked around for a moment when she had gone: a wardrobe, a writing table, a narrow bed, and a radiator which almost scalded his hand as he reached out and touched it slyly to see if it was on.

'There's food in the kitchen, at any time,' Pam said, when he came down again as if to see what she would tell him next. 'When you feel hungry just help yourself. Juana our *au pair* girl will show you where things are. We're all behind you in your strike, and *know* you'll win. Jack will drive you to the power station in the morning so that you'll get there well in time for your picketing.'

'That's very kind,' said Joshua, somewhat misled by such consideration. 'I don't want to put him out. I's'll find it on the bus.'

They stood in the kitchen part of the ground floor waiting for the kettle to boil. 'No, we're glad to help. We have a car, so you'll be taken there. We can't do enough for you really. Your fight is our fight.'

It wasn't easy to know what she meant by this, when you looked around to see what they'd got. But he was glad of such comfort and kindness no matter how it came about. He was tired after the journey, felt as if his leg-bones were rotting, and could find nothing to say, almost as if he'd turned into a kid again. He wished Marriot were with him, but they'd put him in another house down the road. Still, the tea was good here. Whoever she was she brewed a black cup of tea, which opened his eyes and made him feel better.

She asked where he came from, and he told her about it, thinking it impossible she could imagine what it was like. But she'd been there, had become slightly acquainted with such places during sociological research, though she didn't tell him so, being touched by his exaggerating the squalor of it.

He didn't like being given so many questions, but answered them all, till he felt it was his turn, and asked if she had lived 'in this' for long, and whether she'd got any kids?

'Three,' she told him, and he saw from her smile that even though she was turned thirty she still had good teeth. 'They'll be home from school soon. I'm sure they'll be happy to meet you.'

He told her about his own three. 'All married now. But when I look back on it I know me and Jessie enjoyed bringing them up. They were a lot o' trouble, though. But bringing'em up's the best part of it, any road. After that there in't much left, is there?'

He mused on what it would have been like, being married to such a person as her, this dark, thin-faced, straight-haired, slight-bodied woman who seemed able to deal with the world on her own terms yet could at the same time help others who didn't have that wide and happy grasp of things. A few slots of the picture went through his mind with peculiar clarity, and with perfectly easy realism because it hadn't happened and never would. If it had he would have been another person, though the faint sense of regret that their worlds were so different made him smile – which also brought its feeling of righteousness because it would never do to get too close to the last commandment of the Lord on Sinai. No man's wife would ever be his, nor his any other man's. Having told himself this, the conversation became easier again.

She left him drinking his fourth cup of tea and took a pair of towels up to his bedroom. She saw a Bible on the table and wondered where it had come from. It certainly didn't *belong* in her house, and she looked at it with amusement before realizing it was Joshua's, and flicking the pages from cover to cover. They'd thought they were getting a member of the Party, and here was a collier carrying a worn, well-thumbed Bible! It was at this moment only that he seemed really strange. Otherwise he was simply a coalminer whom she could never begin to understand. Her father had been the vicar of a potty little church in the west of England, and she hadn't seen much of Bibles since then – thank God!

It was still light when Joshua walked across Blackheath and on to Greenwich Park for a bit of air. The roar of traffic along the road deafened his brain so that he felt isolated and knew he didn't belong where he was standing while waiting to cross. It also seemed he didn't even belong in Nottinghamshire, so that he was disembodied and floating in a strange sort of spiritual emptiness. He tried hard to picture his village or even his own house, but could hardly remember it, though he'd only left that morning.

But the more he walked into the park and over the grass the less this fact troubled him. On the way back he actually felt good to be away, as if he were on some kind of holiday, while knowing that the serious business of what he had come for would begin in the morning.

Pam was getting the children out of her French car, having just fetched them from school. Barney ran up to Joshua and cried: 'Mummy, is this our new miner?'

Joshua felt himself hugged around the legs, so picked him up. '*We've* got a miner now,' Barney sang out. 'Horrid Jasper Clewes at school was boasting that they had *two* miners at their house, but now I can say ya-ya-ya we have one as well!'

'Do leave him alone and come in,' Pam called, though amused and pleased when Joshua walked up the drive with Jerry on his other arm. Matthew, who was ten, thought himself too old for such treatment, so followed enviously behind.

Joshua walked into the local pub that evening. 'I thought I'd find you lot in 'ere.'

'You must have smelled your way,' said Marriot. 'I suppose you couldn't tear yourself from that cushy billet.'

He ordered a pint and went to their table. 'What's *your* digs like, then?'

'Digs?' said Marriot. 'It's real solidarity. As posh as they come. Me and Tom shares a room. Do you snore, Tom?'

'What the bloody'ell does it matter?' said Tom, who did. 'You ain't going to bloody marry me.'

'Not on the wages you get,' said Marriot, 'in any case.'

'No' mind,' said Tom. 'I'm out for more!'

Marriot turned to Joshua. 'She's nice, your landlady?'

'Very amiable,' he told them. 'She's got some good kids. I ain't met the husband yet.'

He fell silent and they were unable to get any more opinions out of him, knowing in fact that he had few enough. Joshua realized it too. It sometimes even embarrassed him, though mostly for the sake of others, for by now he had grown used to his quiescence. His lack of opinion was covered somewhat by his attraction to the Bible, a book which he allowed to hold them for him, often in a highly fashioned picturesque way. He was too shy to attribute such direct and colourful sentiments to his own make-up, in spite of the fact that he might have held them anyway. He was also too firmly latched into life to tell himself whether the ins and outs of it were right or wrong. They just were, and there seemed little else you could do about it. And if there was nothing you could do, what better than to keep silent?

Jack the husband came down for breakfast. Joshua thought he looked younger than his wife, and saw him with a similar slight dark build as he stood up to shake hands while still in his socks. His face was so full of life that Joshua couldn't imagine him able to exert much authority as a university professor, but he had to admit that he didn't know much about that sort of world. He was easy to get on with, and that was everything.

The three children watched Joshua wrapping a copy of the *Guardian* around each ankle and shin. He did it as meticulously as a 1914 soldier applying his puttees before going on parade, but in this case a full tight wrap of a complete newspaper for each leg, over which he pulled his Wellingtons.

He looked at Barney: 'That's if anybody kicks me, should I get into a scrimmage.'

Jack puffed at his pipe, and laughed. 'Who are you expecting kicks from?'

'As if we couldn't guess,' said Pam, who came into the room with a briefcase and a bundle of papers.

'It's not what you expect,' said Joshua. 'It's what you get, though. Or might get, shall we say.'

'They put newspaper there, in case the police kick them,' said Matthew. 'That's what we talk about at school.'

'You sound like a good learner,' Joshua said.

'Can I kick you?' Barney asked.

'As a sort of test, you mean?'

Jack poured himself more tea and frowned. 'That's no way to treat a guest, Barney. We have to bring them up on the right side,' he said, as if someone might doubt his basic principles.

'Come on then,' Joshua said to Barney, 'have a go. If I feel it, I'll give yer a penny.'

Barney took a run, a charge of unconscious buckled-down energy from the other side of the room. His foot struck the boot, and he fell back, toes slightly hurt.

Joshua pulled him close: 'You're a brave lad. I think you deserve a shilling for that. But don't do it every day, will yer?'

Pam said a shilling was too much to give a child, who had twenty pence a week pocket money anyway. Joshua coloured faintly, in case they thought him too mean to give such a fair amount. He put a coin into Barney's hand: 'Now you can tell your smarmy school pals that you've got a collier as well.'

The Kent pickets had organized a Flying Column of thirty cars with six men in each, and ten outriding motorbikes with a pillion passenger – a force of two hundred which both employers and police found hard to handle.

Fighting on 'interior lines', the Flying Column raced from one power station to another as soon as information reached them (generally from their fellow workers inside) that a load of coal was due to be delivered.

News came one morning, after a week at the Thames power station, that 'they' were trying to get coal out of the port gates at Medway. Joshua and the Notts lot got into cars for a great dash along fifty miles of dual carriage-way linking the two rivers. Each man wore the same knee-high Wellingtons that he used down pit, reinforced with a newspaper that turned them to concrete should anyone try to engage in a game of kickshins. This was why, when Joshua found himself in the front rank of the two hundred at Medway dock gates, the policeman shouted with pain on trying to get in a good kick at the collier in front who was pushing a bit too hard for law and order.

The police had been 'thumping the guts' out of the few miners blocking the gate since early morning, but now drew back their lines at the sudden vociferous reinforcement of the Flying Column. Two men had been arrested further along the line, and the inspector who heard the Welsh voice exhort Joshua to 'Get your false teeth into his knackers' swung his track violently into the crush shouting: 'If you come near me, you lousy Welsh Baptist bastard, I'll knock *your* false teeth down your throat.'

It acted on the Welshman like a psychological nail-bomb. But he stayed cool, edged towards the inspector and, apparently out of nowhere, got him around the neck. The crowd opened to let them fight, but another part of it, to which Joshua belonged, got a grip on the Welshman, as friendly as could be had under the circumstances, and pulled him off. Meanwhile a couple of constables took hold of the police officer and dragged him away.

This was the ugliest moment of the morning, and perhaps the inspector realized his mistake, for he made his way to the van parked by the kerb to consult with other officers who had just arrived. Certainly the colliers knew that if he had tried any more wild talk with the Welshman the riot would have completed itself into what neither police nor union officials would have found easy to stop.

A policeman went across to the lorry trying to get out of the docks and ordered the driver back inside. The gates were then closed, and the miners informed that they would not be opened again until the strike was settled. So they might as well go home.

'Spin me another,' said Marriot, sitting down on the kerb. 'It's a real fight, Josh, every bit o' the way. They can't tell me it's over yet – not by a long fart.'

Joshua rolled a cigarette. 'I expect we'll laugh at it one day. I don't like it, though. There could be a threat to life and limb in it. The Lord's got nowt to do wi' this. It's the Devil, more like.'

'They're devils,' Marriot nodded. 'Give us the Sermon on the Mount, Joshua.'

'I don't read that. I stop at the Prophets.'

'I expect we'll go back to Greenwich,' said Marriot, sounding as if he'd be glad of a rest. 'I need to set my watch anyway.' He pointed across the road: 'Just bloody look at that, will yer' – where a police canteen van was providing tea, and a few miners were standing around drinking from paper cups the police must have given them. 'What a bloody lot of scroungers. They'd scrounge owt, the boggers. They'd scrounge milk out of a virgin's tit, they would.'

'Don't go on about it,' Joshua said, blinking. 'I suppose the coppers have got soft hearts as well, some of 'em. They're only like us, if you tek that false raiment off their backs.'

Marriot's eyes were sharp for other things, and beamed on a gate further along the road which the majority of pickets had somehow neglected. A huge lorry with high wooden sides, and laden with small pieces of coal, steered out and made off along the road towards the motorway as fast as it was possible to accelerate.

'Come on,' Marriot cried, leaping up.

They ran to the nearest car. A driver was already at the wheel, but so many others were trying to get in that it was almost a minute before it drew away with a clattering roar.

Joshua was by the driver, peering through traffic for a glimpse of the lorry, which seemed to have totally avoided them. 'There ain't much we can do even if we catch it up,' Marriot said from the back seat. 'They pulled a bloody fast one on us all right, the sly gets. Some blokes 'ud sell their souls for a barrel of beer and a kipper.'

'Maybe only a cup o' tea,' said Joshua, who felt himself sweating from sudden heat in the car. His heart beat nervously from the chase. 'Just keep looking.'

It was impossible for him to be comfortable with the Bible so sharp at his back pocket, but now he was almost trying to stand with the effort of looking along the road ahead.

'He's turned off somewhere,' Marriot suggested.

'That's more than he dare do,' said Joshua. 'We'd corner him then like a rat. He'll keep straight on, yo' see.'

'Not that he'll find it easy to drive his load into any power station, man,' the Welsh driver said, overtaking a car and a bus. 'The boys are waiting for the likes of him.'

'They might have another secret gate for him to get into,' said Joshua. 'We must nab him on the way there.' But nobody knew how.

The lorry was labouring up a slip road leading to the motorway. They saw it. The car was faster and more agile, and was soon behind, under the towering rear wall of it.

'Only wish he don't start rolling back,' said the driver. 'Be the end of my promising career' – and his words made them laugh, a near hysterical chorus which sharply ceased when they began wondering what to do.

It was drizzling, and he flicked the wipers on to get rid of grit and oil-slick coming at them from the big wheels. 'We're so close on his tail,' said Marriot, 'that he don't know we're there.'

The driver of their car changed to bottom gear. 'He's crawling like a worm. Packed everything on, the greedy swine.'

'He'll get a fat bonus,' said Marriot. 'Right up his arse, I hope. The thing is, though: What do we do now?'

'How fast is he going?' Joshua asked

'Same as us,' said the Kentish Welshman. 'About ten, I would say.' Joshua opened the door. 'Leave it to me.'

'You'll kill your bloody self,' Marriot shouted.

'I'll be all right. Can you keep a bit back from the lorry, Taffy? As long as the Lord stays with me. I don't want my guts crushing in. Just a bit behind. Then watch.'

Taffy nodded, his face plainly worried when Joshua got out of the car and closed the door quietly as if the lorry-driver in front might hear it. He ran alongside in great strides, like a giraffe.

His breath grated as he worked, hoping the slope was long enough to keep the lorry going slow while he did what was in his mind. The steel pin along the bottom of the wooden back wall was stiff as he tried to loosen it.

It was no use tugging at the bar, for it was solidly in position, so he first lifted the end up and down to try and ease it. His Wellingtons were a liability, as if they were full of wet sand. Black grit from the lorry wheels sprayed out and over, almost blinding him, so that he was continually wiping it away, working with a permanent squint.

He saw a vision of the Lord, fire on Mount Pisgah, and knew the strength of the walls of Jericho. His hands slipped on the cold metal, but it became easier, and with one hard pull in which all his muscle and breath was used, he began to draw it away.

Then it stuck for what seemed the rest of his life, and he saw the Angel of Death, and ten thousand Egyptian chariots ready to fall and sweep him into the blood-red sea of blackness.

It seemed as if he'd taken on more than he could handle, and he felt for a moment at the Bible banging loose in his trousers behind. Then he ran to catch up with the lorry of the Pharisees, and work harder than he'd ever worked in his life.

The bar was a quarter of the way across and he planned his leap clear should the avalanche of coal come down from the sky, aimed as it would be straight at his head and vulnerable body which seemed small enough to him now. He thought of the car trailing a few yards from his heels, but daren't look at it, knowing beyond doubt that they'd seen his renewed hope and further progress.

It was raining more heavily, but in a way he welcomed it because the icy sloosh cooled and comforted him, eating up the hot sweat from his face as he ran. The bar was half-way across, and at three quarters over he could leap clear because it would come the rest of the way by itself. A few lumps of coal were already banging on to his Wellingtons.

With the finest show of timing, born of knowing when the creak of the Doughty prop was at the breaking point and one had to scramble clear, he left the bar to do its own work, for it was down at the road and striking sparks from it. Half a hundredweight of best power-station coal had already fallen. He glanced over his shoulder, a look which Marriot said later was full of rabbit-panic.

The car was close by, yet it was out of his grasp, a mile away, and impossible to reach. As the coal fell he had a feeling of death, of dropping also into an emptiness so wide and complete that his consciousness was for a moment obliterated. Sky, road, and coal no longer existed. It was like going to sleep on the job: when you came out of it a hundred years might have passed, but in reality it was only a second. Something went into his mind during that short vacuum of time, and he didn't know what it was, only that in all his years down the pit he'd never been so close to it before.

He had pins and needles in front of the eyes, an aching clarity that made him want to shut out the sharp detail of the lorry-back. Then he saw Marriot looking from the car and beckoning madly. He nipped to the side and pulled at the half-open door as it drew level.

Nobody spoke as he got into his seat. Hearts and eyes were fixed on the menacing wall of the lorry shedding its coal, now breaking on them. The driver, with a soft and melodious curse (followed by a prayer for their safety) turned the wheel and eased on to the outer lane to avoid the avalanche.

They followed in this position till the whole of several tons had fallen, and paved the road behind for a good mile. The driver inside the lorry, still perhaps full of his triumph at out-witting the colliers, and thinking of the promised bonus, drove without realizing the unexpected twist that had befallen him.

They got on to the motorway, and put on speed to seventy miles an hour. Ten miles must have passed before the driver reached over to Joshua, his hand outstretched: 'Shake it, there's a good man. I've never seen anything like it.'

Marriot was laughing hysterically in the back, already thinking of telling it that night to the others in the pub. He knew he would have a monopoly of the tale, because Joshua wouldn't say much about it.

Joshua took the Welshman's hand, and held it as if they were both children who needed the solid reassurance of love that only children can give each other. Then he let go and felt behind him. The angular sharpness had gone from his back pocket. He'd no longer got his Bible – the old, only, long-loved book of life and leisure bought as a youth from a stall in Workshop market place. It must have jumped out during his frantic work, and been buried under thousands of black coal-lumps. He felt like a mountain crumbling into sleep.

The pay terms were announced, and accepted. They had got what they wanted. The government had given in. With so many troops in Northern Ireland it could not afford to fight the miners as well.

Joshua was neither glad nor disappointed. They could beat Caesar any time. But he wanted to get back, back to where he came from so that he could feel real again. He felt a need to get himself back into the pit and rip out that coal from under the earth.

He sat in the kitchen, having packed two carrier-bags with his things. Pam came in to give him a meal before the journey north. She would be sorry to see him go. It was as if he had lived in the house for a long time. He belonged to it almost.

'Are they your things, Josh?'

'That's 'em.'

'Do you have your Bible?'

He coloured slightly. She wondered why he was embarrassed at her mentioning it, when he hadn't been before. He didn't know she knew he'd lost it, because he'd mentioned it to no one. 'It got misplaced,' he said, seeing no reason for secrets.

'I hear you lost it in a scrimmage,' she said.

He laughed, and she was surprised to see an elderly man so shy. It made him look young: 'I'll get another sort of Bible, I expect. I'm never too old to learn.'

'It's true,' she said.

He nodded. 'I suppose it would have been better to have learned things a bit younger, though. We can get 'em on the run any time o' day or night. It's been a bit of an education, you might say.'

His carrier-bags weren't packed neatly enough, so he bent down to rearrange the things inside. Pam went out, and came back with a suitcase: 'Put your things in this.'

'It's done,' he told her.

'I hope you'll come and see us when you're in London. We'll never forget you. Especially the children. Barney cried last night when I told him you had to go.'

She took a platter of chops from the oven. It was the *au pair*'s day off. 'Jack and I are so glad about it all.'

'We had a lot of help,' he said, beginning to eat.

She put his things in the suitcase, determined that he should take it, having talked it over with her husband the night before. 'You'll need it when you come down again – or go anywhere else on your travels.'

'There's no need,' he said, but seeing he was embarrassing her by refusing he added: 'It's very good of you.'

He was glad she repacked his things out in the hall because he'd be able to eat without being looked at. Marriot would be round with the car in half an hour. The only woman he could bear to have looking at him while he was eating was Jessie. It was marvellous how people stuck together during a strike. He didn't feel young any more. There was more to life than that. He'd not forget the different men from coalmines around the country he'd met. It certainly was one land when you thought of it like that. All he'd known was the black guts he sweated in among the dust and shale. Now he knew a bit more about the top of it.

When he thought of the coal he'd spilled over the road he couldn't believe he was still alive, though it seemed a terrible waste. There was some malice when he brought back the memory and laughed over it. With so many endings in life it was good to have a happy one for a change.

But all he wanted to do was rip more coal out of the earth, now that Caesar had been put in his place – for a while.

Storm Petrel

Romesh Gunesekera

Introduction

Romesh Gunesekera was born in Colombo, Sri Lanka (which then still bore its British-colonial name, Ceylon), in 1954. His father worked for the Central Bank of Ceylon, and the family was part of an English-speaking middle class, although Romesh's schooling was conducted in Sinhala, which, as the language of the majority ethnic group who populate most of the south and east of the island, was favoured by nationalist policies of post-independence Sri Lanka. Romesh grew up partly in the Philippines with his father, who spent five years there setting up the Asian Development Bank, before emigrating to Britain in the early 1970s. He studied English and Philosophy at Liverpool University, and then worked for the British Council in London for a number of years before becoming a full-time writer in 1996.

Gunesekera is a poet as well as a fiction-writer and has won a number of poetry prizes in addition to awards for his novels and short stories. His first book was the collection of short stories, *Monkfish Moon* (1992), in which 'Storm Petrel' appears. Some of the nine stories are set in Sri Lanka, some in Britain, but all are coloured in various ways by the political and ethnic tensions that have dominated Sri Lankan history since independence in 1948. Similar concerns emerge in Gunesekera's first novel, *Reef* (1994), which was short-listed for both the Booker Prize and the *Guardian* Fiction Prize. Most of the novel's action is set in Sri Lanka during the turbulent decades from the 1960s through to the 1980s, though the narrator, Triton, finally becomes a kind of refugee in London, numbly facing a future 'without a past, without a name'[1]. Gunesekera has published three further novels, *The Sandglass* (1998), which follows the histories of two Sri Lankan families in the post-independence era, *Heaven's Edge* (2002), set in a post-nuclear future, and *The Match* (2006), in which the South Asian passion for cricket provides an overall framework.

London is now Gunesekera's home, but he travels extensively, often appearing at literary festivals and participating in writing workshops. He has also held writing residencies in Denmark, Singapore and Hong Kong. A number of his short stories have been broadcast on national radio – 'Storm Petrel', for example, was read on BBC Radio Scotland in 2000. In 2004 he was elected a Fellow of the Royal Society of Literature, and in 2005 he received a national honour, a Ranjana, from the President of Sri Lanka.

'Storm Petrel', the briefest of the stories in *Monkfish Moon*, is a superficially simple account of a chance conversation between two Sri Lankan expatriates in London. But the date of this spring-time conversation, very precisely established as May 1983, is just two months before the eruption of civil war between the Sri Lankan government and the Liberation Tigers of Tamil Eelam (the 'Tamil Tigers'), a separatist organization that, since the 1970s, has been fighting for an independent state in the north and east of the island. Through Gunesekera's spare, delicate prose, we perceive the fragility both of the contemporary world and of the idea of 'home'. The story was originally to be titled 'Jerath's Beach' but 'Storm Petrel' evokes metaphoric associations, in much the same way that 'Reef', as the title of his first novel, denotes not simply the delicate eco-system of the living coral disappearing from Sri Lanka's beautiful coast but also the erosion of human and social stability. Storm petrels are small sea-birds, found all around the world, that sailors used to believe brought warning of storms because they shelter in the lee of ships during bad weather.

Note

1. R. Gunesekera, *Reef* (London: *Granta*, 1994), p. 180.

Storm Petrel

I was going up Woburn Walk to a second-hand bookshop when I bumped into CK coming out of a travel agency. CK was a small thin man in his late forties; he wore a brown tweed jacket with a bright red woollen tie. He was startled, but then we recognized each other.

'How are you?' he asked quickly, looking rather pleased.

I mumbled something.

'I have been back home, to Sri Lanka!' His winter skin had been warmed, the brown was deep; he looked healthy.

'Oh yes.' I nodded.

'Yes! Yes!' he said excitedly, 'Just before the hot weather. Wonderful. When . . . ' he pushed back the spectacles sliding down his nose, 'when did you last go back? To Sri Lanka?' Now he was beaming.

I had to think hard. I am useless at measuring time. 'About four years,' I guessed.

'I went about then also. 'Seventy-nine. How different! You can't imagine. Then ten rupees, even five rupees, was good money. You had something you know. But now! Everybody has fists of money. Fifty rupees, hundred rupees, it's just nothing. Nothing!' He shook his head in amazement but did not elaborate on whether this was inflation or prosperity, whether he approved or disapproved.

His sense of amazement was infectious. The grim wet May air suddenly cleared and the midday sun flooded the little alley we were in. The air lost its chill and the warm buds and curled green leaves of the plants in the pavement tubs seemed to open before us.

CK carried on like one of those indefatigable South Asian steam engines. 'East Coast, West Coast, North, I went everywhere. I also went to India you know. The South. Madras, Trivandrum, Goa, you know Goa? Cochin. All nice. Goa and Cochin especially. But Ceylon . . . ' he took a deep breath and tightly crumpled his mouth so that what was his smile hovered only in his eyes. He slowly shook his head. 'Ceylon is now very prosperous. You know they are building houses all over the place. And very modern too. And tourists all over. All over the place. East Coast, West Coast, all over. You can't go a hundred yards – tourists! India is even more full of them,' he added, in case I planned to offer a comparison. 'In India young people, not hippies and all, but just young people are roaming all over. All kinds of young people, boys and girls sleeping anywhere. You won't believe how happy they are! I asked them, you know, What are you doing? Do you like this sort of wandering?' His voice pitched high, rising uphill. 'But you know it's very good. They love it! They come from Norway, Sweden, Germany, and they don't want to go back. It is really amazing. They sleep on the street or station and can eat for two rupees. What more is there in life, huh? They are looking for *dharma*. I also slept in a station in India.' CK cocked his head and smiled, almost forgetting me in his contemplation of that hot night in a southern station, sharing a platform with a bevy of sweaty moon-eyed wanderers.

I was impressed. CK was so enthusiastic, and seemed to have travelled with such wonderful curiosity, talking to everyone about their lives, their hopes and their migrant dreams. *And are you happy*? I could so easily imagine him interviewing them with his large open smile creasing an already quite wrinkled narrow face. I could see him peering forward and asking earnestly for the *really true* answers. Their responses he would settle in his head by patting his grey temples very gently.

'You know I'm going back,' he said, as if clinching some complex argument. I did not react. I was not altogether there with him. I was in India. He repeated his statement, 'I am going back – home to Sri Lanka!'

'You mean for good?' I asked, catching up.

He sighed longingly, 'Yes soon. I just now was inquiring about tickets!' He nodded at the travel agency.

'I went on this last trip really to view things you know: the prospects. That is why I went to India as well. People say it is picking up there also. But back home is even better, now.' He looked over my shoulder into the distance at the many possibilities: London, Madras, Batticaloa. 'I have more or less made up my mind. You know what I will do? I will go to the East Coast and open a little guest house there.' This must have been a thought that had occurred, or even a decision made, minutes before our encounter but which had quickly assumed the appearance of a lifelong dream. It must have been what caused that wonderful exuberance which filled the air when he first spoke. But the full potential of his happy vision seemed to hit him only as he continued. 'Yes, you know what I mean?' He looked appealingly. Then, almost in a dream, he said, 'Just a little place. A sort of *guest house*.' The last two words were worked around his mouth to savour every last drop of magic in them. Already he had a proprietorial air about him basking in London's spring noon.

A rich spice smell drifted from the samosa counter a few yards away to add to our exotic shared vision of CK on the East Coast.

'Are you going to build it? Like a hotel?' I asked.

CK looked surprised. Then with a benign smile he explained 'No, no. Not a hotel, but a simple guest house you know.'

I felt sheepish. Of course not a hotel. A hotel in Sri Lanka has hundreds of rooms, swimming pools and cocktail bars. It has concrete; waiters in crisp white sarongs; Sunday curry buffets; conspicuous Bar-B-Q dances; three-day-island-tours; Serendip gem stores; batik dresses and shy girls employed for their simple faces and bare midriffs. Hotels are built by international conglomerates, not individuals you meet on the street.

'Actually maybe *cabanas* would be better. That's what these tourists like nowadays. You know what I mean?'

I said I did, but he insisted on clarifying the meaning.

'You see, it is really just a cabin. Very simple. I will have it like a hut. Some cement, and you know our coconut thatch? *Cadjan*. I will put that. Costs very, very little. And the less it has nowadays, the more these tourists like it. They pay more in fact for less!' He beamed again. 'So I will just have a few of those. That is all.'

He was already there, sitting on the veranda of his own modern bungalow enjoying a panoramic view of the Indian Ocean and his plot of *cadjan cabanas*. I too gazed longingly at the mile-long line of white surf rolling on CK's beach.

Then he had another idea.

'You know there is no problem about food. Always there is a *kadé* nearby where you can get rice and curry for a few rupees. And these tourists, they like that.'

'Ah good,' I said, 'I was wondering about the food.'

I was thinking to myself that it would be worth opening a restaurant near CK's beach. It would be a better idea than the *cabanas*; you could live without a thatched hut but you wouldn't last long, even in paradise, without food.

'I also went to the small towns, you know.' CK lifted his eyebrows and with the same action lifted his whole scalp. 'It has changed so much. There's no denying, it has certainly changed. We have developed a lot you know. You should see the houses there now.'

He was so persuasive I wanted to return immediately with him.

'The houses are just like in Colombo now, much better than in this place.' His face became very serious, his mouth purposefully turned down at both ends. 'You know what the reason is? Everybody now has somebody in the Middle East. Working there. Earning pots of money. Then they get everything. You know, TVs – televisions – cassettes, videos, motorcycles, the works! And still the *kadé* is there with our *thosai* and sweet tea. Unbelievable, no? But . . . ' CK then smiled again as if he was passing over a secret, 'in some ways nothing has changed. You know what I mean?'

I knew what he meant. It reminded me of the happy times when, as a child, I would smuggle home spicy sweet packets: mixes of cardamom, gram, almonds, saffron and silver coated sugar pearls. A deep impossibly personal pleasure.

'You know the real things are still there. That is why I have decided to go. Have you been to the East Coast? You know beyond the lagoon and all: Nilaveli, Kuchchaveli. Around there is where I'm thinking of. Good sea, white sand. And very warm.'

We were both silent for a while. The salt in the sea air lulled us almost to a sleep. Overhead the sea breeze echoed the roar of the surf as coconut trees brushed their heads together, whispering like giants planning our destiny. The sun was hot. CK was going over each step of his dream. But in just two months the whole island would be engulfed in flames: the East Coast like the North would become a blazing battleground. Mined and strafed and bombed and pulverized, CK's beach, the dry-zone scrub land – disputed mother earth – would be dug up, exploded and exhumed. The carnage in Colombo, massacres in Vavuniya, the battle of Elephant Pass were all to come. But that day in the middle of London in the middle of May we knew none of that.

Eventually I asked CK about his schedule, 'So when exactly are you going back?'

This innocent question stopped his whole happy train of thought. Suddenly he was thrown back from the Land Registry office in

Trincomalee to our sunny walkway in Bloomsbury. But the wheels soon turned smoothly again.

'I am thinking of going back in about six months time. I have a few things to settle, then I think the time will be right for me to go. You see you can't rush these things. You know how it is, going home. But definitely by next year I think I will be there.' He looked at me as if for confirmation.

Involuntarily I nodded my approval. I could see he was pleased. The plan was falling into place under a logic of its own; there was a kind of effortless imagination at work. He said he felt he was a lucky man. For ten years his imagination had soured slipping on the spinning rungs of the clerical grades in his Euston office. His expectations, even his dreams, had learned to conform to a fixed and finite set of small increments. Now, suddenly, he felt he had a new dimension – a free future – to explore. He seemed twenty years younger in a world of his own making. He looked at me and said, 'You know, I am already a happy man now.'

Then the sun slipped behind a cloud and shadows rushed the ground; we both became aware that it was late. Our lunch plans had become distorted. We nodded vigorously to each other and parted company. CK craned his thin neck like a bird searching for the sea while I hurried on to my bookshop.

Squatter

Rohinton Mistry

Introduction

Rohinton Mistry was born in Bombay (now Mumbai), India, in 1952. His family was part of the Parsi Zoroastrian community, a dwindling group originally from Persia, where they had suffered religious persecution in the eighth century. The Parsis prospered under British rule in India, but they became unpopular after the British left in 1947, and a westward tide of emigration began. Mistry took a degree in Mathematics and Economics at the University of Bombay before emigrating to Canada himself, with his wife, at the age of 23. By then, he said, 'I had been fully formed by my own culture and my own family', and although life in Canada was, to an unexpected degree, 'strange and new', it was also 'navigable'.[1]

After settling in Toronto, Mistry worked as a bank clerk, but later resumed his studies part-time, and completed a second degree, in English and Philosophy, in 1982. It was while he was at the University of Toronto that he began writing fiction, and his early short stories won a number of prizes. By the mid-1980s, with the help of a Canada Council grant, he was able to leave his bank job to become a full-time writer. He is now a naturalized Canadian citizen.

Mistry's first short story collection was published in Canada under the title *Swimming Lessons and Other Stories from Firozsha Baag* in 1987, and in the UK as *Tales from Firozsha Baag* in 1992. A 'baag' (colony) is an apartment complex with a communal courtyard, characteristic of Bombay, and the fictitious baag that provides the setting for Mistry's eleven inter-linked stories is peopled by Parsis struggling, in various ways, to reconcile the demands of tradition and modernity. The stories are told from a number of different perspectives, but the last story suggests a more definite link between them as the childhood memories of one of the younger characters who has since moved to Canada.

Mistry has published three novels to date, all of which have been critically acclaimed. He continues to write not about Canada but about India, with a precise and detailed realism that produces extraordinarily rich effects. His first novel, *Such a Long Journey* (1991), is set at the time of the war between India and Pakistan in 1971, over what was to become Bangladesh, and centres on the moral dilemmas of a middle-aged Bombay bank clerk. The novel won several awards, including Canada's Governor General's Award for Fiction and the Commonwealth Writers' Award for Best Book of the Year; it was short-listed for the Booker Prize, and was later made into a film, under the same title (1998). In his second novel, *A Fine Balance* (1996), Mistry moves forward to the period of India's state of emergency under Indira Ghandi in 1975, but this time the sweep of the novel is more panoramic. The third novel, *Family Matters* (2002), is again set in Bombay, but in the 1990s, and its main character is an elderly Parsi widower living with his step-children; this novel, too, was short-listed for the Booker Prize.

In some respects *Family Matters* recalls the world of Firozsha Baag, though the earlier tales perhaps demonstrate Mistry's wry humour more strongly. The narrator of 'Squatter' is Firozsha Baag's respected story-teller Nariman Hansotia, who transfixes his young audience with two contrasting stories, laced with satire. The subject of emigration in 'Squatter' is exposed as an insoluble dilemma, with ambition and cultural expectations on the one hand set against the emigrant's inevitable sense of guilt at leaving his homeland.

Note

1. S. Nasta (ed.), *Writing Across Worlds: Contemporary Writers Talk* (London: Routledge, 2004), p. 199.

Squatter

Whenever Nariman Hansotia returned in the evening from the Cawasji Framji Memorial Library in a good mood the signs were plainly evident.

First, he parked his 1932 Mercedes-Benz (he called it the apple of his eye) outside A Block, directly in front of his ground-floor veranda window, and beeped the horn three long times. It annoyed Rustomji who also had a ground-floor flat in A Block. Ever since he had defied Nariman in the matter of painting the exterior of the building, Rustomji was convinced that nothing the old coot did was untainted by the thought of vengeance and harassment, his retirement pastime.

But the beeping was merely Nariman's signal to let Hirabai inside know that though he was back he would not step indoors for a while. Then he raised the hood, whistling "Rose Marie," and leaned his tall frame over the engine. He checked the oil, wiped here and there with a rag, tightened the radiator cap, and lowered the hood. Finally, he polished the Mercedes star and let the whistling modulate into the march from *The Bridge On The River Kwai*. The boys playing in the compound knew that Nariman was ready now to tell a story. They started to gather round.

"*Sahibji*, Nariman Uncle," someone said tentatively and Nariman nodded, careful not to lose his whistle, his bulbous nose flaring slightly. The pursed lips had temporarily raised and reshaped his Clark Gable moustache. More boys walked up. One called out, "How about a story, Nariman Uncle?" at which point Nariman's eyes began to twinkle, and he imparted increased energy to the polishing. The cry was taken up by others, "Yes, yes, Nariman Uncle, a story!" He swung into a final verse of the march. Then the lips relinquished the whistle, the Clark Gable moustache descended. The rag was put away, and he began.

"You boys know the great cricketers: Contractor, Polly Umrigar, and recently, the young chap, Farokh Engineer. Cricket *aficionados*, that's what you all are." Nariman liked to use new words, especially big ones, in the stories he told, believing it was his duty to expose young minds to as shimmering and varied a vocabulary as possible;

if they could not spend their days at the Cawasji Framji Memorial Library then he, at least, could carry bits of the library out to them.

The boys nodded; the names of the cricketers were familiar.

"But does any one know about Savukshaw, the greatest of them all?" They shook their heads in unison.

"This, then, is the story about Savukshaw, how he saved the Indian team from a humiliating defeat when they were touring in England." Nariman sat on the steps of A Block. The few diehards who had continued with their games could not resist any longer when they saw the gathering circle, and ran up to listen. They asked their neighbours in whispers what the story was about, and were told: Savukshaw the greatest cricketer. The whispering died down and Nariman began.

"The Indian team was to play the indomitable MCC as part of its tour of England. Contractor was our captain. Now the MCC being the strongest team they had to face, Contractor was almost certain of defeat. To add to Contractor's troubles, one of his star batsmen, Nadkarni, had caught influenza early in the tour, and would definitely not be well enough to play against the MCC. By the way, does anyone know what those letters stand for? You, Kersi, you wanted to be a cricketer once."

Kersi shook his head. None of the boys knew, even though they had heard the MCC mentioned in radio commentaries, because the full name was hardly ever used.

Then Jehangir Bulsara spoke up, or Bulsara Bookworm, as the boys called him. The name given by Pesi *paadmaroo* had stuck even though it was now more than four years since Pesi had been sent away to boarding-school, and over two years since the death of Dr Mody. Jehangir was still unliked by the boys in the Baag, though they had come to accept his aloofness and respect his knowledge and intellect. They were not surprised that he knew the answer to Nariman's question: "Marylebone Cricket Club."

"Absolutely correct," said Nariman, and continued with the story. "The MCC won the toss and elected to bat. They scored four hundred and ninety-seven runs in the first inning before our spinners could get them out. Early in the second day's play our team was dismissed for one hundred and nine runs, and the extra who had taken Nadkarni's place was injured by a vicious bumper that opened a gash on his forehead." Nariman indicated the spot and the length of the gash on his furrowed brow. "Contractor's worst fears were coming true. The MCC waived their own second inning and gave the Indian team a follow-on, wanting to inflict an inning's defeat. And this time he had to use the second extra. The second extra was a certain Savukshaw."

The younger boys listened attentively; some of them, like the two sons of the chartered accountant in B Block, had only recently been deemed old enough by their parents to come out and play in the compound, and had not received any exposure to Nariman's stories. But the others like Jehangir, Kersi, and Viraf were familiar with Nariman's technique.

Once, Jehangir had overheard them discussing Nariman's stories, and he could not help expressing his opinion: that unpredictability was the brush he used to paint his tales with, and ambiguity the palette he mixed his colours in. The others looked at him with admiration. Then Viraf asked what exactly he meant by that. Jehangir said that Nariman sometimes told a funny incident in a very serious way, or expressed a significant matter in a light and playful manner. And these were only two rough divisions, in between were lots of subtle gradations of tone and texture. Which, then, was the funny story and which the serious? Their opinions were divided, but ultimately, said Jehangir, it was up to the listener to decide.

"So," continued Nariman, "Contractor first sent out his two regular openers, convinced that it was all hopeless. But after five wickets were lost for just another thirty-eight runs, out came Savukshaw the extra. Nothing mattered any more."

The street lights outside the compound came on, illuminating the iron gate where the watchman stood. It was a load off the watchman's mind when Nariman told a story. It meant an early end to the hectic vigil during which he had to ensure that none of the children ran out on the main road, or tried to jump over the wall. For although keeping out riff-raff was his duty, keeping in the boys was as important if he wanted to retain the job.

"The first ball Savukshaw faced was wide outside the off stump. He just lifted his bat and ignored it. But with what style! What panache! As if to say, come on, you blighters, play some polished cricket. The next ball was also wide, but not as much as the first. It missed the off stump narrowly. Again Savukshaw lifted his bat, boredom written all over him. Everyone was now watching closely. The bowler was annoyed by Savukshaw's arrogance, and the third delivery was a vicious fast pitch, right down on the middle stump.

"Savukshaw was ready, quick as lightning. No one even saw the stroke of his bat, but the ball went like a bullet towards square leg.

"Fielding at square leg was a giant of a fellow, about six feet seven, weighing two hundred and fifty pounds, a veritable Brobdingnagian, with arms like branches and hands like a pair of huge *sapaal*, the kind that Dr Mody used to wear, you remember what big feet Dr Mody had." Jehangir was the only one who did; he nodded. "Just to see him standing there was scary. Not one ball had got past him, and he had taken some great catches. Savukshaw purposely aimed his shot right at him. But he was as quick as Savukshaw, and stuck out his huge *sapaal* of a hand to stop the ball. What do you think happened then, boys?"

The older boys knew what Nariman wanted to hear at this point. They asked, "What happened, Nariman Uncle, what happened?" Satisfied, Nariman continued.

"A howl is what happened. A howl from the giant fielder, a howl that rang through the entire stadium, that soared like the cry of a banshee right up to the cheapest seats in the furthest, highest corners, a howl that echoed from the scoreboard and into the pavilion, into the kitchen, startling the chap inside who was preparing tea and scones for after the match, who spilled boiling water all over himself and was severely hurt. But not nearly as bad as the giant fielder at square leg. Never at any English stadium was a howl heard like that one, not in the whole history of cricket. And why do you think he was howling, boys?"

The chorus asked, "Why, Nariman Uncle, why?"

"Because of Savukshaw's bullet-like shot, of course. The hand he had reached out to stop it, he now held up for all to see, and *dhur-dhur, dhur-dhur* the blood was gushing like a fountain in an Italian piazza, like a burst water-main from the Vihar-Powai reservoir, dripping onto his shirt and his white pants, and sprinkling the green grass, and only because he was such a giant of a fellow could he suffer so much blood loss and not faint. But even he could not last forever; eventually, he felt dizzy, and was helped off the field. And where do you think the ball was, boys, that Savukshaw had smacked so hard?"

And the chorus rang out again on the now dark steps of A Block: "Where, Nariman Uncle, where?"

"Past the boundary line, of course. Lying near the fence. Rent asunder. Into two perfect leather hemispheres. All the stitches had ripped, and some of the insides had spilled out. So the umpires sent for a new one, and the game resumed. Now none of the fielders dared to touch any ball that Savukshaw hit. Every shot went to the boundary, all the way for four runs. Single-handedly, Savukshaw wiped out the deficit, and had it not been for loss of time due to rain, he would have taken the Indian team to a thumping victory against the MCC. As it was, the match ended in a draw."

Nariman was pleased with the awed faces of the youngest ones around him. Kersi and Viraf were grinning away and whispering something. From one of the flats the smell of frying fish swam out to explore the night air, and tickled Nariman's nostrils. He sniffed appreciatively, aware that it was in his good wife Hirabai's pan that the frying was taking place. This morning, he had seen the pomfret she had purchased at the door, waiting to be cleaned, its mouth open and eyes wide, like the eyes of some of these youngsters. It was time to wind up the story.

"The MCC will not forget the number of new balls they had to produce that day because of Savukshaw's deadly strokes. Their annual ball budget was thrown badly out of balance. Any other bat would have cracked under the strain, but Savukshaw's was seasoned with a special combination of oils, a secret formula given to him by a *sadhu* who had seen him one day playing cricket when he was a small boy. But Savukshaw used to say his real secret was practice, lots of practice, that was the advice he gave to any young lad who wanted to play cricket."

The story was now clearly finished, but none of the boys showed any sign of dispersing. "Tell us about more matches that Savukshaw played in," they said.

"More nothing. This was his greatest match. Anyway, he did not play cricket for long because soon after the match against the MCC he became a champion bicyclist, the fastest human on two wheels. And later, a pole-vaulter – when he glided over on his pole, so graceful, it was like watching a bird in flight. But he gave that up, too, and became a hunter, the mightiest hunter ever known, absolutely fearless, and so skilful, with a gun he could have, from the third floor of A Block, shaved the whisker of a cat in the backyard of C Block."

"Tell us about that," they said, "about Savukshaw the hunter!"

The fat ayah, Jaakaylee, arrived to take the chartered accountant's two children home. But they refused to go without hearing about Savukshaw the hunter. When she scolded them and things became a little hysterical, some other boys tried to resurrect the ghost she had once seen: "Ayah *bhoot*! Ayah *bhoot*!" Nariman raised a finger in warning – that subject was still taboo in Firozsha Baag; none of the adults was in a hurry to relive the wild and rampageous days that Pesi *paadmaroo* had ushered in, once upon a time, with the *bhoot* games.

Jaakaylee sat down, unwilling to return without the children, and whispered to Nariman to make it short. The smell of frying fish which had tickled Nariman's nostrils ventured into and awakened his stomach. But the story of Savukshaw the hunter was one he had wanted to tell for a long time.

"Savukshaw always went hunting alone, he preferred it that way. There are many incidents in the life of Savukshaw the hunter, but the one I am telling you about involves a terrifying situation. Terrifying for us, of course; Savukshaw was never terrified of anything. What happened was, one night he set up camp, started a fire and warmed up his bowl of chicken-*dhansaak*."

The frying fish had precipitated famishment upon Nariman, and the subject of chicken-*dhansaak* suited him well. His own mouth watering, he elaborated: "Mrs Savukshaw was as famous for her *dhansaak* as Mr was for hunting. She used to put in tamarind and brinjal, coriander and cumin, cloves and cinnamon, and dozens of other spices no one knows about. Women used to come from miles around to stand outside her window while she cooked it, to enjoy the fragrance and try to penetrate her secret, hoping to identify the ingredients as the aroma floated out, layer by layer, growing more complex and delicious. But always, the delectable fragrance enveloped the women and they just surrendered to the ecstasy, forgetting what they had come for. Mrs Savukshaw's secret was safe."

Jaakaylee motioned to Nariman to hurry up, it was past the children's dinner-time. He continued: "The aroma of savoury spices soon filled the night air in the jungle, and when the *dhansaak* was piping hot he started to eat, his rifle beside him. But as soon as he lifted the first morsel to his lips, a tiger's eyes flashed in the bushes! Not twelve feet from him! He emerged licking his chops! What do you think happened then, boys?"

"What, what, Nariman Uncle?"

Before he could tell them, the door of his flat opened. Hirabai put her head out and said, "*Chaalo ni*, Nariman, it's time. Then if it gets cold you won't like it."

That decided the matter. To let Hirabai's fried fish, crisp on the outside, yet tender and juicy inside, marinated in turmeric and cayenne – to let that get cold would be something that *Khoedaiji* above would not easily forgive. "Sorry boys, have to go. Next time about Savukshaw and the tiger."

There were some groans of disappointment. They hoped Nariman's good spirits would extend into the morrow when he returned from the Memorial Library, or the story would get cold.

But a whole week elapsed before Nariman again parked the apple of his eye outside his ground-floor flat and beeped the horn three times. When he had raised the hood, checked the oil, polished the star and swung into the "Colonel Bogie March," the boys began drifting towards A Block.

Some of them recalled the incomplete story of Savukshaw and the tiger, but they knew better than to remind him. It was never wise to prompt Nariman until he had dropped the first hint himself, or things would turn out badly.

Nariman inspected the faces: the two who stood at the back, always looking superior and wise, were missing. So was the quiet Bulsara boy, the intelligent one. "Call Kersi, Viraf, and Jehangir," he said, "I want them to listen to today's story."

Jehangir was sitting alone on the stone steps of C Block. The others were chatting by the compound gate with the watchman. Someone went to fetch them.

"Sorry to disturb your conference, boys, and your meditation, Jehangir," Nariman said facetiously, "but I thought you would like to hear this story. Especially since some of you are planning to go abroad."

This was not strictly accurate, but Kersi and Viraf did talk a lot about America and Canada. Kersi had started writing to universities there since his final high-school year, and had also sent letters of inquiry to the Canadian High Commission in New Delhi and to the US Consulate at Breach Candy. But so far he had not made any progress. He and Viraf replied with as much sarcasm as their unripe years allowed, "Oh yes, next week, just have to pack our bags."

"Riiiight," drawled Nariman. Although he spoke perfect English, this was the one word with which he allowed himself sometimes to take liberties, indulging in a broadness of vowel more American than anything else. "But before we go on with today's story, what did you learn about Savukshaw, from last week's story?"

"That he was a very talented man," said someone.

"What else?"

"He was also a very lucky man, to have so many talents," said Viraf.

"Yes, but what else?"

There was silence for a few moments. Then Jehangir said, timidly: "He was a man searching for happiness, by trying all kinds of different things."

"Exactly! And he never found it. He kept looking for new experiences, and though he was very successful at everything he attempted, it did not bring him happiness. Remember this, success alone does not bring happiness. Nor does failure have to bring unhappiness. Keep it in mind when you listen to today's story."

A chant started somewhere in the back: "We-want-a-story! We-want-a-story!"

"Riiiight," said Nariman. "Now, everyone remembers Vera and Dolly, daughters of Najamai from C Block." There were whistles and hoots; Viraf nudged Kersi with his elbow, who was smiling wistfully. Nariman held up his hand: "Now now, boys, behave yourselves. Those two girls went abroad for studies many years ago, and never came back. They settled there happily.

"And like them, a fellow called Sarosh also went abroad, to Toronto, but did not find happiness there. This story is about him.

You probably don't know him, he does not live in Firozsha Baag, though he is related to someone who does."

"Who? Who?"

"Curiosity killed the cat," said Nariman, running a finger over each branch of his moustache, "and what's important is the tale. So let us continue. This Sarosh began calling himself Sid after living in Toronto for a few months, but in our story he will be Sarosh and nothing but Sarosh, for that is his proper Parsi name. Besides, that was his own stipulation when he entrusted me with the sad but instructive chronicle of his recent life." Nariman polished his glasses with his handkerchief, put them on again, and began.

"At the point where our story commences, Sarosh had been living in Toronto for ten years. We find him depressed and miserable, perched on top of the toilet, crouching on his haunches, feet planted firmly for balance upon the white plastic oval of the toilet seat.

"Daily for a decade had Sarosh suffered this position. Morning after morning, he had no choice but to climb up and simulate the squat of our Indian latrines. If he sat down, no amount of exertion could produce success.

"At first, this inability was no more than mildly incommodious. As time went by, however, the frustrated attempts caused him grave anxiety. And when the failure stretched unbroken over ten years, it began to torment and haunt all his waking hours."

Some of the boys struggled hard to keep straight faces. They suspected that Nariman was not telling just a funny story, because if he intended them to laugh there was always some unmistakable way to let them know. Only the thought of displeasing Nariman and prematurely terminating the story kept their paroxysms of mirth from bursting forth unchecked.

Nariman continued: "You see, ten years was the time Sarosh had set himself to achieve complete adaptation to the new country. But how could he claim adaptation with any honesty if the acceptable catharsis continually failed to favour him? Obtaining his new citizenship had not helped either. He remained dependent on the old way, and this unalterable fact, strengthened afresh every morning of his life in the new country, suffocated him.

"The ten-year time limit was more an accident than anything else. But it hung over him with the awesome presence and sharpness of a guillotine. Careless words, boys, careless words in a moment of lightheartedness, as is so often the case with us all, had led to it.

"Ten years before, Sarosh had returned triumphantly to Bombay after fulfilling the immigration requirements of the Canadian High Commission in New Delhi. News of his imminent departure spread amongst relatives and friends. A farewell party was organized. In fact, it was given by his relatives in Firozsha Baag. Most of you will be too young to remember it, but it was a very loud party, went on till late in the night. Very lengthy and heated arguments took place, which is not the thing to do at a party. It started like this: Sarosh was told by some what a smart decision he had made, that his whole life would change for the better; others said he was making a mistake, emigration was all wrong, but if he wanted to be unhappy that was his business, they wished him well.

"By and by, after substantial amounts of Scotch and soda and rum and Coke had disappeared, a fierce debate started between the two groups. To this day Sarosh does not know what made him raise his glass and announce: 'My dear family, my dear friends, if I do not become completely Canadian in exactly ten years from the time I land there, then I will come back. I promise. So please, no more arguments. Enjoy the party.' His words were greeted with cheers and shouts of hear! hear! They told him never to fear embarrassment; there was no shame if he decided to return to the country of his birth.

"But shortly, his poor worried mother pulled him aside. She led him to the back room and withdrew her worn and aged prayer book from her purse, saying, 'I want you to place your hand upon the *Avesta* and swear that you will keep that promise.'

"He told her not to be silly, that it was just a joke. But she insisted: '*Kassum khà* – on the *Avesta*. One last thing for your mother. Who knows when you will see me again?' and her voice grew tremulous as it always did when she turned deeply emotional. Sarosh complied, and the prayer book was returned to her purse.

"His mother continued: 'It is better to live in want among your family and your friends, who love you and care for you, than to be unhappy surrounded by vacuum cleaners and dishwashers and big shiny motor cars.' She hugged him. Then they joined the celebration in progress.

"And Sarosh's careless words spoken at the party gradually forged themselves into a commitment as much to himself as to his mother and the others. It stayed with him all his years in the new land, reminding him every morning of what must happen at the end of the tenth, as it reminded him now while he descended from his perch."

Jehangir wished the titters and chortles around him would settle down, he found them annoying. When Nariman structured his sentences so carefully and chose his words with extreme care as he was doing now, Jehangir found it most pleasurable to listen. Sometimes, he remembered certain words Nariman had used, or combinations of words, and repeated them to himself, enjoying again the beauty of their sounds when he went for his walks to the Hanging Gardens or was sitting alone on the stone steps of C Block. Mumbling to himself did nothing to mitigate the isolation which the other boys in the Baag had dropped around him like a heavy cloak, but he had grown used to all that by now.

Nariman continued: "In his own apartment Sarosh squatted barefoot. Elsewhere, if he had to go with his shoes on, he would carefully cover the seat with toilet paper before climbing up. He learnt to do this after the first time, when his shoes had left telltale footprints on the seat. He had had to clean it with a wet paper towel. Luckily, no one had seen him.

"But there was not much he could keep secret about his ways. The world of washrooms is private and at the same time very public. The absence of feet below the stall door, the smell of faeces, the rustle of paper, glimpses caught through the narrow crack between stall door and jamb – all these added up to only one thing: a foreign presence in the stall, not doing things in the conventional way. And if the one outside could receive the fetor of Sarosh's business wafting through the door, poor unhappy Sarosh too could detect something malodorous in the air: the presence of xenophobia and hostility."

What a feast, thought Jehangir, what a feast of words! This would be the finest story Nariman had ever told, he just knew it.

"But Sarosh did not give up trying. Each morning he seated himself to push and grunt, grunt and push, squirming and writhing unavailingly on the white plastic oval. Exhausted, he then hopped up, expert at balancing now, and completed the movement quite effortlessly.

"The long morning hours in the washroom created new difficulties. He was late going to work on several occasions, and one such day, the supervisor called him in: 'Here's your time-sheet for this month. You've been late eleven times. What's the problem?' "

Here, Nariman stopped because his neighbour Rustomji's door creaked open. Rustomji peered out, scowling, and muttered: "*Saala* loafers, sitting all evening outside people's houses, making a nuisance, and being encouraged by grownups at that."

He stood there a moment longer, fingering the greying chest hair that was easily accessible through his *sudra*, then went inside. The boys immediately took up a soft and low chant: "Rustomji-the-curmudgeon! Rustomji-the-curmudgeon!"

Nariman held up his hand disapprovingly. But secretly, he was pleased that the name was still popular, the name he had given Rustomji when the latter had refused to pay his share for painting the building. "Quiet, quiet!" said he. "Do you want me to continue or not?"

"Yes, yes!" The chanting died away, and Nariman resumed the story.

"So Sarosh was told by his supervisor that he was coming late to work too often. What could poor Sarosh say?"

"What, Nariman Uncle?" rose the refrain.

"Nothing, of course. The supervisor, noting his silence, continued: 'If it keeps up, the consequences could be serious as far as your career is concerned.'

"Sarosh decided to speak. He said embarrassedly, 'It's a different kind of problem. I ... I don't know how to explain ... it's an immigration-related problem.'

"Now this supervisor must have had experience with other immigrants, because right away he told Sarosh, 'No problem. Just contact your Immigrant Aid Society. They should be able to help you. Every ethnic group has one: Vietnamese, Chinese – I'm certain that one exists for Indians. If you need time off to go there, no problem. That can be arranged, no problem. As long as you do something about your lateness, there's no problem.' That's the way they talk over there, nothing is ever a problem.

"So Sarosh thanked him and went to his desk. For the umpteenth time he bitterly rued his oversight. Could fate have plotted it, concealing the western toilet behind that shroud of anxieties which had appeared out of nowhere to beset him just before he left India? After all, he had readied himself meticulously for the new life. Even for the great, merciless Canadian cold he had heard so much about. How could he have overlooked preparation for the western toilet with its matutinal demands unless fate had conspired? In Bombay, you know that offices of foreign businesses offer both options in their bathrooms. So do all hotels with three stars or more. By practising in familiar surroundings, Sarosh was convinced he could have mastered a seated evacuation before departure.

"But perhaps there was something in what the supervisor said. Sarosh found a telephone number for the Indian Immigrant Aid Society and made an appointment. That afternoon, he met Mrs Maha-Lepate at the Society's office."

Kersi and Viraf looked at each other and smiled. Nariman Uncle had a nerve, there was more *lepate* in his own stories than anywhere else.

"Mrs Maha-Lepate was very understanding, and made Sarosh feel at ease despite the very personal nature of his problem. She said, 'Yes, we get many referrals. There was a man here last month who couldn't eat Wonder Bread – it made him throw up.'

"By the way, boys, Wonder Bread is a Canadian bread which all happy families eat to be happy in the same way; the unhappy families are unhappy in their own fashion by eating other brands." Jehangir was the only one who understood, and murmured: "Tolstoy," at Nariman's little joke. Nariman noticed it, pleased. He continued.

"Mrs Maha-Lepate told Sarosh about that case: 'Our immigrant specialist, Dr No-Ilaaz, recommended that the patient eat cake instead. He explained that Wonder Bread caused vomiting because the digestive system was used to Indian bread only, made with Indian flour in the village he came from. However, since his system was unfamiliar with cake, Canadian or otherwise, it did not react but was digested as a newfound food. In this way he got used to Canadian flour first in cake form. Just yesterday we received a report from Dr No-Ilaaz. The patient successfully ate his first slice of whole-wheat Wonder Bread with no ill effects. The ultimate goal is pure white Wonder Bread.'

"Like a polite Parsi boy, Sarosh said, 'That's very interesting.' The garrulous Mrs Maha-Lepate was about to continue, and he tried to interject: 'But I – ' but Mrs Maha-Lepate was too quick for him: 'Oh, there are so many interesting cases I could tell you about. Like the woman from Sri Lanka – referred to us because they don't have their own Society – who could not drink the water here. Dr No-Ilaaz said it was due to the different mineral content. So he started her on Coca-Cola and then began diluting it with water, bit by bit. Six weeks later she took her first sip of unadulterated Canadian water and managed to keep it down.'

"Sarosh could not halt Mrs Maha-Lepate as she launched from one case history into another: 'Right now, Dr No-Ilaaz is working on a very unusual case. Involves a whole Pakistani family. Ever since immigrating to Canada, none of them can swallow. They choke on their own saliva, and have to spit constantly. But we are confident that Dr No-Ilaaz will find a remedy. He has never been stumped by any immigrant problem. Besides, we have an information network with other third-world Immigrant Aid Societies. We all seem to share a history of similar maladies, and regularly compare notes. Some of us thought these problems were linked to retention of original citizenship. But this was a false lead.'

"Sarosh, out of his own experience, vigorously nodded agreement. By now he was truly fascinated by Mrs Maha-Lepate's wealth of information. Reluctantly, he interrupted: 'But will Dr No-Ilaaz be able to solve my problem?'

" 'I have every confidence that he will,' replied Mrs Maha-Lepate in great earnest. 'And if he has no remedy for you right away, he will be delighted to start working on one. He loves to take up new projects.' "

Nariman halted to blow his nose, and a clear shrill voice travelled the night air of the Firozsha Baag compound from C Block to where the boys had collected around Nariman in A Block: "Jehangoo! O Jehangoo! Eight o'clock! Upstairs now!"

Jehangir stared at his feet in embarrassment. Nariman looked at his watch and said, "Yes, it's eight." But Jehangir did not move, so he continued.

"Mrs Maha-Lepate was able to arrange an appointment while Sarosh waited, and he went directly to the doctor's office. What he had heard so far sounded quite promising. Then he cautioned himself not to get overly optimistic, that was the worst mistake he could make. But along the way to the doctor's, he could not help thinking what a lovely city Toronto was. It was the same way he had felt when he first saw it ten years ago, before all the joy had dissolved in the acid of his anxieties."

Once again that shrill voice travelled through the clear night: "*Arré* Jehangoo! *Muà*, do I have to come down and drag you upstairs!"

Jehangir's mortification was now complete. Nariman made it easy for him, though: "The first part of the story is over. Second part continues tomorrow. Same time, same place." The boys were surprised, Nariman did not make such commitments. But never before had he told such a long story. They began drifting back to their homes.

As Jehangir strode hurriedly to C Block, falsettos and piercing shrieks followed him in the darkness: "*Arré* Jehangoo! *Muà* Jehangoo! Bulsara Bookworm! Eight o'clock Jehangoo!" Shaking his head, Nariman went indoors to Hirabai.

Next evening, the story punctually resumed when Nariman took his place on the topmost step of A Block: "You remember that we left Sarosh on his way to see the Immigrant Aid Society's doctor. Well, Dr No-Ilaaz listened patiently to Sarosh's concerns, then said, 'As a matter of fact, there is a remedy which is so new even the IAS does not know about it. Not even that Mrs Maha-Lepate who knows it all,' he added drolly, twirling his stethoscope like a stunted lasso. He slipped it on around his neck before continuing: 'It involves a minor operation which was developed with financial assistance from the Multicultural Department. A small device, *Crappus Non Interruptus*, or CNI as we call it, is implanted in the bowel. The device is controlled by an external handheld transmitter similar to the ones used for automatic garage door-openers – you may have seen them in hardware stores.' "

Nariman noticed that most of the boys wore puzzled looks and realized he had to make some things clearer. "The Multicultural Department is a Canadian invention. It is supposed to ensure that ethnic cultures are able to flourish, so that Canadian society will consist of a mosaic of cultures – that's their favourite word, mosaic – instead of one uniform mix, like the American melting pot. If you ask me, mosaic and melting pot are both nonsense, and ethnic is a polite way of saying bloody foreigner. But anyway, you understand Multicultural Department? Good. So Sarosh nodded, and Dr No-Ilaaz went on: 'You can encode the handheld transmitter with a personal ten-digit code. Then all you do is position yourself on the toilet seat and activate your transmitter. Just like a garage door, your bowel will open without pushing or grunting.' "

There was some snickering in the audience, and Nariman raised his eyebrows, whereupon they covered up their mouths with their hands. "The doctor asked Sarosh if he had any questions. Sarosh thought for a moment, then asked if it required any maintenance.

"Dr No-Ilaaz replied: 'CNI is semi-permanent and operates on solar energy. Which means you would have to make it a point to get some sun periodically, or it would cease and lead to constipation. However, you don't have to strip for a tan. Exposing ten percent of your skin surface once a week during summer will let the device store sufficient energy for year-round operation.'

"Sarosh's next question was: 'Is there any hope that someday the bowels can work on their own, without operating the device?' at which Dr No-Ilaaz grimly shook his head: 'I'm afraid not. You must think very, very carefully before making a decision. Once CNI is implanted, you can never pass a motion in the natural way – neither sitting nor squatting.'

"He stopped to allow Sarosh time to think it over, then continued: 'And you must understand what that means. You will never be able to live a normal life again. You will be permanently different from your family and friends because of this basic internal modification. In fact, in this country or that, it will set you apart from your fellow countrymen. So you must consider the whole thing most carefully.'

"Dr No-Ilaaz paused, toyed with his stethoscope, shuffled some papers on his desk, then resumed: 'There are other dangers you should know about. Just as a garage door can be accidentally opened by a neighbour's transmitter on the same frequency, CNI can also be activated by someone with similar apparatus.' To ease the tension he attempted a quick laugh and said, 'Very embarrassing, eh, if it happened at the wrong place and time. Mind you, the risk is not so great at present, because the chances of finding yourself within a fifty-foot radius of another transmitter on the same frequency are infinitesimal. But what about the future? What if CNI becomes very popular? Sufficient permutations may not be available for trans-mitter frequencies and you could be sharing the code with others. Then the risk of accidents becomes greater.' "

Something landed with a loud thud in the yard behind A Block, making Nariman startle. Immediately, a yowling and screeching and caterwauling went up from the stray cats there, and the *kuchrawalli's* dog started barking. Some of the boys went around the side of A Block to peer over the fence into the backyard. But the commotion soon died down of its own accord. The boys returned and, once again, Nariman's voice was the only sound to be heard.

"By now, Sarosh was on the verge of deciding against the oper-ation. Dr No-Ilaaz observed this and was pleased. He took pride in being able to dissuade his patients from following the very remedies which he first so painstakingly described. True to his name, Dr No-Ilaaz believed no remedy is the best remedy, rather than prescribing this-mycin and that-mycin for every little ailment. So he continued: 'And what about our sons and daughters? And the quality of their lives? We still don't know the long-term effects of CNI. Some researchers speculate that it could generate a genetic defi-ciency, that the offspring of a CNI parent would also require CNI. On the other hand, they could be perfectly healthy toilet seat-users, without any congenital defects. We just don't know at this stage.'

"Sarosh rose from his chair: 'Thank you very much for your time, Dr No-Ilaaz. But I don't think I want to take such a drastic step. As you suggest, I will think it over very carefully.'

" 'Good, good,' said Dr No-Ilaaz, 'I was hoping you would say that. There is one more thing. The operation is extremely expensive, and is not covered by the province's Health Insurance Plan. Many immig-rant groups are lobbying to obtain coverage for special immigration-related health problems. If they succeed, then good for you.'

"Sarosh left Dr No-Ilaaz's office with his mind made up. Time was running out. There had been a time when it was perfectly natural to squat. Now it seemed a grotesquely aberrant thing to do. Wherever he went he was reminded of the ignominy of his way. If he could not be westernized in all respects, he was nothing but a failure in this land – a failure not just in the washrooms of the nation but everywhere. He knew what he must do if he was to be true to himself and to the decade-old commitment. So what do you think Sarosh did next?"

"What, Nariman Uncle?"

"He went to the travel agent specializing in tickets to India. He bought a fully refundable ticket to Bombay for the day when he would complete exactly ten immigrant years – if he succeeded even once before that day dawned, he would cancel the booking.

"The travel agent asked sympathetically, 'Trouble at home?' His name was Mr Rawaana, and he was from Bombay too.

" 'No,' said Sarosh, 'trouble in Toronto.'

" 'That's a shame,' said Mr Rawaana. 'I don't want to poke my nose into your business, but in my line of work I meet so many people who are going back to their homeland because of problems here. Sometimes I forget I'm a travel agent, that my interest is to convince them to travel. Instead, I tell them: don't give up, God is great, stay and try again. It's bad for my profits but gives me a different, a spiritual kind of satisfaction when I succeed. And I succeed about half the time. Which means,' he added with a wry laugh, 'I could double my profits if I minded my own business.'

"After the lengthy sessions with Mrs Maha-Lepate and Dr No-Ilaaz, Sarosh felt he had listened to enough advice and kind words. Much as he disliked doing it, he had to hurt Mr Rawaana's feelings and leave his predicament undiscussed: 'I'm sorry, but I'm in a hurry. Will you be able to look after the booking?'

" 'Well, okay,' said Mr Rawaana, a trifle crestfallen; he did not relish the travel business as much as he did counselling immigrants. 'Hope you solve your problem. I will be happy to refund your fare, believe me.'

"Sarosh hurried home. With only four weeks to departure, every spare minute, every possible method had to be concentrated on a final attempt at adaptation.

"He tried laxatives, crunching down the tablets with a prayer that these would assist the sitting position. Changing brands did not help, and neither did various types of suppositories. He spent long stretches on the toilet seat each morning. The supervisor continued to reprimand him for tardiness. To make matters worse, Sarosh left his desk every time he felt the slightest urge, hoping: maybe this time.

"The working hours expended in the washroom were noted with unflagging vigilance by the supervisor. More counselling sessions followed. Sarosh refused to extinguish his last hope, and the supervisor punctiliously recorded 'No Improvement' in his daily log. Finally, Sarosh was fired. It would soon have been time to resign in any case, and he could not care less.

"Now whole days went by seated on the toilet, and he stubbornly refused to relieve himself the other way. The doorbell would ring only to be ignored. The telephone went unanswered. Sometimes, he would awake suddenly in the dark hours before dawn and rush to the washroom like a madman."

Without warning, Rustomji flung open his door and stormed: "Ridiculous nonsense this is becoming! Two days in a row, whole Firozsha Baag gathers here! This is not Chaupatty beach, this is not a squatters' colony, this is a building, people want to live here in peace and quiet!" Then just as suddenly, he stamped inside and slammed the door. Right on cue, Nariman continued, before the boys could say anything.

"Time for meals was the only time Sarosh allowed himself off the seat. Even in his desperation he remembered that if he did not eat well, he was doomed – the downward pressure on his gut was essential if there was to be any chance of success.

"But the ineluctable day of departure dawned, with grey skies and the scent of rain, while success remained out of sight. At the airport Sarosh checked in and went to the dreary lounge. Out of sheer habit he started towards the washroom. Then he realized the hopelessness of it and returned to the cold, clammy plastic of the lounge seats. Airport seats are the same almost anywhere in the world.

"The boarding announcement was made, and Sarosh was the first to step onto the plane. The skies were darker now. Out of the window he saw a flash of lightning fork through the clouds. For some reason, everything he'd learned years ago in St Xavier's about sheet light-ning and forked lightning went through his mind. He wished it would change to sheet, there was something sinister and unpropi-tious about forked lightning."

Kersi, absorbedly listening, began cracking his knuckles quite unconsciously. His childhood habit still persisted. Jehangir frowned at the disturbance, and Viraf nudged Kersi to stop it.

"Sarosh fastened his seat-belt and attempted to turn his thoughts towards the long journey home: to the questions he would be expected to answer, the sympathy and criticism that would be thrust upon him. But what remained uppermost in his mind was the present moment – him in the plane, dark skies lowering, lightning on the horizon – irrevocably spelling out: defeat.

"But wait. Something else was happening now. A tiny rumble. Inside him. Or was it his imagination? Was it really thunder outside which, in his present disoriented state, he was internalizing? No, there it was again. He had to go.

"He reached the washroom, and almost immediately the sign flashed to 'Please return to seat and fasten seat-belts.' Sarosh debated whether to squat and finish the business quickly, abandoning the perfunctory seated attempt. But the plane started to move and that decided him; it would be difficult now to balance while squatting.

"He pushed. The plane continued to move. He pushed again, trembling with the effort. The seat-belt sign flashed quicker and brighter now. The plane moved faster and faster. And Sarosh pushed hard, harder than he had ever pushed before, harder than in all his ten years of trying in the new land. And the memories of Bombay, the immigration interview in New Delhi, the farewell party, his mother's tattered prayer book, all these, of their own accord, emerged from beyond the region of the ten years to push with him and give him newfound strength."

Nariman paused and cleared his throat. Dusk was falling, and the frequency of B.E.S.T. buses plying the main road outside Firozsha Baag had dropped. Bats began to fly madly from one end of the compound to the other, silent shadows engaged in endless laps over the buildings.

"With a thunderous clap the rain started to fall. Sarosh felt a splash under him. Could it really be? He glanced down to make certain. Yes, it was. He had succeeded!

"But was it already too late? The plane waited at its assigned position on the runway, jet engines at full thrust. Rain was falling in torrents and takeoff could be delayed. Perhaps even now they would allow him to cancel his flight, to disembark. He lurched out of the constricting cubicle.

"A stewardess hurried towards him: 'Excuse me, sir, but you must return to your seat immediately and fasten your belt.'

" 'You don't understand!' Sarosh shouted excitedly. 'I must get off the plane! Everything is all right, I don't have to go any more . . . '

" 'That's impossible, sir!' said the stewardess, aghast. 'No one can leave now. Takeoff procedures are in progress!' The wild look in his sleepless eyes, and the dark rings around them scared her. She beckoned for help.

"Sarosh continued to argue, and a steward and the chief stewardess hurried over: 'What seems to be the problem, sir? You *must* resume your seat. We are authorized, if necessary, to forcibly restrain you, sir.'

"The plane began to move again, and suddenly Sarosh felt all the urgency leaving him. His feverish mind, the product of nightmarish days and torturous nights, was filled again with the calm which had fled a decade ago, and he spoke softly now: 'That . . . that will not be necessary . . . it's okay, I understand.' He readily returned to his seat.

"As the aircraft sped down the runway, Sarosh's first reaction was one of joy. The process of adaptation was complete. But later, he could not help wondering if success came before or after the ten-year limit had expired. And since he had already passed through the customs and security check, was he really an immigrant in every sense of the word at the moment of achievement?

"But such questions were merely academic. Or were they? He could not decide. If he returned, what would it be like? Ten years ago, the immigration officer who had stamped his passport had said, 'Welcome to Canada.' It was one of Sarosh's dearest memories, and thinking of it, he fell asleep.

"The plane was flying above the rainclouds. Sunshine streamed into the cabin. A few raindrops were still clinging miraculously to the windows, reminders of what was happening below. They sparkled as the sunlight caught them."

Some of the boys made as if to leave, thinking the story was finally over. Clearly, they had not found this one as interesting as the others Nariman had told. What dolts, thought Jehangir, they cannot recognize a masterpiece when they hear one. Nariman motioned with his hand for silence.

"But our story does not end there. There was a welcome-home party for Sarosh a few days after he arrived in Bombay. It was not in Firozsha Baag this time because his relatives in the Baag had a serious sickness in the house. But I was invited to it anyway. Sarosh's family and friends were considerate enough to wait till the jet lag had worked its way out of his system. They wanted him to really enjoy this one.

"Drinks began to flow freely again in his honour: Scotch and soda, rum and Coke, brandy. Sarosh noticed that during his absence all the brand names had changed – the labels were different and unfamiliar. Even for the mixes. Instead of Coke there was Thums-Up, and he remembered reading in the papers about Coca-Cola being kicked out by the Indian Government for refusing to reveal their secret formula.

"People slapped him on the back and shook his hand vigorously, over and over, right through the evening. They said: 'Telling the truth, you made the right decision, look how happy your mother is to live to see this day;' or they asked: 'Well, bossy, what changed your mind?' Sarosh smiled and nodded his way through it all, passing around Canadian currency at the insistence of some of the curious ones who, egged on by his mother, also pestered him to display his Canadian passport and citizenship card. She had been badgering him since his arrival to tell her the real reason: '*Saachoo kahé*, what brought you back?' and was hoping that tonight, among his friends, he might raise his glass and reveal something. But she remained disappointed.

"Weeks went by and Sarosh found himself desperately searching for his old place in the pattern of life he had vacated ten years ago. Friends who had organized the welcome-home party gradually disappeared. He went walking in the evenings along Marine Drive, by the sea-wall, where the old crowd used to congregate. But the people who sat on the parapet while waves crashed behind their backs were strangers. The tetrapods were still there, staunchly protecting the reclaimed land from the fury of the sea. He had watched as a kid when cranes had lowered these cement and concrete hulks of respectable grey into the water. They were grimy black now, and from their angularities rose the distinct stench of human excrement. The old pattern was never found by Sarosh; he searched in vain. Patterns of life are selfish and unforgiving.

"Then one day, as I was driving past Marine Drive, I saw someone sitting alone. He looked familiar, so I stopped. For a moment I did not recognize Sarosh, so forlorn and woebegone was his countenance. I parked the apple of my eye and went to him, saying, 'Hullo, Sid, what are you doing here on your lonesome?' And he said, 'No no! No more Sid, please, that name reminds me of all my troubles.' Then, on the parapet at Marine Drive, he told me his unhappy and wretched tale, with the waves battering away at the tetrapods, and around us the hawkers screaming about coconut-water and sugar-cane juice and *paan*.

"When he finished, he said that he had related to me the whole sad saga because he knew how I told stories to boys in the Baag, and he wanted me to tell this one, especially to those who were planning to go abroad. 'Tell them,' said Sarosh, 'that the world can be a bewildering place, and dreams and ambitions are often paths to the most pernicious of traps.' As he spoke, I could see that Sarosh was somewhere far away, perhaps in New Delhi at his immigration interview, seeing himself as he was then, with what he thought was a life of hope and promise stretching endlessly before him. Poor Sarosh. Then he was back beside me on the parapet.

" 'I pray you, in your stories,' said Sarosh, his old sense of humour returning as he deepened his voice for his favourite *Othello* lines" – and here, Nariman produced a basso profundo of his own – " 'When you shall these unlucky deeds relate, speak of me as I am; nothing extenuate, nor set down aught in malice: tell them that in Toronto once there lived a Parsi boy as best as he could. Set you down this; and say, besides, that for some it was good and for some it was bad, but for me life in the land of milk and honey was just a pain in the posterior.' "

And now, Nariman allowed his low-pitched rumbles to turn into chuckles. The boys broke into cheers and loud applause and cries of "Encore!" and "More!" Finally, Nariman had to silence them by pointing warningly at Rustomji-the-curmudgeon's door.

While Kersi and Viraf were joking and wondering what to make of it all, Jehangir edged forward and told Nariman this was the best story he had ever told. Nariman patted his shoulder and smiled. Jehangir left, wondering if Nariman would have been as popular if Dr Mody was still alive. Probably, since the two were liked for different reasons: Dr Mody used to be constantly jovial, whereas Nariman had his periodic story-telling urges.

Now the group of boys who had really enjoyed the Savukshaw story during the previous week spoke up. Capitalizing on Nariman's extraordinarily good mood, they began clamouring for more Savukshaw: "Nariman Uncle, tell the one about Savukshaw the hunter, the one you had started that day."

"What hunter? I don't know which one you mean." He refused to be reminded of it, and got up to leave. But there was loud protest, and the boys started chanting, "We-want-Savukshaw! We-want-Savukshaw!"

Nariman looked fearfully towards Rustomji's door and held up his hands placatingly: "All right, all right! Next time it will be Savukshaw again. Savukshaw the artist. The story of the Parsi Picasso."

One out of Many

V. S. Naipaul

Introduction

Vidiadhar Surajprasad Naipaul was born in Chaguanas, Trinidad, in 1932. His mother, Droapatie Capildeo, came from a prominent family of orthodox Trinidadian Hindus, and his father, Seepersad, was a journalist who also wrote some short stories about the Asian Indian community in Trinidad, *The Adventures of Gurudeva and Other Stories*. In an essay entitled 'Prologue to an Autobiography' V. S. Naipaul wrote that as a child in Trinidad he had little sense of the kind of personal history that had brought his grandparents' generation to the West Indies: 'The India where Gandhi and Nehru and the others operated was historical and real. The India from which we had come was impossibly remote, almost as legendary as the land of the *Ramayana*, our Hindu epic.'[1] Out of this blankness there would later come acute scrutiny not just of the past and histories of colonization, but also of the de-colonized world of the second half of the twentieth century.

When he was eighteen, Naipaul moved to England on a university scholarship, with the ambition of becoming a writer. 'I was travelling from the periphery, the margin,' he later wrote, 'to what to me was the centre. . . . I always recognized, in England in the 1950s, that as someone with a writing vocation there was nowhere else for me to go.'[2] After completing his course at Oxford, Naipaul worked part-time for the BBC on a World Service programme called *Caribbean Voices*. While he was there he began writing the short stories that would eventually be published as *Miguel Street* (1959), winning the Somerset Maugham award. Before that he published two comic novels set in Trinidad, but it was his fourth book, *A House for Mr Biswas* (1961), an imaginative reconstruction of his father's life in Trinidad, that established his reputation as a major international writer.

After the success of *Mr Biswas*, Naipaul began travelling, going back first to the Caribbean, then to India and then many other parts of the world, staying for extended periods and writing about the places he travelled to. His work has often been controversial, and he has attracted criticism for his portrayal ('unsympathetic' or 'unflinching', depending on one's point of view) of some Third World countries. But he is in many quarters a highly respected figure; he accepted a knighthood in 1990 and was awarded the Nobel Prize for Literature in 2001. He continues to be based in England.

Naipaul's published work divides almost equally into fiction (besides the linked short stories of *Miguel Street*, there is more short fiction in *A Flag on the Island* (1967), as well as about a dozen novels) and non-fiction (especially travel-writing). Some of his later works, such as *The Enigma of Arrival* (1987) and *A Way in the World* (1994), straddle the borderline between fiction and non-fiction, though the first movements in this direction are evident in his Booker Prize-winning *In a Free State* (1971). The title novella, set in Africa, is preceded by two shorter stories, 'One out of Many' and 'Tell Me Who to Kill', but the whole sequence is set within a documentary-style framework, with a Prologue and Epilogue '*from a Journal*' – narrated by Naipaul-the-traveller. All five sections of the book are about characters who are in some sense displaced, and although the tonal range is wide, there are connecting threads such as the meanings, and contradictions, of being 'free', and a sense of violence which is always threatening or erupting into the action.

In 'One out of Many', narrated by a Bombay servant, Santosh, who accompanies his Indian employer to the United States, the humour that distinguished Naipaul's earlier fiction is still apparent, although it is overlaid with a sense of tragedy. Searching for connections in Washington, DC, Santosh at first mistakes a group of hippies for fellow-Hindus, and is troubled by the presence of African-Americans (he refers to them by the Urdu word 'hubshi', meaning Ethiopian) who, according to his cultural norms, are unclean. The burning of the city that Santosh and his employer watch on TV occurred in 1968, when race riots followed the assassination of the black civil rights leader Martin Luther King, Jr. The title of the story alludes to the traditional motto of the USA, *E Pluribus Unum* ('from many, one').

Notes

1. V. S. Naipaul, *Finding the Centre: Two Narratives* (Harmondsworth: Penguin, 1984), pp. 51–2.
2. V. S. Naipaul, Our Universal Civilization [1992], in *The Writer and the World* (London: Picador, 2002).

One out of Many

I am now an American citizen and I live in Washington, capital of the world. Many people, both here and in India, will feel that I have done well. But.

I was so happy in Bombay. I was respected, I had a certain position. I worked for an important man. The highest in the land came to our bachelor chambers and enjoyed my food and showered compliments on me. I also had my friends. We met in the evenings on the pavement below the gallery of our chambers. Some of us, like the tailor's bearer and myself, were domestics who lived in the street. The others were people who came to that bit of pavement to sleep. Respectable people; we didn't encourage riff-raff.

In the evenings it was cool. There were few passers-by and, apart from an occasional double-decker bus or taxi, little traffic. The pavement was swept and sprinkled, bedding brought out from daytime hiding-places, little oil-lamps lit. While the folk upstairs chattered and laughed, on the pavement we read newspapers, played cards, told stories and smoked. The clay pipe passed from friend to friend; we became drowsy. Except of course during the monsoon, I preferred to sleep on the pavement with my friends, although in our chambers a whole cupboard below the staircase was reserved for my personal use.

It was good after a healthy night in the open to rise before the sun and before the sweepers came. Sometimes I saw the street lights go off. Bedding was rolled up; no one spoke much; and soon my friends were hurrying in silent competition to secluded lanes and alleys and open lots to relieve themselves. I was spared this competition; in our chambers I had facilities.

Afterwards for half an hour or so I was free simply to stroll. I liked walking beside the Arabian Sea, waiting for the sun to come up. Then the city and the ocean gleamed like gold. Alas for those morning walks, that sudden ocean dazzle, the moist salt breeze on my face, the flap of my shirt, that first cup of hot sweet tea from a stall, the taste of the first leaf-cigarette.

Observe the workings of fate. The respect and security I enjoyed were due to the importance of my employer. It was this very importance which now all at once destroyed the pattern of my life.

My employer was seconded by his firm to Government service and was posted to Washington. I was happy for his sake but frightened for mine. He was to be away for some years and there was nobody in Bombay he could second me to. Soon, therefore, I was to be out of a job and out of the chambers. For many years I had considered my life as settled. I had served my apprenticeship, known my hard times. I didn't feel I could start again. I despaired. Was there a job for me in Bombay? I saw myself having to return to my village in the hills, to my wife and children there, not just for a holiday but for good. I saw myself again becoming a porter during the tourist season, racing after the buses as they arrived at the station and shouting with forty or fifty others for luggage. Indian luggage, not this lightweight American stuff! Heavy metal trunks!

I could have cried. It was no longer the sort of life for which I was fitted. I had grown soft in Bombay and I was no longer young. I had acquired possessions, I was used to the privacy of my cupboard. I had become a city man, used to certain comforts.

My employer said, 'Washington is not Bombay! Santosh. Washington is expensive. Even if I was able to raise your fare, you wouldn't be able to live over there in anything like your present style.'

But to be barefoot in the hills, after Bombay! The shock, the disgrace! I couldn't face my friends. I stopped sleeping on the pavement and spent as much of my free time as possible in my cupboard among my possessions, as among things which were soon to be taken from me.

My employer said, 'Santosh, my heart bleeds for you.'

I said, 'Sahib, if I look a little concerned it is only because I worry about you. You have always been fussy, and I don't see how you will manage in Washington.'

'It won't be easy. But it's the principle. Does the representative of a poor country like ours travel about with his cook? Will that create a good impression?'

'You will always do what is right, sahib.'

He went silent.

After some days he said, 'There's not only the expense, Santosh. There's the question of foreign exchange. Our rupee isn't what it was.'

'I understand, sahib. Duty is duty.'

A fortnight later, when I had almost given up hope, he said, 'Santosh, I have consulted Government. You will accompany me. Government has sanctioned, will arrange accommodation. But not expenses. You will get your passport and your P form. But I want you to think, Santosh. Washington is not Bombay.'

I went down to the pavement that night with my bedding.

I said, blowing down my shirt, 'Bombay gets hotter and hotter.'

'Do you know what you are doing?' the tailor's bearer said. 'Will the Americans smoke with you? Will they sit and talk with you in the evenings? Will they hold you by the hand and walk with you beside the ocean?'

It pleased me that he was jealous. My last days in Bombay were very happy.

* * *

I packed my employer's two suitcases and bundled up my own belongings in lengths of old cotton. At the airport they made a fuss about my bundles. They said they couldn't accept them as luggage for the hold because they didn't like the responsibility. So when the time came I had to climb up to the aircraft with all my bundles. The girl at the top, who was smiling at everybody else, stopped smiling when she saw me. She made me go right to the back of the plane, far from my employer. Most of the seats there were empty, though, and I was able to spread my bundles around and, well, it was comfortable.

It was bright and hot outside, cool inside. The plane started, rose up in the air, and Bombay and the ocean tilted this way and that. It was very nice. When we settled down I looked around for people like myself, but I could see no one among the Indians or the foreigners who looked like a domestic. Worse, they were all dressed as though they were going to a wedding and, brother, I soon saw it wasn't they who were conspicuous. I was in my ordinary Bombay clothes, the loose long-tailed shirt, the wide-waisted pants held up with a piece of string. Perfectly respectable domestic's wear, neither dirty nor clean, and in Bombay no one would have looked. But now on the plane I felt heads turning whenever I stood up.

I was anxious. I slipped off my shoes, tight even without the laces, and drew my feet up. That made me feel better. I made myself a little betel-nut mixture and that made me feel better still. Half the pleasure of betel, though, is the spitting; and it was only when I had worked up a good mouthful that I saw I had a problem. The airline girl saw too. That girl didn't like me at all. She spoke roughly to me. My mouth was full, my cheeks were bursting, and I couldn't say anything. I could only look at her. She went and called a man in uniform and he came and stood over me. I put my shoes back on and swallowed the betel juice. It made me feel quite ill.

The girl and the man, the two of them, pushed a little trolley of drinks down the aisle. The girl didn't look at me but the man said, 'You want a drink, chum?' He wasn't a bad fellow. I pointed at random to a bottle. It was a kind of soda drink, nice and sharp at first but then not so nice. I was worrying about it when the girl said, 'Five shillings sterling or sixty cents U.S.' That took me by surprise. I had no money, only a few rupees. The girl stamped, and I thought she was going to hit me with her pad when I stood up to show her who my employer was.

Presently my employer came down the aisle. He didn't look very well. He said, without stopping, 'Champagne, Santosh? Already we are overdoing?' He went on to the lavatory. When he passed back he said, 'Foreign exchange, Santosh! Foreign exchange!' That was all. Poor fellow, he was suffering too.

The journey became miserable for me. Soon, with the wine I had drunk, the betel juice, the movement and the noise of the aeroplane, I was vomiting all over my bundles, and I didn't care what the girl said or did. Later there were more urgent and terrible needs. I felt I would choke in the tiny, hissing room at the back. I had a shock when I saw my face in the mirror. In the fluorescent light it was the colour of a corpse. My eyes were strained, the sharp air hurt my nose and seemed to get into my brain. I climbed up on the lavatory seat and squatted. I lost control of myself. As quickly as I could I ran back out into the comparative openness of the cabin and hoped no one had noticed. The lights were dim now; some people had taken off their jackets and were sleeping. I hoped the plane would crash.

The girl woke me up. She was almost screaming, 'It's you, isn't it? Isn't it?'

I thought she was going to tear the shirt off me. I pulled back and leaned hard on the window. She burst into tears and nearly tripped on her sari as she ran up the aisle to get the man in uniform.

Nightmare. And all I knew was that somewhere at the end, after the airports and the crowded lounges where everybody was dressed up, after all those take-offs and touchdowns, was the city of Washington. I wanted the journey to end but I couldn't say I wanted to arrive at Washington. I was already a little scared of that city, to tell the truth. I wanted only to be off the plane and to be in the open again, to stand on the ground and breathe and to try to understand what time of day it was.

At last we arrived. I was in a daze. The burden of those bundles! There were more closed rooms and electric lights. There were questions from officials.

'Is he diplomatic?'

'He's only a domestic,' my employer said.

'Is that his luggage? What's in that pocket?'

I was ashamed.

'Santosh,' my employer said.

I pulled out the little packets of pepper and salt, the sweets, the envelopes with scented napkins, the toy tubes of mustard. Airline trinkets. I had been collecting them throughout the journey, seizing a handful, whatever my condition, every time I passed the galley.

'He's a cook,' my employer said.

'Does he always travel with his condiments?'

'Santosh, Santosh,' my employer said in the car afterwards, 'in Bombay it didn't matter what you did. Over here you represent your country. I must say I cannot understand why your behaviour has already gone so much out of character.'

'I am sorry, sahib.'

'Look at it like this, Santosh. Over here you don't only represent your country, you represent me.'

For the people of Washington it was late afternoon or early evening, I couldn't say which. The time and the light didn't match, as they did in Bombay. Of that drive I remember green fields, wide roads, many motor cars travelling fast, making a steady hiss, hiss, which wasn't at all like our Bombay traffic noise. I remember big buildings and wide parks; many bazaar areas; then smaller houses without fences and with gardens like bush, with the *hubshi* standing about or sitting down, more usually sitting down, everywhere. Especially I remember the *hubshi*. I had heard about them in stories and had seen one or two in Bombay. But I had never dreamt that this wild race existed in such numbers in Washington and were permitted to roam the streets so freely. O father, what was this place I had come to?

I wanted, I say, to be in the open, to breathe, to come to myself, to reflect. But there was to be no openness for me that evening. From the aeroplane to the airport building to the motor car to the apartment block to the elevator to the corridor to the apartment itself, I was forever enclosed, forever in the hissing, hissing sound of air-conditioners.

I was too dazed to take stock of the apartment. I saw it as only another halting place. My employer went to bed at once, completely exhausted, poor fellow. I looked around for my room. I couldn't find it and gave up. Aching for the Bombay ways, I spread my bedding in the carpeted corridor just outside our apartment door. The corridor was long: doors, doors. The illuminated ceiling was decorated with stars of different sizes; the colours were grey and blue and gold. Below that imitation sky I felt like a prisoner.

* * *

Waking, looking up at the ceiling, I thought just for a second that I had fallen asleep on the pavement below the gallery of our Bombay chambers. Then I realized my loss. I couldn't tell how much time had passed or whether it was night or day. The only clue was that newspapers now lay outside some doors. It disturbed me to think that while I had been sleeping, alone and defenceless, I had been observed by a stranger and perhaps by more than one stranger.

I tried the apartment door and found I had locked myself out. I didn't want to disturb my employer. I thought I would get out into the open, go for a walk. I remembered where the elevator was. I got in and pressed the button. The elevator dropped fast and silently and it was like being in the aeroplane again. When the elevator stopped and the blue metal door slid open I saw plain concrete corridors and blank walls. The noise of machinery was very loud. I knew I was in the basement and the main floor was not far above me. But I no longer wanted to try; I gave up ideas of the open air. I thought I would just go back up to the apartment. But I hadn't noted the number and didn't even know what floor we were on. My courage flowed out of me. I sat on the floor of the elevator and felt the tears come to my eyes. Almost without noise the elevator door closed, and I found I was being taken up silently at great speed.

The elevator stopped and the door opened. It was my employer, his hair uncombed, yesterday's dirty shirt partly unbuttoned. He looked frightened.

'Santosh, where have you been at this hour of morning? Without your shoes.'

I could have embraced him. He hurried me back past the newspapers to our apartment and I took the bedding inside. The wide window showed the early morning sky, the big city; we were high up, way above the trees.

I said, 'I couldn't find my room.'

'Government sanctioned,' my employer said. 'Are you sure you've looked?'

We looked together. One little corridor led past the bathroom to his bedroom; another, shorter, corridor led to the big room and the kitchen. There was nothing else.

'Government sanctioned,' my employer said, moving about the kitchen and opening cupboard doors. 'Separate entrance, shelving. I have the correspondence.' He opened another door and looked inside. 'Santosh, do you think it is possible that this is what Government meant?'

The cupboard he had opened was as high as the rest of the apartment and as wide as the kitchen, about six feet. It was about three feet deep. It had two doors. One door opened into the kitchen; another door, directly opposite, opened into the corridor.

'Separate entrance,' my employer said. 'Shelving, electric light, power point, fitted carpet.'

'This must be my room, sahib.'

'Santosh, some enemy in Government has done this to me.'

'Oh no, sahib. You mustn't say that. Besides, it is very big. I will be able to make myself very comfortable. It is much bigger than my little cubby-hole in the chambers. And it has a nice flat ceiling. I wouldn't hit my head.'

'You don't understand, Santosh. Bombay is Bombay. Here if we start living in cupboards we give the wrong impression. They will think we all live in cupboards in Bombay.'

'O sahib, but they can just look at me and see I am dirt.'

'You are very good, Santosh. But these people are malicious. Still, if you are happy, then I am happy.'

'I am very happy, sahib.'

And after all the upset, I was. It was nice to crawl in that evening, spread my bedding and feel protected and hidden. I slept very well.

*   *   *

In the morning my employer said, 'We must talk about money, Santosh. Your salary is one hundred rupees a month. But Washington isn't Bombay. Everything is a little bit more expensive here, and I am going to give you a Dearness Allowance. As from today you are getting one hundred and fifty rupees.'

'Sahib.'

'And I'm giving you a fortnight's pay in advance. In foreign exchange. Seventy-five rupees. Ten cents to the rupees, seven hundred and fifty cents. Seven fifty U.S. Here, Santosh. This afternoon you go out and have a little walk and enjoy. But be careful. We are not among friends, remember.'

So at last, rested, with money in my pocket, I went out in the open. And of course the city wasn't a quarter as frightening as I had thought. The buildings weren't particularly big, not all the streets were busy, and there were many lovely trees. A lot of the *hubshi* were about, very wild-looking some of them, with dark glasses and their hair frizzed out, but it seemed that if you didn't trouble them they didn't attack you.

I was looking for a café or a tea-stall where perhaps domestics congregated. But I saw no domestics, and I was chased away from the place I did eventually go into. The girl said, after I had been waiting some time, 'Can't you read? We don't serve hippies or bare feet here.'

O father! I had come out without my shoes. But what a country, I thought, walking briskly away, where people are never allowed to dress normally but must forever wear their very best! Why must they wear out shoes and fine clothes for no purpose? What occasion are they honouring? What waste, what presumption! Who do they think is noticing them all the time?

And even while these thoughts were in my head I found I had come to a roundabout with trees and a fountain where – and it was like a fulfilment in a dream, not easy to believe – there were many people who looked like my own people. I tightened the string around my loose pants, held down my flapping shirt and ran through the traffic to the green circle.

Some of the *hubshi* were there, playing musical instruments and looking quite happy in their way. There were some Americans sitting about on the grass and the fountain and the kerb. Many of them were in rough, friendly-looking clothes; some were without shoes; and I felt I had been over-hasty in condemning the entire race. But it wasn't these people who had attracted me to the circle. It was the dancers. The men were bearded, bare-footed and in saffron robes, and the girls were in saris and canvas shoes that looked like our own Bata shoes. They were shaking little cymbals and chanting and lifting their heads up and down and going round in a circle, making a lot of dust. It was a little bit like a Red Indian dance in a cowboy movie, but they were chanting Sanskrit words in praise of Lord Krishna.

I was very pleased. But then a disturbing thought came to me. It might have been because of the half-caste appearance of the dancers; it might have been their bad Sanskrit pronunciation and their accent. I thought that these people were now strangers, but that perhaps once upon a time they had been like me. Perhaps, as in some story, they had been brought here among the *hubshi* as captives a long time ago and had become a lost people, like our own wandering gipsy folk, and had forgotten who they were. When I thought that, I lost my pleasure in the dancing; and I felt for the dancers the sort of distaste we feel when we are faced with something that should be kin but turns out not to be, turns out to be degraded, like a deformed man, or like a leper, who from a distance looks whole.

I didn't stay. Not far from the circle I saw a café which appeared to be serving bare feet. I went in, had a coffee and a nice piece of cake and bought a pack of cigarettes; matches they gave me free with the cigarettes. It was all right, but then the bare feet began looking at me, and one bearded fellow came and sniffed loudly at me and smiled and spoke some sort of gibberish, and then some others of the bare feet came and sniffed at me. They weren't unfriendly, but I didn't appreciate the behaviour; and it was a little frightening to find, when I left the place, that two or three of them appeared to be following me. They weren't unfriendly, but I didn't want to take any chances. I passed a cinema; I went in. It was something I wanted to do anyway. In Bombay I used to go once a week.

And that was all right. The movie had already started. It was in English, not too easy for me to follow, and it gave me time to think. It was only there, in the darkness, that I thought about the money I had been spending. The prices had seemed to me very reasonable, like Bombay prices. Three for the movie ticket, one fifty in the café, with tip. But I had been thinking in rupees and paying in dollars. In less than an hour I had spent nine days' pay.

I couldn't watch the movie after that. I went out and began to make my way back to the apartment block. Many more of the *hubshi* were about now and I saw that where they congregated the pavement was wet, and dangerous with broken glass and bottles. I couldn't think of cooking when I got back to the apartment. I couldn't bear to look at the view. I spread my bedding in the cupboard, lay down in the darkness and waited for my employer to return.

When he did I said, 'Sahib, I want to go home.'

'Santosh, I've paid five thousand rupees to bring you here. If I send you back now, you will have to work for six or seven years without salary to pay me back.'

I burst into tears.

'My poor Santosh, something has happened. Tell me what has happened?'

'Sahib, I've spent more than half the advance you gave me this morning. I went out and had a coffee and cake and then I went to a movie.'

His eyes went small and twinkly behind his glasses. He bit the inside of his top lip, scraped at his moustache with his lower teeth, and he said, 'You see, you see. I told you it was expensive.'

* * *

I understood I was a prisoner. I accepted this and adjusted. I learned to live within the apartment, and I was even calm.

My employer was a man of taste and he soon had the apartment looking like something in a magazine, with books and Indian paintings and Indian fabrics and pieces of sculpture and bronze statues of our gods. I was careful to take no delight in it. It was of course very pretty, especially with the view. But the view remained foreign and I never felt that the apartment was real, like the shabby old Bombay chambers with the cane chairs, or that it had anything to do with me.

When people came to dinner I did my duty. At the appropriate time I would bid the company goodnight, close off the kitchen behind its folding screen and pretend I was leaving the apartment. Then I would lie down quietly in my cupboard and smoke. I was free to go out; I had my separate entrance. But I didn't like being out of the apartment. I didn't even like going down to the laundry room in the basement.

Once or twice a week I went to the supermarket on our street. I always had to walk past groups of *hubshi* men and children. I tried not to look, but it was hard. They sat on the pavement, on steps and in the bush around their redbrick houses, some of which had boarded-up windows. They appeared to be very much a people of the open air, with little to do; even in the mornings some of the men were drunk.

Scattered among the *hubshi* houses were others just as old but with gas-lamps that burned night and day in the entrance. These were the houses of the Americans. I seldom saw these people; they didn't spend much time on the street. The lighted gas-lamp was the American way of saying that though a house looked old outside it was nice and new inside. I also felt that it was like a warning to the *hubshi* to keep off.

Outside the supermarket there was always a policeman with a gun. Inside, there were always a couple of *hubshi* guards with truncheons, and, behind the cashiers, some old *hubshi* beggar men in rags. There were also many young *hubshi* boys, small but muscular, waiting to carry parcels, as once in the hills I had waited to carry Indian tourists' luggage.

These trips to the supermarket were my only outings, and I was always glad to get back to the apartment. The work there was light. I watched a lot of television and my English improved. I grew to like certain commercials very much. It was in these commercials I saw the Americans whom in real life I so seldom saw and knew only by their gas-lamps. Up there in the apartment, with a view of the white domes and towers and greenery of the famous city, I entered the homes of the Americans and saw them cleaning those homes. I saw them cleaning floors and dishes. I saw them buying clothes and cleaning clothes, buying motor cars and cleaning motor cars. I saw them cleaning, cleaning.

The effect of all this television on me was curious. If by some chance I saw an American on the street I tried to fit him or her into the commercials; and I felt I had caught the person in an interval between his television duties. So to some extent Americans have remained to me, as people not quite real, as people temporarily absent from television.

Sometimes a *hubshi* came on the screen, not to talk of *hubshi* things, but to do a little cleaning of his own. That wasn't the same. He was too different from the *hubshi* I saw on the street and I knew he was an actor. I knew that his television duties were only make-believe and that he would soon have to return to the street.

* * *

One day at the supermarket, when the *hubshi* girl took my money, she sniffed and said, 'You always smell sweet, baby.'

She was friendly, and I was at last able to clear up that mystery, of my smell. It was the poor country weed I smoked. It was a peasant taste of which I was slightly ashamed, to tell the truth; but the cashier was encouraging. As it happened, I had brought a quantity of the weed with me from Bombay in one of my bundles, together with a hundred razor blades, believing both weed and blades to be purely Indian things. I made an offering to the girl. In return she taught me a few words of English. 'Me black and beautiful' was the first thing she taught me. Then she pointed to the policeman with the gun outside and taught me: 'He pig.'

My English lessons were taken a stage further by the *hubshi* maid who worked for someone on our floor in the apartment block. She too was attracted by my smell, but I soon began to feel that she was also attracted by my smallness and strangeness. She herself was a big woman, broad in the face, with high cheeks and bold eyes and lips that were full but not pendulous. Her largeness disturbed me; I found it better to concentrate on her face. She misunderstood; there were times when she frolicked with me in a violent way. I didn't like it, because I couldn't fight her off as well as I would have liked and because in spite of myself I was fascinated by her appearance. Her smell mixed with the perfumes she used could have made me forget myself.

She was always coming into the apartment. She disturbed me while I was watching the Americans on television. I feared the smell she left behind. Sweat, perfume, my own weed: the smells lay thick in the room, and I prayed to the bronze gods my employer had installed as living-room ornaments that I would not be dishonoured. Dishonoured, I say; and I know that this might seem strange to people over here, who have permitted the *hubshi* to settle among them in such large numbers and must therefore esteem them in certain ways. But in our country we frankly do not care for the *hubshi*. It is written in our books, both holy and not so holy, that it is indecent and wrong for a man of our blood to embrace the *hubshi* woman. To be dishonoured in this life, to be born a cat or a monkey or a *hubshi* in the next!

But I was falling. Was it idleness and solitude? I was found attractive: I wanted to know why. I began to go to the bathroom of the apartment simply to study my face in the mirror. I cannot easily believe it myself now, but in Bombay a week or a month could pass without my looking in the mirror; and then it wasn't to consider my looks but to check whether the barber had cut off too much hair or whether a pimple was about to burst. Slowly I made a discovery. My face was handsome. I had never thought of myself in this way. I had thought of myself as unnoticeable, with features that served as identification alone.

The discovery of my good looks brought its strains. I became obsessed with my appearance, with a wish to see myself. It was like an illness. I would be watching television, for instance, and I would be surprised by the thought: are you as handsome as that man? I would have to get up and go to the bathroom and look in the mirror.

I thought back to the time when these matters hadn't interested me, and I saw how ragged I must have looked, on the aeroplane, in the airport, in that café for bare feet, with the rough and dirty clothes I wore, without doubt or question, as clothes befitting a servant. I was choked with shame. I saw, too, how good people in Washington had been, to have seen me in rags and yet to have taken me for a man.

I was glad I had a place to hide. I had thought of myself as a prisoner. Now I was glad I had so little of Washington to cope with: the apartment, my cupboard, the television set, my employer, the walk to the supermarket, the *hubshi* woman. And one day I found I no longer knew whether I wanted to go back to Bombay. Up there, in the apartment, I no longer knew what I wanted to do.

*   *   *

I became more careful of my appearance. There wasn't much I could do. I bought laces for my old black shoes, socks, a belt. Then some money came my way. I had understood that the weed I smoked was of value to the *hubshi* and the bare feet; I disposed of what I had, disadvantageously as I now know, through the *hubshi* girl at the supermarket. I got just under two hundred dollars. Then, as anxiously as I had got rid of my weed, I went out and bought some clothes.

I still have the things I bought that morning. A green hat, a green suit. The suit was always too big for me. Ignorance, inexperience; but I also remember the feeling of presumption. The salesman wanted to talk, to do his job. I didn't want to listen. I took the first suit he showed me and went into the cubicle and changed. I couldn't think about size and fit. When I considered all that cloth and all that tailoring I was proposing to adorn my simple body with, that body that needed so little, I felt I was asking to be destroyed. I changed back quickly, went out of the cubicle and said I would take the green suit. The salesman began to talk; I cut him short; I asked for a hat. When I got back to the apartment I felt quite weak and had to lie down for a while in my cupboard.

I never hung the suit up. Even in the shop, even while counting out the precious dollars, I had known it was a mistake. I kept the suit folded in the box with all its pieces of tissue paper. Three or four times I put it on and walked about the apartment and sat down on chairs and lit cigarettes and crossed my legs, practising. But I couldn't bring myself to wear the suit out of doors. Later I wore the pants, but never the jacket. I never bought another suit; I soon began wearing the sort of clothes I wear today, pants with some sort of zippered jacket.

Once I had had no secrets from my employer; it was so much simpler not to have secrets. But some instinct told me now it would be better not to let him know about the green suit or the few dollars I had, just as instinct had already told me I should keep my own growing knowledge of English to myself.

Once my employer had been to me only a presence. I used to tell him then that beside him I was as dirt. It was only a way of talking, one of the courtesies of our language, but it had something of truth. I meant that he was the man who adventured in the world for me, that I experienced the world through him, that I was content to be a small part of his presence. I was content, sleeping on the Bombay pavement with my friends, to hear the talk of my employer and his guests upstairs. I was more than content, late at night, to be identified among the sleepers and greeted by some of those guests before they drove away.

Now I found that, without wishing it, I was ceasing to see myself as part of my employer's presence, and beginning at the same time to see him as an outsider might see him, as perhaps the people who came to dinner in the apartment saw him. I saw that he was a man of my own age, around thirty-five; it astonished me that I hadn't noticed this before. I saw that he was plump, in need of exercise, that he moved with short, fussy steps; a man with glasses, thinning hair, and that habit, during conversation, of scraping at his moustache with his teeth and nibbling at the inside of his top lip; a man who was frequently anxious, took pains over his work, was subjected at his own table to unkind remarks by his office colleagues; a man who looked as uneasy in Washington as I felt, who acted as cautiously as I had learned to act.

I remember an American who came to dinner. He looked at the pieces of sculpture in the apartment and said he had himself brought back a whole head from one of our ancient temples; he had got the guide to hack it off.

I could see that my employer was offended. He said, 'But that's illegal.'

'That's why I had to give the guide two dollars. If I had a bottle of whisky he would have pulled down the whole temple for me.'

My employer's face went blank. He continued to do his duties as host but he was unhappy throughout the dinner. I grieved for him.

Afterwards he knocked on my cupboard. I knew he wanted to talk. I was in my underclothes but I didn't feel underdressed, with the American gone. I stood in the door of my cupboard; my employer paced up and down the small kitchen; the apartment felt sad.

'Did you hear that person, Santosh?'

I pretended I hadn't understood, and when he explained I tried to console him. I said, 'Sahib, but we know these people are Franks and barbarians.'

'They are malicious people, Santosh. They think that because we are a poor country we are all the same. They think an official in Government is just the same as some poor guide scraping together a few rupees to keep body and soul together, poor fellow.'

I saw that he had taken the insult only in a personal way, and I was disappointed. I thought he had been thinking of the temple.

* * *

A few days later I had my adventure. The *hubshi* woman came in, moving among my employer's ornaments like a bull. I was greatly provoked. The smell was too much; so was the sight of her armpits. I fell. She dragged me down on the couch, on the saffron spread which was one of my employer's nicest pieces of Punjabi folk-weaving. I saw the moment, helplessly, as one of dishonour. I saw her as Kali, goddess of death and destruction, coal-black, with a red tongue and white eyeballs and many powerful arms. I expected her to be wild and fierce; but she added insult to injury by being very playful, as though, because I was small and strange, the act was not real. She laughed all the time. I would have liked to withdraw, but the act took over and completed itself. And then I felt dreadful.

I wanted to be forgiven, I wanted to be cleansed, I wanted her to go. Nothing frightened me more than the way she had ceased to be a visitor in the apartment and behaved as though she possessed it. I looked at the sculpture and the fabrics and thought of my poor employer, suffering in his office somewhere.

I bathed and bathed afterwards. The smell would not leave me. I fancied that the woman's oil was still on that poor part of my poor body. It occurred to me to rub it down with half a lemon. Penance and cleansing; but it didn't hurt as much as I expected, and I extended the penance by rolling about naked on the floor of the bathroom and the sitting-room and howling. At last the tears came, real tears, and I was comforted.

It was cool in the apartment; the air-conditioning always hummed; but I could see that it was hot outside, like one of our own summer days in the hills. The urge came upon me to dress as I might have done in my village on a religious occasion. In one of my bundles I had a dhoti-length of new cotton, a gift from the tailor's bearer that I had never used. I draped this around my waist and between my legs, lit incense sticks, sat down crosslegged on the floor and tried to meditate and become still. Soon I began to feel hungry. That made me happy; I decided to fast.

Unexpectedly my employer came in. I didn't mind being caught in the attitude and garb of prayer; it could have been so much worse. But I wasn't expecting him till late afternoon.

'Santosh, what has happened?'

Pride got the better of me. I said, 'Sahib, it is what I do from time to time.'

But I didn't find merit in his eyes. He was far too agitated to notice me properly. He took off his lightweight fawn jacket, dropped it on the saffron spread, went to the refrigerator and drank two tumblers of orange juice, one after the other. Then he looked out at the view, scraping at his moustache.

'Oh, my poor Santosh, what are we doing in this place? Why do we have to come here?'

I looked with him. I saw nothing unusual. The wide window showed the colours of the hot day: the pale-blue sky, the white, almost colourless, domes of famous buildings rising out of dead-green foliage; the untidy roofs of apartment blocks where on Saturday and Sunday mornings people sunbathed; and, below, the fronts and backs of houses on the tree-lined street down which I walked to the supermarket.

My employer turned off the air-conditioning and all noise was absent from the room. An instant later I began to hear the noises outside: sirens far and near. When my employer slid the window open the roar of the disturbed city rushed into the room. He closed the window and there was near-silence again. Not far from the supermarket I saw black smoke, uncurling, rising, swiftly turning colourless. This was not the smoke which some of the apartment blocks gave off all day. This was the smoke of a real fire.

'The *hubshi* have gone wild, Santosh. They are burning down Washington.'

I didn't mind at all. Indeed, in my mood of prayer and repentance, the news was even welcome. And it was with a feeling of release that I watched and heard the city burn that afternoon and watched it burn that night. I watched it burn again and again on television; and I watched it burn in the morning. It burned like a famous city and I didn't want it to stop burning. I wanted the fire to spread and spread and I wanted everything in the city, even the apartment block, even the apartment, even myself, to be destroyed and consumed. I wanted escape to be impossible; I wanted the very idea of escape to become absurd. At every sign that the burning was going to stop I felt disappointed and let down.

For four days my employer and I stayed in the apartment and watched the city burn. The television continued to show us what we could see and what, whenever we slid the window back, we could hear. Then it was over. The view from our window hadn't changed. The famous buildings stood; the trees remained. But for the first time since I had understood that I was a prisoner I found that I wanted to be out of the apartment and in the streets.

The destruction lay beyond the supermarket. I had never gone into this part of the city before, and it was strange to walk in those long wide streets for the first time, to see trees and houses and shops and advertisements, everything like a real city, and then to see that every signboard on every shop was burnt or stained with smoke, that the shops themselves were black and broken, that flames had burst through some of the upper windows and scorched the red bricks. For mile after mile it was like that. There were *hubshi* groups about, and at first when I passed them I pretended to be busy, minding my own business, not at all interested in the ruins. But they smiled at me and I found I was smiling back. Happiness was on the faces of the *hubshi*. They were like people amazed they could do so much, that so much lay in their power. They were like people on holiday. I shared their exhilaration.

* * *

The idea of escape was a simple one, but it hadn't occurred to me before. When I adjusted to my imprisonment I had wanted only to get away from Washington and to return to Bombay. But then I had become confused. I had looked in the mirror and seen myself, and I knew it wasn't possible for me to return to Bombay to the sort of job I had had and the life I had lived. I couldn't easily become part of someone else's presence again. Those evening chats on the pavement, those morning walks: happy times, but they were like the happy times of childhood: I didn't want them to return.

I had taken, after the fire, to going for long walks in the city. And one day, when I wasn't even thinking of escape, when I was just enjoying the sights and my new freedom of movement, I found myself in one of those leafy streets where private houses had been turned into business premises. I saw a fellow countryman superintending the raising of a signboard on his gallery. The signboard told me that the building was a restaurant, and I assumed that the man in charge was the owner. He looked worried and slightly ashamed, and he smiled at me. This was unusual, because the Indians I had seen on the streets of Washington pretended they hadn't seen me; they made me feel that they didn't like the competition of my presence or didn't want me to start asking them difficult questions.

I complimented the worried man on his signboard and wished him good luck in his business. He was a small man of about fifty and he was wearing a double-breasted suit with old-fashioned wide lapels. He had dark hollows below his eyes and he looked as though he had recently lost a little weight. I could see that in our country he had been a man of some standing, not quite the sort of person who would go into the restaurant business. I felt at one with him. He invited me in to look around, asked my name and gave his. It was Priya.

Just past the gallery was the loveliest and richest room I had ever seen. The wallapaper was like velvet; I wanted to pass my hand over it. The brass lamps that hung from the ceiling were in a lovely cut-out pattern and the bulbs were of many colours. Priya looked with me, and the hollows under his eyes grew darker, as though my admiration was increasing his worry at his extravagance. The restaurant hadn't yet opened for customers and on a shelf in one corner I saw Priya's collection of good-luck objects: a brass plate with a heap of uncooked rice, for prosperity; a little copybook and a little diary pencil, for good luck with the accounts; a little clay lamp, for general good luck.

'What do you think, Santosh? You think it will be all right?'

'It is bound to be all right, Priya.'

'But I have enemies, you know, Santosh. The Indian restaurant people are not going to appreciate me. All mine, you know, Santosh. Cash paid. No mortgage or anything like that. I don't believe in mortgages. Cash or nothing.'

I understood him to mean that he had tried to get a mortgage and failed, and was anxious about money.

'But what are you doing here, Santosh? You used to be in Government or something?'

'You could say that, Priya.'

'Like me. They have a saying here. If you can't beat them, join them. I joined them. They are still beating me.' He sighed and spread his arms on the top of the red wall-seat. 'Ah, Santosh, why do we do it? Why don't we renounce and go and meditate on the riverbank?' He waved about the room. 'The yemblems of the world, Santosh. Just yemblems.'

I didn't know the English word he used, but I understood its meaning; and for a moment it was like being back in Bombay, exchanging stories and philosophies with the tailor's bearer and others in the evening.

'But I am forgetting, Santosh. You will have some tea or coffee or something?'

I shook my head from side to side to indicate that I was agreeable, and he called out in a strange harsh language to someone behind the kitchen door.

'Yes, Santosh. Yem-*blems*!' And he sighed and slapped the red seat hard.

A man came out from the kitchen with a tray. At first he looked like a fellow countryman, but in a second I could tell he was a stranger.

'You are right,' Priya said, when the stranger went back to the kitchen. 'He is not of Bharat. He is a Mexican. But what can I do? You get fellow countrymen, you fix up their papers and everything, green card and everything. And then? Then they run away. Run-run-runaway. Crooks this side, crooks that side, I can't tell you. Listen, Santosh. I was in cloth business before. Buy for fifty rupees that side, sell for fifty dollars this side. Easy. But then. Caftan, everybody wants caftan. Caftan-aftan, I say, I will settle your caftan. I buy one thousand, Santosh. Delays India-side, of course. They come one year later. Nobody wants caftan then. We're not organized, Santosh. We don't do enough consumer research. That's what the fellows at the embassy tell me. But if I do consumer research, when will I do my business? The trouble, you know, Santosh, is that this shopkeeping is not in my blood. The damn thing goes *against* my blood. When I was in cloth business I used to hide sometimes for shame when a customer came in. Sometimes I used to pretend I was a shopper myself. Consumer research! These people make us dance, Santosh. You and I, we will renounce. We will go together and walk beside Potomac and meditate.'

I loved his talk. I hadn't heard anything so sweet and philosophical since the Bombay days. I said, 'Priya, I will cook for you, if you want a cook.'

'I feel I've known you a long time, Santosh. I feel you are like a member of my own family. I will give you a place to sleep, a little food to eat and a little pocket money, as much as I can afford.'

I said, 'Show me the place to sleep.'

He led me out of the pretty room and up a carpeted staircase. I was expecting the carpet and the new paint to stop somewhere, but it was nice and new all the way. We entered a room that was like a smaller version of my employer's apartment.

'Built-in cupboards and everything, you see, Santosh.'

I went to the cupboard. It had a folding door that opened outward. I said, 'Priya, it is too small. There is room on the shelf for my belongings. But I don't see how I can spread my bedding inside here. It is far too narrow.'

He giggled nervously. 'Santosh, you are a joker. I feel that we are of the same family already.'

Then it came to me that I was being offered the whole room. I was stunned.

Priya looked stunned too. He sat down on the edge of the soft bed. The dark hollows under his eyes were almost black and he looked very small in his double-breasted jacket. 'This is how they make us dance over here, Santosh. You say staff quarters and they say staff quarters. This is what they mean.'

For some seconds we sat silently, I fearful, he gloomy, meditating on the ways of this new world.

Someone called from downstairs, 'Priya!'

His gloom gone, smiling in advance, winking at me, Priya called back in an accent of the country, 'Hi, Bab!'

I followed him down.

'Priya,' the American said, 'I've brought over the menus.'

He was a tall man in a leather jacket, with jeans that rode up above thick white socks and big rubber-soled shoes. He looked like someone about to run in a race. The menus were enormous; on the cover there was a drawing of a fat man with a moustache and a plumed turban, something like the man in the airline advertisements.

'They look great, Bab.'

'I like them myself. But what's that, Priya? What's that shelf doing there?'

Moving like the front part of a horse, Bab walked to the shelf with the rice and the brass plate and the little clay lamp. It was only then that I saw that the shelf was very roughly made.

Priya looked penitent and it was clear he had put the shelf up himself. It was also clear he didn't intend to take it down.

'Well, it's yours,' Bab said. 'I suppose we had to have a touch of the East somewhere. Now, Priya –'

'Money-money-money, is it?' Priya said, racing the words together as though he was making a joke to amuse a child. 'But, Bab, how can *you* ask *me* for money? Anybody hearing you would believe that this restaurant is mine. But this restaurant isn't mine, Bab. This restaurant is yours.'

It was only one of our courtesies, but it puzzled Bab and he allowed himself to be led to other matters.

I saw that, for all his talk of renunciation and business failure, and for all his jumpiness, Priya was able to cope with Washington. I admired this strength in him as much as I admired the richness of his talk. I didn't know how much to believe of his stories, but I liked having to guess about him. I liked having to play with his words in my mind. I liked the mystery of the man. The mystery came from his solidity. I knew where I was with him. After the apartment and the green suit and the *hubshi* woman and the city burning for four days, to be with Priya was to feel safe. For the first time since I had come to Washington I felt safe.

I can't say that I moved in. I simply stayed. I didn't want to go back to the apartment even to collect my belongings. I was afraid that something might happen to keep me a prisoner there. My employer might turn up and demand his five thousand rupees. The *hubshi* woman might claim me for her own; I might be condemned to a life among the *hubshi*. And it wasn't as if I was leaving behind anything of value in the apartment. The green suit I was even happy to forget. But.

* * *

Priya paid me forty dollars a week. After what I was getting, three dollars and seventy-five cents, it seemed a lot; and it was more than enough for my needs. I didn't have much temptation to spend, to tell the truth. I knew that my old employer and the *hubshi* woman would be wondering about me in their respective ways and I thought I should keep off the streets for a while. That was no hardship; it was what I was used to in Washington. Besides, my days at the restaurant were pretty full; for the first time in my life I had little leisure.

The restaurant was a success from the start, and Priya was fussy. He was always bursting into the kitchen with one of those big menus in his hand, saying in English, 'Prestige job, Santosh, prestige.' I didn't mind. I liked to feel I had to do things perfectly; I felt I was earning my freedom. Though I was in hiding, and though I worked every day until midnight, I felt I was much more in charge of myself than I had ever been.

Many of our waiters were Mexicans, but when we put turbans on them they could pass. They came and went, like the Indian staff. I didn't get on with these people. They were frightened and jealous of one another and very treacherous. Their talk amid the biryanis and the pillaus was all of papers and green cards. They were always about to get green cards or they had been cheated out of green cards or they had just got green cards. At first I didn't know what they were talking about. When I understood I was more than depressed.

I understood that because I had escaped from my employer I had made myself illegal in America. At any moment I could be denounced, seized, jailed, deported, disgraced. It was a complication. I had no green card; I didn't know how to set about getting one; and there was no one I could talk to.

I felt burdened by my secrets. Once I had none; now I had so many. I couldn't tell Priya I had no green card. I couldn't tell him I had broken faith with my old employer and dishonored myself with a *hubshi* woman and lived in fear of retribution. I couldn't tell him that I was afraid to leave the restaurant and that nowadays when I saw an Indian I hid from him as anxiously as the Indian hid from me. I would have felt foolish to confess. With Priya, right from the start, I had pretended to be strong; and I wanted it to remain like that. Instead, when we talked now, and he grew philosophical, I tried to find bigger causes for being sad. My mind fastened on to these causes, and the effect of this was that my sadness became like a sickness of the soul.

It was worse than being in the apartment, because now the responsibility was mine and mine alone. I had decided to be free, to act for myself. It pained me to think of the exhilaration I had felt during the days of the fire; and I felt mocked when I remembered that in the early days of my escape I had thought I was in charge of myself.

The year turned. The snow came and melted. I was more afraid than ever of going out. The sickness was bigger than all the causes. I saw the future as a hole into which I was dropping. Sometimes at night when I awakened my body would burn and I would feel the hot perspiration break all over.

I leaned on Priya. He was my only hope, my only link with what was real. He went out; he brought back stories. He went out especially to eat in the restaurants of our competitors.

He said, 'Santosh, I never believed that running a restaurant was a way to God. But it is true. I eat like a scientist. Every day I eat like a scientist. I feel I have already renounced.'

This was Priya. This was how his talk ensnared me and gave me the bigger causes that steadily weakened me. I became more and more detached from the men in the kitchen. When they spoke of their green cards and the jobs they were about to get I felt like asking them: Why? Why?

And every day the mirror told its own tale. Without exercise, with the sickening of my heart and my mind, I was losing my looks. My face had become pudgy and sallow and full of spots; it was becoming ugly. I could have cried for that, discovering my good looks only to lose them. It was like a punishment for my presumption, the punishment I had feared when I bought the green suit.

Priya said, 'Santosh, you must get some exercise. You are not looking well. Your eyes are getting like mine. What are you pining for? Are you pining for Bombay or your family in the hills?'

But now, even in my mind, I was a stranger in those places.

Priya said one Sunday morning, 'Santosh, I am going to take you to see a Hindi movie today. All the Indians of Washington will be there, domestics and everybody else.'

I was very frightened. I didn't want to go and I couldn't tell him why. He insisted. My heart began to beat fast as soon as I got into the car. Soon there were no more houses with gas-lamps in the entrance, just those long wide burnt-out *hubshi* streets, now with fresh leaves on the trees, heaps of rubble on bulldozed, fenced-in lots, boarded-up shop windows, and old smoke-stained signboards announcing what was no longer true. Cars raced along the wide roads; there was life only on the roads. I thought I would vomit with fear.

I said, 'Take me back, *sahib*.'

I had used the wrong word. Once I had used the word a hundred times a day. But then I had considered myself a small part of my employer's presence, and the word was not servile; it was more like a name, like a reassuring sound, part of my employer's dignity and therefore part of mine. But Priya's dignity could never be mine; that was not our relationship. Priya I had always called Priya; it was his wish, the American way, man to man. With Priya the word was servile. And he responded to the word. He did as I asked; he drove me back to the restaurant. I never called him by his name again.

I was good-looking; I had lost my looks. I was a free man; I had lost my freedom.

*　*　*

One of the Mexican waiters came into the kitchen late one evening and said, 'There is a man outside who wants to see the chef.'

No one had made this request before, and Priya was at once agitated. 'Is he an American? Some enemy has sent him here. Sanitary-anitary, health-ealth, they can inspect my kitchens at any time.'

'He is an Indian,' the Mexican said.

I was alarmed. I thought it was my old employer; that quiet approach was like him. Priya thought it was a rival. Though Priya regularly ate in the restaurants of his rivals he thought it unfair when they came to eat in his. We both went to the door and peeked through the glass window into the dimly lit dining-room.

'Do you know that person, Santosh?'

'Yes, sahib.'

It wasn't my old employer. It was one of his Bombay friends, a big man in Government, whom I had often served in the chambers. He was by himself and seemed to have just arrived in Washington. He had a new Bombay haircut, very close, and a stiff dark suit, Bombay tailoring. His shirt looked blue, but in the dim multi-coloured light of the dining-room everything white looked blue. He didn't look unhappy with what he had eaten. Both his elbows were on the curry-spotted tablecloth and he was picking his teeth, half closing his eyes and hiding his mouth with his cupped left hand.

'I don't like him,' Priya said. 'Still, big man in Government and so on. You must go to him, Santosh.'

But I couldn't go.

'Put on your apron, Santosh. And that chef's cap. Prestige. You must go, Santosh.'

Priya went out to the dining-room and I heard him say in English that I was coming.

I ran up to my room, put some oil on my hair, combed my hair, put on my best pants and shirt and my shining shoes. It was so, as a man about town rather than as a cook, I went to the dining-room.

The man from Bombay was as astonished as Priya. We exchanged the old courtesies, and I waited. But, to my relief, there seemed little more to say. No difficult questions were put to me; I was grateful to the man from Bombay for his tact. I avoided talk as much as possible. I smiled. The man from Bombay smiled back. Priya smiled uneasily at both of us. So for a while we were, smiling in the dim blue-red light and waiting.

The man from Bombay said to Priya, 'Brother, I just have a few words to say to my old friend Santosh.'

Priya didn't like it, but he left us.

I waited for those words. But they were not the words I feared. The man from Bombay didn't speak of my old employer. We continued to exchange courtesies. Yes, I was well and he was well and everybody else we knew was well; and I was doing well and he was doing well. That was all. Then, secretively, the man from Bombay gave me a dollar. A dollar, ten rupees, an enormous tip for Bombay. But, from him, much more than a tip: an act of graciousness, part of the sweetness of the old days. Once it would have meant so much to me. Now it meant so little. I was saddened and embarrassed. And I had been anticipating hostility!

Priya was waiting behind the kitchen door. His little face was tight and serious, and I knew he had seen the money pass. Now, quickly, he read my own face, and without saying anything to me he hurried out into the dining-room.

I heard him say in English to the man from Bombay, 'Santosh is a good fellow. He's got his own room with bath and everything. I am giving him a hundred dollars a week from next week. A thousand rupees a week. This is a first-class establishment.'

A thousand chips a week! I was staggered. It was much more than any man in Government got, and I was sure the man from Bombay was also staggered, and perhaps regretting his good gesture and that precious dollar of foreign exchange.

'Santosh,' Priya said, when the restaurant closed that evening, 'that man was an enemy. I knew it from the moment I saw him. And because he was an enemy I did something very bad, Santosh.'

'Sahib.'

'I lied, Santosh. To protect you. I told him, Santosh, that I was going to give you seventy-five dollars a week after Christmas.'

'Sahib.'

'And now I have to make that lie true. But, Santosh, you know that is money we can't afford. I don't have to tell you about overheads and things like that. Santosh, I will give you sixty.'

I said, 'Sahib, I couldn't stay on for less than a hundred and twenty-five.'

Priya's eyes went shiny and the hollows below his eyes darkened. He giggled and pressed out his lips. At the end of that week I got a hundred dollars. And Priya, good man that he was, bore me no grudge.

* * *

Now here was a victory. It was only after it happened that I realized how badly I had needed such a victory, how far, gaining my freedom, I had begun to accept death not as the end but as the goal. I revived. Or rather, my senses revived. But in this city what was there to feed my senses? There were no walks to be taken, no idle conversations with understanding friends. I could buy new clothes. But then? Would I just look at myself in the mirror? Would I go walking, inviting passers-by to look at me and my clothes? No, the whole business of clothes and dressing up only threw me back into myself.

There was a Swiss or German woman in the cake-shop some doors away, and there was a Filipino woman in the kitchen. They were neither of them attractive, to tell the truth. The Swiss or German could have broken my back with a slap, and the Filipino, though young, was remarkably like one of our older hill women. Still, I felt I owed something to the senses, and I thought I might frolic with these women. But then I was frightened of the responsibility. Goodness, I had learned that a woman is not just a roll and a frolic but a big creature weighing a hundred-and-so-many pounds who is going to be around afterwards.

So the moment of victory passed, without celebration. And it was strange, I thought, that sorrow lasts and can make a man look forward to death, but the mood of victory fills a moment and then is over. When my moment of victory was over I discovered below it, as if waiting for me, all my old sickness and fears: fear of my illegality, my former employer, my presumption, the *hubshi* woman. I saw then that the victory I had had was not something I had worked for, but luck; and that luck was only fate's cheating, giving an illusion of power.

But that illusion lingered, and I became restless. I decided to act, to challenge fate. I decided I would no longer stay in my room and hide. I began to go out walking in the afternoons. I gained courage; every afternoon I walked a little farther. It became my ambition to walk to that green circle with the fountain where, on my first day out in Washington, I had come upon those people in Hindu costumes, like domestics abandoned a long time ago, singing their Sanskrit gibberish and doing their strange Red Indian dance. And one day I got there.

One day I crossed the road to the circle and sat down on a bench. The *hubshi* were there, and the bare feet, and the dancers in saris and the saffron robes. It was mid-afternoon, very hot, and no one was active. I remembered how magical and inexplicable that circle had seemed to me the first time I saw it. Now it seemed so ordinary and tired: the roads, the motor cars, the shops, the trees, the careful policemen: so much part of the waste and futility that was our world. There was no longer a mystery. I felt I knew where everybody had come from and where those cars were going. But I also felt that everybody there felt like me, and that was soothing. I took to going to the circle every day after the lunch rush and sitting until it was time to go back to Priya's for the dinners.

Late one afternoon, among the dancers and the musicians, the *hubshi* and the bare feet, the singers and the police, I saw her. The *hubshi* woman. And again I wondered at her size; my memory had not exaggerated. I decided to stay where I was. She saw me and smiled. Then, as if remembering anger, she gave me a look of great hatred; and again I saw her as Kali, many-armed, goddess of death and destruction. She looked hard at my face; she considered my clothes. I thought: is it for this I bought these clothes? She got up. She was very big and her tight pants made her much more appalling. She moved towards me. I got up and ran. I ran across the road and then, not looking back, hurried by devious ways to the restaurant.

Priya was doing his accounts. He always looked older when he was doing his accounts, not worried, just older, like a man to whom life could bring no further surprises. I envied him.

'Santosh, some friend brought a parcel for you.'

It was a big parcel wrapped in brown paper. He handed it to me, and I thought how calm he was, with his bills and pieces of paper, and the pen with which he made his neat figures, and the book in which he would write every day until that book was exhausted and he would begin a new one.

I took the parcel up to my room and opened it. Inside there was a cardboard box; and inside that, still in its tissue paper, was the green suit.

*   *   *

I felt a hole in my stomach. I couldn't think. I was glad I had to go down almost immediately to the kitchen, glad to be busy until midnight. But then I had to go up to my room again, and I was alone. I hadn't escaped; I had never been free. I had been abandoned. I was like nothing; I had made myself nothing. And I couldn't turn back.

In the morning Priya said, 'You don't look very well, Santosh.'

His concern weakened me further. He was the only man I could talk to and I didn't know what I could say to him. I felt tears coming to my eyes. At that moment I would have liked the whole world to be reduced to tears. I said, 'Sahib, I cannot stay with you any longer.'

They were just words, part of my mood, part of my wish for tears and relief. But Priya didn't soften. He didn't even look surprised. 'Where will you go, Santosh?'

How could I answer his serious question?

'Will it be different where you go?'

He had freed himself of me. I could no longer think of tears. I said, 'Sahib, I have enemies.'

He giggled. 'You are a joker, Santosh. How can a man like yourself have enemies? There would be no profit in it. *I* have enemies. It is part of your happiness and part of the equity of the world that you cannot have enemies. That's why you can run-run-runaway.' He smiled and made the running gesture with his extended palm.

So, at last, I told him my story. I told him about my old employer and my escape and the green suit. He made me feel I was telling him nothing he hadn't already known. I told him about the *hubshi* woman. I was hoping for some rebuke. A rebuke would have meant that he was concerned for my honour, that I could lean on him, that rescue was possible.

But he said, 'Santosh, you have no problems. Marry the *hubshi*. That will automatically make you a citizen. Then you will be a free man.'

It wasn't what I was expecting. He was asking me to be alone for ever. I said, 'Sahib, I have a wife and children in the hills at home.'

'But this is your home, Santosh. Wife and children in the hills, that is very nice and that is always there. But that is over. You have to do what is best for you here. You are alone here. *Hubshi-ubshi*, nobody worries about that here, if that is your choice. This isn't Bombay. Nobody looks at you when you walk down the street. Nobody cares what you do.'

He was right. I was a free man; I could do anything I wanted. I could, if it were possible for me to turn back, go to the apartment and beg my old employer for forgiveness. I could, if it were possible for me to become again what I once was, go to the police and say, 'I am an illegal immigrant here. Please deport me to Bombay.' I could run away, hang myself, surrender, confess, hide. It didn't matter what I did, because I was alone. And I didn't know what I wanted to do. It was like the time when I felt my senses revive and I wanted to go out and enjoy and I found there was nothing to enjoy.

To be empty is not to be sad. To be empty is to be calm. It is to renounce. Priya said no more to me; he was always busy in the mornings. I left him and went up to my room. It was still a bare room, still like a room that in half an hour could be someone else's. I had never thought of it as mine. I was frightened of its spotless painted walls and had been careful to keep them spotless. For just such a moment.

I tried to think of the particular moment in my life, the particular action, that had brought me to that room. Was it the moment with the *hubshi* woman, or was it when the American came to dinner and insulted my employer? Was it the moment of my escape, my sight of Priya in the gallery, or was it when I looked in the mirror and bought the green suit? Or was it much earlier, in that other life, in Bombay, in the hills? I could find no one moment; every moment seemed important. An endless chain of action had brought me to

that room. It was frightening; it was burdensome. It was not a time
for new decisions. It was time to call a halt.

I lay on the bed watching the ceiling, watching the sky. The door
was pushed open. It was Priya.

'My goodness, Santosh! How long have you been here? You have
been so quiet I forgot about you.'

He looked about the room. He went into the bathroom and came
out again.

'Are you all right, Santosh?'

He sat on the edge of the bed and the longer he stayed the
more I realized how glad I was to see him. There was this: when
I tried to think of him rushing into the room I couldn't place it
in time; it seemed to have occurred only in my mind. He sat with
me. Time became real again. I felt a great love for him. Soon I
could have laughed at his agitation. And later, indeed, we laughed
together.

I said, 'Sahib, you must excuse me this morning. I want to go for
a walk. I will come back about tea time.'

He looked hard at me, and we both knew I had spoken truly.

'Yes, yes, Santosh. You go for a good long walk. Make yourself
hungry with walking. You will feel much better.'

Walking, through streets that were now so simple to me, I thought
how nice it would be if the people in Hindu costumes in the circle
were real. Then I might have joined them. We would have taken to
the road; at midday we would have halted in the shade of big trees;
in the late afternoon the sinking sun would have turned the dust
clouds to gold; and every evening at some village there would have
been welcome, water, food, a fire in the night. But that was a dream
of another life. I had watched the people in the circle long enough
to know that they were of their city; that their television life awaited
them; that their renunciation was not like mine. No television life
awaited me. It didn't matter. In this city I was alone and it didn't
matter what I did.

As magical as the circle with the fountain the apartment block
had once been to me. Now I saw that it was plain, not very tall,
and faced with small white tiles. A glass door; four tiled steps down;
the desk to the right, letters and keys in the pigeonholes; a carpet
to the left, upholstered chairs, a low table with paper flowers in the

vase; the blue door of the swift, silent elevator. I saw the simplicity of all these things. I knew the floor I wanted. In the corridor, with its illuminated star-decorated ceiling, an imitation sky, the colours were blue, grey and gold. I knew the door I wanted. I knocked.

The *hubshi* woman opened. I saw the apartment where she worked. I had never seen it before and was expecting something like my old employer's apartment, which was on the same floor. Instead, for the first time, I saw something arranged for a television life.

I thought she might have been angry. She looked only puzzled. I was grateful for that.

I said to her in English, 'Will you marry me?'

And there, it was done.

'It is for the best, Santosh,' Priya said, giving me tea when I got back to the restaurant. 'You will be a free man. A citizen. You will have the whole world before you.'

I was pleased that he was pleased.

* * *

So I am now a citizen, my presence is legal, and I live in Washington. I am still with Priya. We do not talk together as much as we did. The restaurant is one world, the parks and green streets of Washington are another, and every evening some of these streets take me to a third. Burnt-out brick houses, broken fences, overgrown gardens; in a levelled lot between the high brick walls of two houses, a sort of artistic children's playground which the *hubshi* children never use; and then the dark house in which I now live.

Its smells are strange, everything in it is strange. But my strength in this house is that I am a stranger. I have closed my mind and heart to the English language, to newspapers and radio and television, to the pictures of *hubshi* runners and boxers and musicians on the wall. I do not want to understand or learn any more.

I am a simple man who decided to act and see for himself, and it is as though I have had several lives. I do not wish to add to these. Some afternoons I walk to the circle with the fountain. I see the dancers but they are separated from me as by glass. Once, when there were rumours of new burnings, someone scrawled in white paint on the pavement outside my house: *Soul Brother.* I understand the words;

but I feel, brother to what or to whom? I was once part of the flow, never thinking of myself as a presence. Then I looked in the mirror and decided to be free. All that my freedom has brought me is the knowledge that I have a face and have a body, that I must feed this body and clothe this body for a certain number of years. Then it will be over.

Selected Further Reading

The reader who wants to explore more works by any of the writers represented in this book should find useful starting-points in the separate introductions to each writer. The brief selection of titles here provides suggestions for more general further reading.

Other collections of international short stories

Gordimer, N. (ed.), *Telling Tales* (London: Bloomsbury, 2004)
Halpern, D. (ed.), *The Art of the Short Story* (New York: Viking, 1999)
Scholes, R. (ed.), *Elements of Fiction: An Anthology* (New York, Oxford: Oxford University Press, 1981)

Critical works on the short story

Bardolph, J. (ed.), *Telling Stories: Postcolonial Short Fiction in English* (Amsterdam; Atlanta, GA: Rodopi, 2001)
Fallon, E. *et al.* (eds), *A Reader's Companion to the Short Story in English* (London, Chicago: Fitzroy Dearborn, 2001)
Hanson, C. (ed.), *Re-reading the Short Story* (Basingstoke: Macmillan, 1989)
May, C. E., *The Short Story: The Reality of Artifice* (New York: Twayne, 1995)
O'Connor, F., *The Lonely Voice: A Study of the Short Story* (Hoboken, New Jersey: Melville Publishing, 2004 [1963])

Literary perspectives on the 'Cultural Encounters' theme

Boehmer, E., *Colonial and Postcolonial Literature: Migrant Metaphors*, 2nd edn (Oxford, New York: Oxford University Press, 2005)

Naipaul, V.S., *A Writer's People: Ways of Looking and Feeling* (Basingstoke, Oxford: Picador, 2007)

Nasta, S. (ed.), *Writing Across Worlds: Contemporary Writers Talk* (London: Routledge, 2004)

Phillips, C. (ed.), *Extravagant Strangers: A Literature of Belonging* (London, Boston: Faber and Faber, 1997)

Rushdie, S., *Imaginary Homelands: Essays and Criticism, 1981–1991* (Harmondsworth: Granta Books in association with Penguin, 1991)